# Lecture Notes in Computer Science

# Lecture Notes in Computer Science

Edited by G. Goos and J. Hartmanis

## 216

Christer Fernstrom
Ivan Kruzela
Bertil Svensson

# LUCAS
## Associative Array Processor
Design, Programming and Application Studies

Springer-Verlag
Berlin Heidelberg New York Tokyo

**Authors**

Christer Fernstrom
Ivan Kruzela
Bertil Svensson
Department of Computer Engineering, University of Lund
P.O. Box 118, 22100 Lund, Sweden

CR Subject Classifications (1985): B.1.4, B.2.1, B.3.2, C.1.2, D.3, F.2.1, G.2.2,
H.2.6, I.4.0, I.4.3, I.4.6, I.4.7


ISBN 3-540-16445-6 Springer-Verlag Berlin Heidelberg New York Tokyo
ISBN 0-387-16445-6 Springer-Verlag New York Heidelberg Berlin Tokyo

Printing and binding: Beltz Offsetdruck, Hemsbach/Bergstr.
2145/3140-543210

# PREFACE

Performance requirements for computers are steadily increasing. New application areas are considered that pose performance requirements earlier thought unrealistic. In the history of computing, growing demands have to a substantial degree been met through increased circuit speed. However, in the most powerful computers of each time parallelism has also been introduced because improvements in circuit speed alone have not been sufficient to produce the required performance.

The 40 year history of computing shows that concepts introduced in high-performance computers often become part of the design of more moderately sized (or at least more moderately priced) wide-spread computers a few years later. The rapid progress of Very Large Scale Integration (VLSI) technology also helped increase the use of parallelism.

New computer architectures often originate from the need to efficiently solve problems arising in some specific application areas. They are, in a way, tuned specifically to these problem classes. However, many architectures are of a general purpose kind or demonstrate great similarities with each other. Thus, the need to discover efficient algorithms for solving problems from different areas on specific classes of parallel machines is evident. Existing programming languages are strongly influenced by classical computer architecture and thus not suited for expressing these algorithms. Therefore a need for new languages is also evident.

The necessity of abandoning the von Neumann architecture in the design of high-performance systems has been advocated by many authors. One of the most prominent is John Backus. He maintains that we are also hampered in our way of designing algorithms by the habit of always breaking them down into sequential form: "It is an intellectual bottleneck that has kept us tied to word-at-a-time thinking instead of encouraging us to think in terms of the larger conceptual units of the task at hand" [Backus78].

This view points to the importance of implementing radically new computer architectures and using them in practice. Many computational problems have engaged a large number of computer scientists for decades due to the continued relevance of these problems. With new architectures, some of these problems may be less important while others will become essential. For example, when working with a highly parallel computer, we may find sorting to be of little interest, yet the problem of routing large amounts of data between different parts of the machine without conflict now becomes a salient problem.

The LUCAS project (Lund University Content Addressable System) is an attempt to design and evaluate a highly parallel system while still keeping its size within the limits necessary for a university research project.

The initial plans, greatly inspired by the monograph "Content Addressable Parallel Processors" by Caxton Foster [Foster76], were drawn in 1978. The project started in autumn of that same year. After simulations and implementation of a prototype, the final design (with 128 processors and a general purpose interconnection network including the perfect shuffle/exchange) was decided upon in 1980 and fully implemented in 1982. In 1983 a dedicated input/output processor was added to the system.

The main objective of LUCAS design and implementation was to allow a research vehicle for the study of architectural principles, programming methodology and applicability of associative array processors. With certain principles and design details fixed (such as bit-serial working mode and the use of conventional memory circuits), the implementation of LUCAS allowed modification of architecture parts to suit certain applications. These parts include the network that interconnects the processing units, the input/output system, and the instruction sets at different architectural levels. The number of processing elements in the design is not limited in itself, but has been fixed to 128 in the implemented version used for application studies.

The algorithms that have been programmed and evaluated on the machine mainly concern three large areas - image processing, signal processing, and database processing. New programming tools and languages were developed to express parallelism and associativity.

This book is an attempt to compile the underlying thoughts, design principles, programming tools and experiences from the project. The greater part of the book is material from three PhD theses published in 1983, [Fernstrom83, Kruzela83, Svensson83a]. Also included is a summing up of continued work on an improved architecture tuned for signal processing, (described in [Ohlsson84]), and on design of a dedicated I/O Processor [Kordina83].

The book is organized as follows:

Part 1, Processor Design, starts with a chapter introducing parallel and associative processing. It continues with a rather detailed description of LUCAS System architecture, followed by an overview of the basic instructions. Part 1 concludes with a comparison of LUCAS to related designs published in the literature.

Part 2 is devoted to programming aspects, both on microprogramming and application programming level. A new microprogramming language which greatly simplifies the mastering of parallel computing structure is presented. A high level language (Pascal/L), suitable for expressing parallel algorithms is also defined. Comparison with other proposed languages is made.

Part 3 of the book comprises three chapters on applications. The first of these - Chapter 7 - treats "some well known problems" implemented on LUCAS. The problems are taken from three important classes of computations, namely matrix multiplication, computation of the discrete Fourier Transform, and solution of graph theoretical problems. Chapter 8 discusses the use of LUCAS in relational data base processing and shows that many of the operations in this field can be efficiently implemented. Chapter 9 shows the implementation of image processing algorithms. Chapters 8 and 9 both compare the results with reported results from other designs.

Part 4, the epilogue, contains conclusions and description of continued research. The proposal for an improved processing element with a bit-serial multiplier is included here, as are the conditions for VLSI implementation of the processor array.

Many people have been helpful during the work that resulted in this book. We want to thank Rolf Johannesson and the staff at the department of Computer Engineering at University of Lund. We are deeply indebted to Lennart Ohlsson and Staffan Kordina for the permission to include their results in the book. Anders Ardo has implemented the text formatting system which greatly simplified the work of preparing the manuscript. The Swedish National Board for Technical Development has provided financial support. Professor Dines Bjorner, who served as scientific advisor to the Board, has given us valuable constructive criticism. We are also grateful for the support from Lund Science Corporation, University of Halmstad and Cap Sogeti Innovation in France for having made the publication of this book possible.

Christer Fernstrom
Ivan Kruzela
Bertil Svensson

# CONTENTS

# Part 1
# PROCESSOR DESIGN

# Chapter 1
# PARALLEL AND ASSOCIATIVE
# PROCESSING


## 1.1 INTRODUCTION

The rapid development of computers during the last decades has pushed the state of the art in two different directions: computers are becoming smaller and they are becoming more powerful.

Advances in different fields have contributed to the development: the technological progress has influenced speed, cost and size of the components, new algorithms have been developed for the basic operations, such as arithmetic operations, and new forms of organizing the entire systems are used, where parallel operation between the system components is exploited.

All these areas have had impact on the development of more powerful machines. Unfortunately we are approaching the speed limits of gates and flip-flops, which means that the enhancement in circuit technology alone will only allow a relatively small gain in speed. It is clear that questions concerning the organization of systems together with the development of new algorithms will play an increasingly important role for further advances.

According to a classification scheme of Flynn [Flynn66], there are four different categories of computer organization. The basis of this scheme is that a processor of any kind processes data by a sequence of instructions. Based on the context of a data stream and an instruction stream, the following possibilities exist:


* SISD - Single Instruction stream Single Data stream

* SIMD - Single Instruction stream Multiple Data stream

* MISD - Multiple Instruction stream Single Data stream

* MIMD - Multiple Instruction stream Multiple Data stream

The von Neumann architecture belongs to the SISD category.  In an SIMD architecture each processing unit executes the same instruction,  but on different data.  In MIMD systems many processors cooperate to solve a common computational task,  but the tasks assigned to the individual processors can all be different.  The exact structure of the MISD architecture is not fully agreed upon.  Some authors put pipelined processors in this category,  others claim that pipelined processors belong to the SIMD category,  in which case the MISD category becomes empty.

We will in the following only deal with the SIMD category of parallel computers.  This class of computers is well suited for applications where the same (often rather simple) operation is performed on a large number of well structured data elements.

Different taxonomies for SIMD computers have been presented.  We will borrow the following definitions from Thurber [Thurber76].

* SIMD  processor - a  computer  architecture  characterized  by  an  SIMD orientation of data and procedure streams.

* Array  processor/Parallel  processor - an  SIMD  processor  in  which  the  cells usually bear some topological relationship to each other.

* Associative  processor - an  SIMD  processor  in  which  the  prime  means  of element activation is an associative process.  (The meaning of this will be explained in Section 1.3.)  Generally the cells of an associative processor have a  loose  topological  relationship  and  are  functionally  very  simple.   The processor  is  usually  designed  around  an  associative  memory  system.

We will use the term associative array processor to denote an associative processor,  as defined by Thurber,  in which a communication network defines a topological relationship between the processing elements.  As proposed by Slotnick [Slotnick82],  we will use the term processing element , or PE for short,  rather than "processing unit",  since this suggests a simpler internal structure,  as is commonly the case in SIMD systems.

We terminate this section with the observation that the name "array processor" sometimes is used to designate a processor which is "suitable for processing arrays".  These "array processors" are usually pipelined back-end computers which serve as attached resources to minicomputers.   In our terminology "array processor" stands for an SIMD organized processor as described above.

## 1.2 PERFORMANCE IN PARALLEL MACHINES

It is the need for larger capacity which is the reason for introducing parallelism in a computer system.    Therefore it is important to have accurate methods to decide the influence of different design parameters on the capacity.

Three aspects of capacity are frequently referenced in the literature,    namely the bandwidth ,  the speedup and the efficiency .  By the bandwidth we mean the number of operations that can be performed in the system per time unit.  The speedup indicates how much faster a computation is done in the parallel machine than if it was executed on a sequential computer.  Efficiency,  finally,  measures the utilization of the parallelism in the machine for a certain computation.

To obtain a value of the bandwidth,  we assume that a computation C consists of n operations which can be performed simultaneously.  We assume further that the operations are independent and can be executed without any form of interaction.  A space-time diagram shows the hardware utilization as a function of time.  Figure 1.1 is a space-time diagram for the computation on an array processor with p processing elements,  where p<n and t is the time needed to execute one instruction.

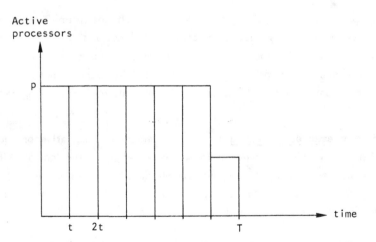

Figure 1.1 Space-time diagram for the computation of C in an array processor with p processors (p<n).

If T is the total time to compute C, then we have

$$T = \lceil n/p \rceil * t$$

and the bandwidth, B, which is equal to the number of instructions that are executed per time unit, can be written:

$$B = n/(\lceil n/p \rceil * t)$$

The speedup is

$$s = n*t/(\lceil n/p \rceil * t) = n/\lceil n/p \rceil$$

The maximum speedup with p processors is p, which is obtained when n is a multiple of p.

The efficiency is the actual speedup divided by the maximum possible speedup:

$$e = s/p$$

An important question when using a parallel computer is how the set up time influences the total speedup of a computation. By set up time, we understand the time needed to initialize the parallel processor plus the time needed to perform all the non-parallel operations. We split the computation into two parts, one sequential part and one parallel part with the parallelism n. The total computation time is T and the time of the sequential part is t. Then we get:

$$s = \frac{t + n*(T-t)}{t + \lceil n/p \rceil *(T-t)} = \frac{t/T + n*(1-t/T)}{t/T + \lceil n/p \rceil *(1-t/T)}$$

Figure 1.2 shows the total speedup as a function of the ratio t/T (the ratio of the total time that is used for set up) for array processors with different number of processing elements. It is assumed that n=p. The figure illustrates the great negative impact any sequential part of an algorithm has on the speedup of the computation. When designing a new parallel machine this fact must be taken into consideration. The architecture should allow set up and parallel computation to be performed simultaneously.

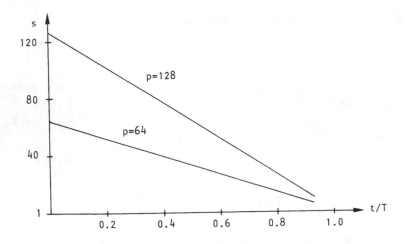

<u>Figure 1.2</u> The speedup as a function of the t/T ratio for different sizes of array processors.

## 1.3 ASSOCIATIVE ARRAY PROCESSORS

In Section 1.1 we defined an associative array processor as a machine with the following properties:

* SIMD processor, i.e. it consists of many processing elements (PEs) and one common control unit.

* Activation of the PEs may be an "associative process", which means that it is not the location or address of a PE that decides if it will execute the instructions from the control unit, but some property of the contents in the memory of the PE.

* A communication network defines a topological relationship between the PEs. They can for example form a linear array or a two-dimensional grid.

In the following we will sometimes use the term <u>associative memory word</u> as a synonym for a processing element together with its local memory. We will start our description of associative array processors by describing an associative memory. By adding computing capabilities to the words of the associative memory we will form an associative processor.

Finally we will present different networks for data communication between the processing elements. The presentation of associative memories and processors is based on the presentation in [Foster76].

## 1 3.1 Associative Memories

An associative memory, or content addressable memory, is a memory where each bit cell contains the necessary logic to compare the stored information with a search argument. Associated with each word is a one bit result register, called the Tag . Outside the memory are three registers of the same size as the width of the memory words: the Commmon , the Mask and the Data registers (see Figure 1.3).

To perform a parallel search, the search argument is loaded into the Common Register and a bit map indicating the bits which will be included in the search is put in the Mask. Before the search operation is initiated, all Tag registers in the words that are to be searched are set to ONE. Now a search is performed by generating the two signals "Match 0" and "Match 1" (see Figure 1.4) in the bit positions where the Mask contains a ONE. A mismatch in one bit position generates a mismatch signal that propagates through the OR-gates and finally causes the corresponding Tag to be set to ZERO (see Figure 1.3).

After a search has been executed it is possible to write data to or read data from the selected words - the words where the Tag contains a ONE. When writing into the memory, the contents in the Data register is copied to all selected words, whereas a read yields the logical OR in each bit position of the selected words.

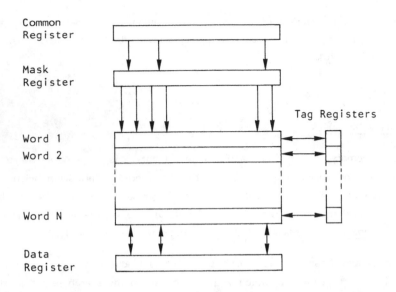

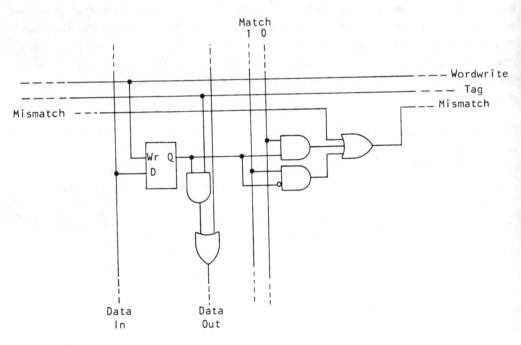

Figure 1.3 Associative memory with detail showing one memory cell.

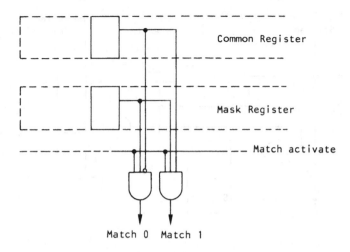

Figure 1.4 Generation of the match signals.

Most likely a unique selection is wanted. This is why a so called multiple match resolver is needed. In its simplest form this is a select first chain, which - when activated - deselects all words except the first one where the Tag contains a ONE (see Figure 1.5). The output from the select first chain can be used as a Some/None indicator (even when the select first funtion is not activated) and shows if a search was successful or not. This implementation of a multiple match resolver suffers from being slow with one gate delay per word. In the description of LUCAS we will see how the select first chain can be speeded up with the use of look-ahead. A general scheme for high speed multiple match resolvers is found in [Anderson74].

In some applications it is desirable to count the numbers of responders to a search operation. Depending on the size of the memory, the speed requirements and the accuracy wanted, different methods may be used. If the size of the memory is moderate and the speed requirements are low or if it is possible to perform the count simultaneously with other activities, one way would be to connect the Tag registers in the form of a shift register, and to shift the Tags n steps, where n is the number of words in the memory, counting the number of ONES.

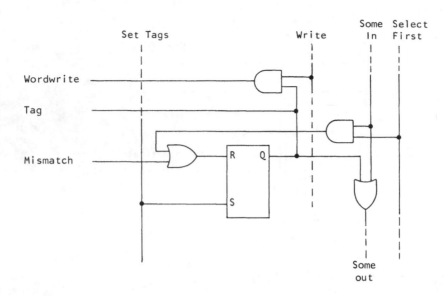

Figure 1.5 The Tag register with a multiple match resolver in the form of a select first chain, which also generates a Some/None signal from the last word.

Another possible way to calculate the number of activated words is with the use of an adder tree (see Figure 1.6). In the first level, groups of tags are processed in combinatorial counters which produce the number of active tags in each group. Assume that g groups are formed, each comprising t tag signals, where g is a power of two. An adder tree of $\log_2 g$ levels is then used to produce the total sum. For example, in an associative memory with 4096 words, 16 tags are grouped together, producing $2^8$ 4-bit numbers after the first level. To produce the total sum, an 8 level adder tree is used.

If the words in the associative memory also can be accessed by address it might be desirable to calculate the address of a responding word. Anderson [Anderson74] proposes a tree-like structure with $\log_2(n)/2$ levels of so called p-generators to produce the result. An elegant method, however, would be to reserve $\log_2 n$ bits in each word, where the word's address is stored. After a search is performed, followed by a multiple match resolution, a readout gives the desired address in the reserved bit positions.

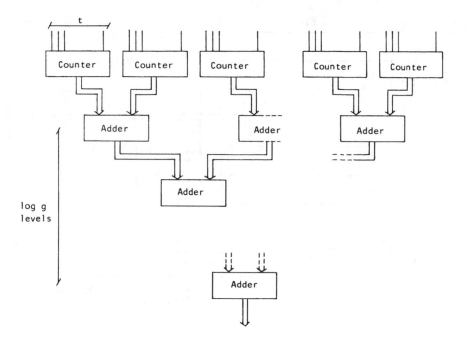

<u>Figure 1.6</u> Count responders network in the form of an adder tree.

h

## 1.3.2 Bit-serial working mode

Recalling Figure 1.3 we see that the complexity of the memory cell in an associative memory is only slightly higher than that of a cell in a memory of random access type. What prevents an efficient implementation is the number of connections to the cells. This makes it possible to integrate only a very limited number of cells per IC package. A way to overcome this problem is to reduce the parallelism in the memory. What we have described can be referred to as a "word-parallel-bit-parallel" memory. If we change the design to a "word-parallel-bit-serial" memory, we lose some speed, but on the other hand this allows integration of the memory in a more efficient manner. As compared to an ordinary random access memory (RAM), we will still have a great advantage, since the number of words that are processed in each computation step largely exceeds the number of bits per word, in applications where this kind of organization is used.

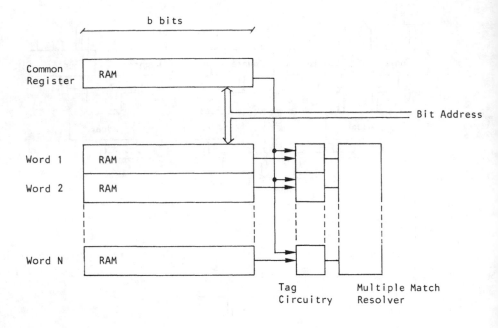

b bits

Common Register — RAM

Bit Address

Word 1 — RAM
Word 2 — RAM
Word N — RAM

Tag Circuitry

Multiple Match Resolver

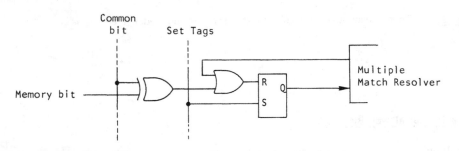

Common bit

Set Tags

Memory bit

Multiple Match Resolver

Figure 1.7 Bit-serial associative memory. Each RAM is a b words by one bit memory.

Now the memory consists either of shift registers or of RAMs that are accessed "perpendiculary" to their normal usage, i.e. a b word by n bit RAM is used as n words by b bits in the associative memory (see Figure 1.7). In the bit-serial working mode, the Mask can be used to decide which bit positions, or bit slices, that are to be processed. Bit positions where the Mask contains a ZERO do not have to be processed at all, which means that the speed of the bit-serial associative memory is not reduced by a factor b as compared to the bit-parallel implementation, but only by a factor according to the length of the search argument.  A discussion of bit-serial working mode is found in [Batcher82].

### 1.3.3 A Bit-serial Associative Processor

The bit-serial associative memory can be transformed into an associative processor by adding bit processing capabilities to the Tag/mismatch circuitry.  This can take the form of a few additional one-bit registers and a Boolean function generator (or ALU).  Inputs to the ALU are the registers,  the PE-memory bit and a bit from the Common register. The ALU produces the new register values.  This extended associative memory will be referred to as an associative array or a processor array .

In addition to the Tag register,  a one-bit result register (R-register) and a carry register (C-register) is a minimum for implementing bit-serial arithmetic operations with reasonable efficiency.  Figure 1.8 shows a possible implementation of a simple PE.  It comprises an ALU and three one-bit registers: T,  R and C.  Input of data to the PE memory,  which is an ordinary RAM,  is handled by the Common register.  The data passes from the common input of the ALU and is loaded into the R register,  from where it may be written into the memory.  Output of data is as follows: the memory output is copied into the R register via the ALU.  When the READ signal is activated,  the data output shows the value of the logical OR function between the R registers of all selected PEs.

A multiple match resolver is implemented in the form of a Some-None/Select-First chain. A central control unit sends the RAM address and the function code to the ALU.  It also controls the Read,  the Write and the Select First functions.

Examples of ALU functions are:

Set        Set all Tags

Mismatch   Reset Tag if mismatch between the Common and the PE memory bit

Add        Add PE memory bit to R and C.  Put result in R (result bit) and C (generated carry)

Load R     Load the R register from the PE memory

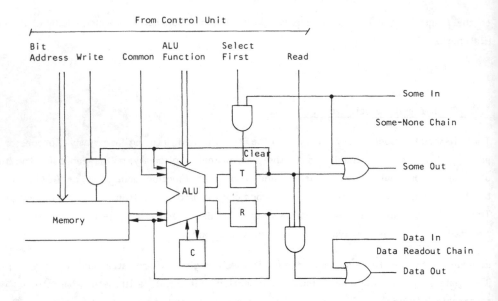

Figure 1.8 Processing element and memory in a bit-serial associative processor.

The control unit plays an important role in a bit-serial implementation of an associative processor. It must be able to accept instructions that operate on data items of various sizes. During the execution it generates the necessary sequence of control signals to the PEs. We call the data items of various formats fields , each field occupying one or several bit slices in the associative memory (see Figure 1.9). The task the control unit performs is basically a transformation of operations on fields to operations on bit slices.

The control unit, which may be microprogrammed, contains a Common register, a Mask register, two or three loop counters, a number of registers to hold the addresses of different bit slices in the associative memory, and logic to load and increment these registers.

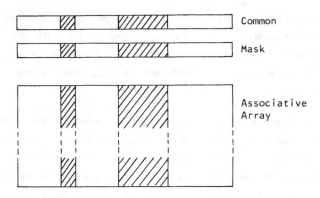

Figure 1.9 Bit slice and Field in the associative memory.


An instruction to the control unit includes specification of the location of the operand fields (their bit slice address) and also the length of the operands.   Examples of such instructions are:

| | |
|---|---|
| ADDCONST | Add the contents of the Common register to a field |
| ADDFIELDS | Add the contents of two fields |
| SEARCH | Compare the contents of the Common register with a field |
| MAX | Select the word which has the maximum value in the specified field |

## 1.4 INTERCONNECTION NETWORKS IN SIMD SYSTEMS


### 1.4.1 Introduction

In many algorithms there is a need to combine array elements with different indices.   In the case of sequential operation this causes no problem.   Since the operands are accessed one after the other,  the same bus can be used to transport data,  even if the operands are located in different memory modules. The problem which arises in an SIMD machine is that all the processing elements must have simultaneous access to the data they need. For this purpose, an interconnection network for parallel data transport between the processing elements is defined. Once the network has been decided, the topology of the processing array has also been settled.

Since only a small subset of all possible interconnections can be included, the choice of these must be guided by the intended applications. In image processing, for example, the most frequently used operations combine the value of a pixel (picture element) with the values of its nearest neighbours to form the new value. In operations on relations in a relational database some algorithm may search two relations with different search keys and then combine the tuples where the search result was affirmative. In signal processing applications, where operations such as the Fast Fourier Transform are common, other ways to combine the operands are needed.

The most simple form of interconnection is when communication is limited to the nearest neighbours. Figure 1.10 shows this form of interconnection in both a one-dimensional and a two-dimensional array. When communication between the elements is needed, the control unit issues an instruction such as READ ABOVE. Now, each active processing element reads the data coming from the neighbour which is situated immediately above in the processing array.

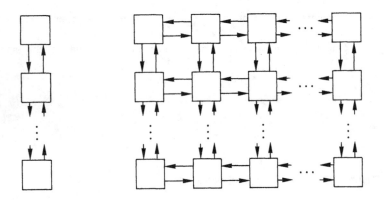

Figure 1.10 One- and two-dimensional processing arrays.

Several machines using the one-dimensional interconnection scheme have been designed:

* RAP, the Relational Array Processor [Ozkarahan et al.75], which is used for relational database processing.

* PEAC, a Peripheral Array Computer [Schomberg77]. Proposed applications are computer assisted tomography and high speed solution of nonlinear partial differential equations.

* PROPAL 2 [Cimsa79], which is used in image processing and general purpose array computing.

Most of the array processors that have actually been built use an interconnection network where neighbours communicate in a two-dimensional array. ILLIAC IV [Barnes et al.68] is built as an 8 by 8 array of PEs, the ICL DAP [Reddaway79] as a 64 by 64 array and the MPP [Batcher80] as a 128 by 128 array. CLIP 4 [Duff79], which is intended for image processing, uses a two-dimensional structure where a PE communicates with its eight neighbours.

In the case of ILLIAC IV, it is true that the topology defined by the network is a quadrant of 8 by 8 processing elements. However, experience has shown that the size of this processing area is too small for most of the problems and that it is more often used as a one-dimensional array with 64 processing elements where the i:th PE communicates with the elements i+1, i-1, i+8 and i-8. The latter two are used to speed up long "shifts" of data.

The advantage of using an interconnection scheme where only neighbours can communicate is of course that it is fairly easy to implement. Physically, all connections can be made short and there is no need for a large bus since all the data movements are local. On the other hand, for many applications the communication is not efficient. It has been shown that the time required to perform an arbitrary permutation in a two-dimensional array of N by N PEs is of the order $O(\sqrt{N} * \log_2 N)$ [Orcutt74].

### 1.4.2 The Perfect Shuffle

Most of the more elaborate schemes for data communication within an SIMD computer are based on the perfect shuffle . The usefulness of the perfect shuffle was demonstrated by Stone [Stone71]. By then, the perfect shuffle had been studied by Golomb [Golomb61], and Pease had shown how it could be used in an efficient calculation of the Fast Fourier Transform on a parallel computer [Pease68]. Batcher later showed how the Flip Network in STARAN [Batcher77, Batcher79] could be redrawn in the form of a perfect shuffle network [Batcher76]. Interconnection networks similar to the perfect shuffle do also have properties which are of great interest to fault-tolerant interconnections [Schlumberger74].

Figure 1.11 shows the perfect shuffle connection between 8 input lines and 8 output lines. We see that the shuffle, S, permutes the input with index i $(i=i_2*2^2 + i_1*2 + i_0)$

according to:

$$S(i) = \begin{array}{ll} 2*i & 0 \le i \le 3 \\ 2*i-7 & 4 \le i \le 7 \end{array} \qquad (1)$$

or, in the general case where we have N inputs and N outputs and $N=2^m$ for some integer m, the input with index i is permuted according to:

$$S(i) = \begin{array}{ll} 2*i & 0 \le i \le N/2 - 1 \\ 2*i+1-N & N/2 \le i \le N-1 \end{array} \qquad (2)$$

We can see from (2) that the index of an output element, o, can be obtained by rotating the index of the input element, i, one step to the left. This is true since in the case where $0 \le i \le (N/2)-1$, o=2*i which is equal to a one-step shift of i and since the most significant bit of i is ZERO, it is also equal to a rotation of i. In the second case, where $N/2 \le i \le N-1$, the most significant bit of i is ONE. Thus 2*i-N is equal to a left <u>shift</u> of i where only m ($m=\log_2 N$) bits are kept. If we <u>rotate</u> i one step, we get 2*i-N+1.

It is now clear that after m shuffles, all the elements will return to their initial positions.

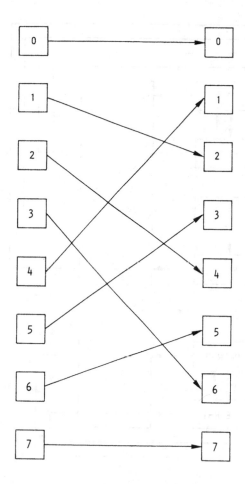

Figure 1.11 The Perfect Shuffle of an 8 element input vector.

One important property of the perfect shuffle is its ability of pairing different operands. Assume we use an array processor with a pairwise interconnection between the processing elements, as in Figure 1.12. Then it is possible to perform parallel operations on pairs of elements whose indices differ in bit 0 only. After one shuffle of the elements, pairs of elements whose indices differ in bit m-1 have come in the right position for parallel operation. After m-1 shuffles, all pairs of elements whose indices differ in only one bit of their binary representation have been in position for parallel operation in the array processor. This scheme is important for the implementation of the Fast Fourier Transform as we will demonstrate in Section 7.3.

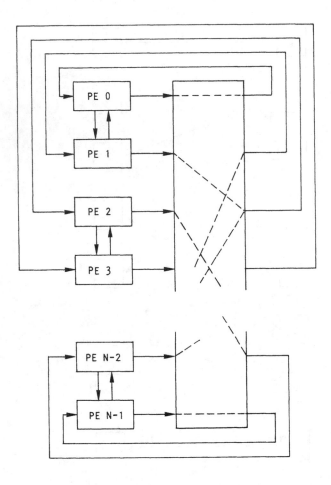

Figure 1.12 N processing elements with a pairwise and a perfect shuffle interconnection.

Accordingly, a drastic improvement of the capabilities of the perfect shuffle interconnection is the inclusion of exchange elements (see Figure 1.13) which allow a pairwise interchange of the outputs from the shuffle network. As we have seen, only $\log_2 N$ different permutations of the original input vector can be obtained with a pure shuffle connection. (Each shuffling of the data rotates the indices one step so that the original order is restored after $\log_2 N$ shuffles.)

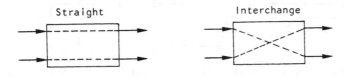

Figure 1.13 Permutations in an exchange element.

Depending on the value of a control signal, the exchange element either gives a straight or an interchanged data connection between its two inputs and outputs. If we allow each of the N/2 exchange elements to be controlled independently of the others, it is in fact possible to obtain any permutation of the N element input vector after a finite number of passes through this shuffle/exchange network.

Shuffle/exchange type networks of this kind can be implemented in the form of a single stage interconnection network (see Figure 1.14), where the input vector is loaded into a register and recirculated through the shuffle/exchange interconnections with different settings of the exchange control signals, until at last the desired permutation is obtained in the register. A multi-stage network consists of several cascaded single-stage networks with or without registers between the stages. If the network includes registers between the stages, data can be pipelined through the network which means that the asymptotic behaviour is like one pass through a single-stage network.

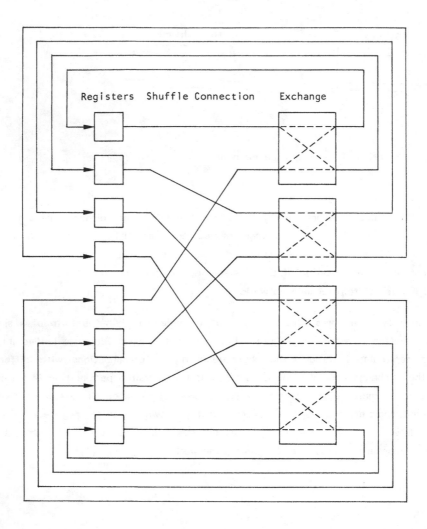

Figure 1.14 One-stage shuffle/exchange network.

In each stage, the exchange elements may either be controlled independently or all have the same setting. We refer to the two methods of switch setting as "individual box control" and "individual stage control", respectively. Individual box control increases the number of possible permutations quite dramatically. Consider for example a network with n stages, where $n=\log_2 N$, such as the Omega network, which is described below. For a given input-output pair in an n-stage network there is one and only one path that connects them [Pease77]. Thus, two different switch settings cannot yield identical permutations, which means that the number of permutations that can be performed is the same as the number of switch settings. For n=4, i.e. 16 PEs, this is $2^{32}$ for a network with individual box control and $2^4$ for a network with individual stage control.

The Omega network, which is a shuffle/exchange network with $\log_2 N$ stages and individual box control (see Figure 1.15), has been analysed by Lawrie [Lawrie75].

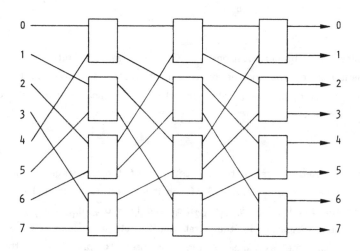

Figure 1.15 The Omega network - a log N-stage shuffle/exchange network, N=8.

Although the Omega network is not capable of performing all possible N! permutations of an N element input vector in one single pass, it is a very powerful interconnection scheme in that many important permutations can be accomplished such as uniform circular shifts (rotations) and flip-permutations, where one or several bits of the indices are inverted (see Figure 1.16).

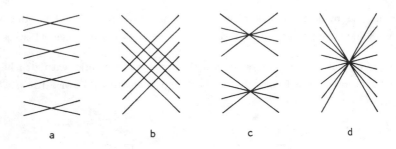

a        b        c        d

<u>Figure 1.16</u> Examples of flip-permutations. One or several bits in the binary representation of the indices of the input vector are inverted ($i = i_2*2^2 + i_1*2 + i_0$). a) $i_0$ inverted, b) $i_2$ inverted, c) $i_1$ and $i_0$ inverted, d) $i_2$, $i_1$ and $i_0$ inverted.

A simple algorithm is used to calculate the settings of the exchange elements in the Omega network. Assume that the element S of the input vector should end up in position D of the output vector and let $S = s_{m-1}s_{m-2}...s_0$ and $D = d_{m-1}d_{m-2}...d_0$ be the binary representations of their indices. In the first shuffle stage S is shifted to position $s_{m-2}s_{m-3}...s_0s_{m-1}$. Now the exchange element is used to place S in the position $s_{m-2}s_{m-3}...s_0d_{m-1}$ by using the bit $d_{m-1}$ of the destination address to control the exchange element: if $d_{m-1}=0$ then S should be connected to the upper output of the exchange element and if $d_{m-1}=1$ to the lower output.

At the inputs of stage i in the network, S has been switched to position $s_{m-i}s_{m-i-1}...d_{m-1}d_{m-2}...d_{m-i+1}$. It is shuffled to position $s_{m-i-1}s_{m-i-2}...d_{m-1}d_{m-2}...d_{m-i+1}s_{m-i}$ and exchanged to position $s_{m-i-1}s_{m-i-2}...d_{m-1}d_{m-2}...d_{m-i+1}d_{m-i}$.

Figure 1.17 shows the settings of the exchange elements for S=010 and D=110. At the first and second stages the lower outputs are selected. At the third stage the upper output is selected.

When the Omega network is used to permute all the N elements of the input vector simultaneously, conflicts occur when the two data elements arriving at an exchange element require connection to the same output. Lawrie has shown which properties of a permutation are necessary for a conflict free solution and has proved that many useful permutations have these properties [Lawrie75].

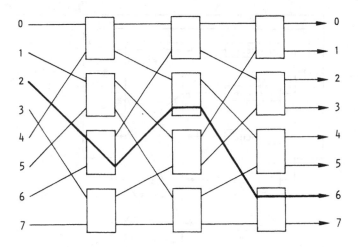

Figure 1.17 The element in position 2 (010) is switched to position 6 (110).

Several people have come up with schemes for enhancing the performance of the Omega network.

Lang [Lang76] starts from a one-stage shuffle/exchange network (as in Figure 1.14). Lawrie's algorithm for setting the exchange elements can of course also be used in a one-stage network since this can be seen as a time multiplexed variant of the Omega network. Lang replaces the exchange elements and the registers by queues, or FIFO registers (see Figure 1.18). Instead of exchanging data elements that appear on the outputs of the shuffle connection, they are placed in the corresponding queue. The difference, as compared to the Omega network, is that both inputs to the exchange stage can be connected to the same output, or rather, more than one data element can be placed in the same queue during a basic permutation step. This corresponds directly to the conflict situation which limits the possibilities of the Omega network.

Each basic permutation step, which is equivalent to one stage in the Omega network, is performed during one or several time steps. In each time step elements are taken from the head of the queues, shuffled and appended to the queues. Associated with each place in a queue is a one-bit flag whose value indicates if the corresponding data element should be shuffled during the current permutation step. A permutation step starts by setting all the flags TRUE and ends when no queue has a TRUE flag in its head element.

Lang shows that the maximum length of the queues is $O(\sqrt{N})$ and that the number of time steps needed to perform an arbitrary permutation also is $O(\sqrt{N})$.

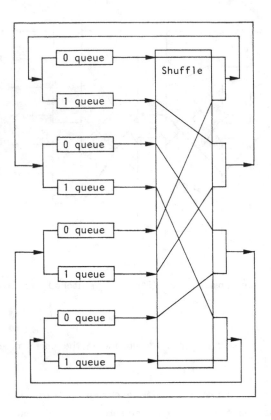

Figure 1.18 The modified one-stage shuffle/exchange network.

Parker has shown that three passes through an Omega network is enough to perform any permutation of the input vector and that six passes is enough for any connection (elements of the input vector could be broadcast to several elements in the output vector) [Parker80]. He also claims that two passes might be enough for permutations - it has been shown for N=4 and a computer simulation for N=8 gives the same result.

Unfortunately no simple algorithm for the settings of the exchange elements has been found to perform permutations in multiple passes through the Omega network.

# Chapter 2
## LUCAS SYSTEM ARCHITECTURE

### 2.1 SYSTEM OVERVIEW

The LUCAS system consists of four parts: the Master Processor, the Control Unit, the Processor Array and the I/O processor (Figure 2.1).

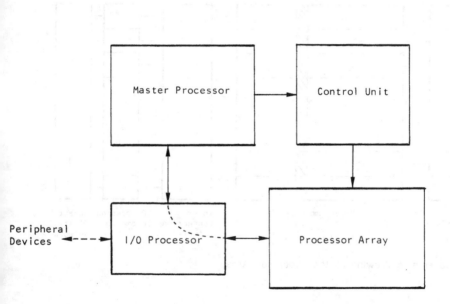

Figure 2.1 Overview of the LUCAS system.

The Master Processor takes care of user interaction, input/output (together with the I/O Processor), file handling and is responsible for sending instructions to the Control Unit. It is interchangeable and an ordinary mini- or microcomputer can be used. Presently a Prolog Z80 microcomputer system is used, which includes a MATROX graphical display processor, a printer with graphic capabilities and a link to the LUNET data communication network at the University of Lund.

The Processor Array, or Associative Array, consists of 128 processors (Figure 2.2). The main parts of a processor are the Memory Module (MM) and the Processing Element (PE). The Memory Module is a 4096 bit memory, where one bit is accessible at a time. All Memory Modules receive the same address from the Control Unit, i.e. a bit-slice of the whole memory area is accessible at a time as indicated in Figure 2.2. The Processing Elements work on one-bit data and have four internal one-bit registers. Most often a PE uses data from "its own" Memory Module. However, an interconnection network is used to route data from the memories to the PEs. This allows data access from other modules as well. The system works in full synchronism and the Processing Elements all get the same control signals each clock cycle from the Control Unit.

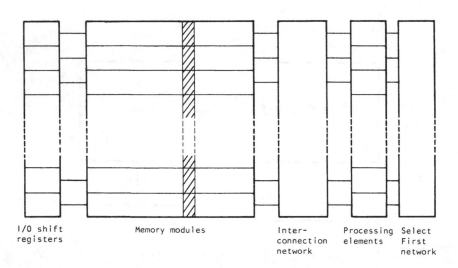

I/O shift            Memory modules           Inter-         Processing  Select
registers                                    connection  elements  First
                                        network                 network

Figure 2.2 Schematic drawing of the Processor Array.

The ensemble of Memory Modules may be seen as one single content addressable memory (associative memory). A typical case when this view is adequate is when a command is issued to all the Processing Elements to compare the memory contents with a certain template. Match/non-match is marked in one of the one-bit registers, the Tag register, in each PE. When a PE has its Tag set to one, we say that the PE is selected . Often, data from the Memory Modules of selected PEs are to be read out to the Master Processor. To allow sequential access to these, a multiple match resolver is included. This takes the form of a Select First network, which keeps the first selected Processing Element and resets the Tag registers in all the following PEs. The Select First network can be used iteratively to select the PEs in sequence.

With every memory module there is an 8-bit shift register, the I/O Register, used for input to and output from the memory module.

The Control Unit (Figure 2.3) receives instructions from the Master Processor and executes these on the Associative Array. Since the PEs work in a bit-serial fashion, the most obvious task for the Control Unit is to translate operations on data items (e.g. 8, 16 or 32 bit words) to sequences of bit operations. The Control Unit is microprogrammable. The microinstructions partly direct the sequencing of the Control Unit itself, partly direct the Processor Array. The set of control signals sent to the Processor Array consists of:

* the bit address to the Memory Modules

* a function code for the PEs

* an interconnection selector code

* control of memory writing, the I/O Registers and the Select First-network

The Instruction Register, IR, holds the current instruction. The locations and length of the operands are specified in the Parameter Registers, PR1...PR4. As an example, parallel addition of two vectors is shown in Figure 2.4. An important feature of LUCAS, illustrated in this example, is the ability to treat operands of different lengths with the same instructions. No extra bits that do not carry any information have to be brought through the computations.

An important part of the Control Unit is the Address Processor, which performs fast computations of addresses to bit-slices in the Memory Modules (increment, decrement, add constant, compare, etc.).

The Control Unit also contains a Common (Comparand) Register and a Mask Register, each 4096 bits wide. The Common Register holds arguments, which are used in the computations by all the PEs, e.g. search arguments or constants to be added to a data item in all the PEs. Through a test input to the Sequencer the contents of the Mask Register may influence the flow of microinstructions. The normal use of the Mask Register is to mask out certain bits in search operations.

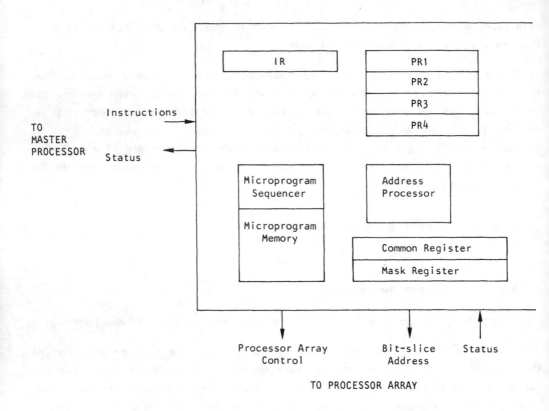

Figure 2.3 LUCAS Control Unit.

In applications where very fast input/output is required the dedicated I/O Processor acts as a microprogrammable interface between various peripheral devices and the Processor Array. The I/O Processor includes a Buffer Memory and an Address Processor. The latter is capable of generating various address sequences to the Buffer Memory in order to reconfigure data according to the input/output conditions at hand.

The Master controls the I/O Processor and the Control Unit in a similar way.

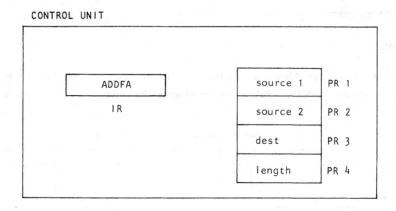

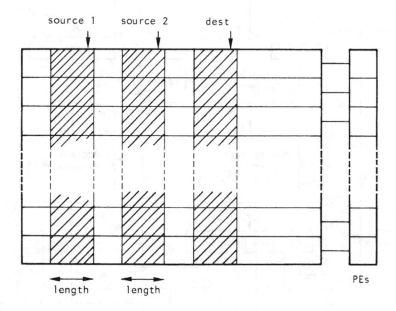

Figure 2.4 Illustration of the four-parameter instruction 'add fields all': ADDFA source1, source2, dest, length.

## 2.2 CONTROL UNIT

### 2.2.1 Overview

The Control Unit, see Figure 2.5, has two parts: an interface to the Master and a microprogrammable execution unit which commands the bit-serial processing in the PEs.

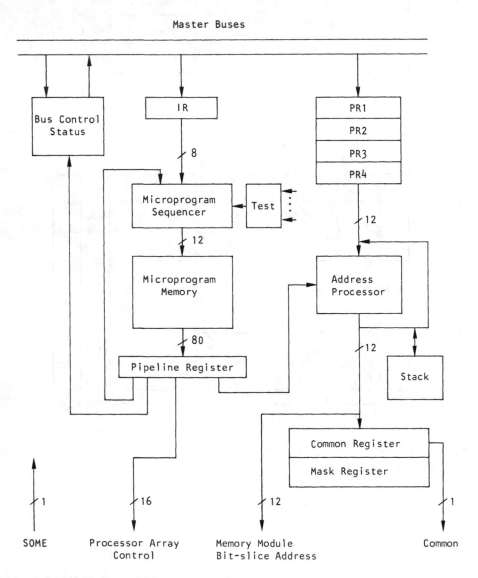

Figure 2.5 LUCAS Control Unit.

LUCAS and the Master communicate via the following registers, which are mapped into the memory space of the Master in the current implementation:

* Instruction Register - IR

* Parameter Registers - PR1 ... PR4

* Status Register

* I/O Buffer Register

* Common I/O Register

* Mask I/O Register

* PE I/O Registers (one in each PE)


The Control Unit is microprogrammable with a microprogram memory of 4 k words.  The microprogram memory works in two modes:

* In run mode,  when it is logically organized as 4096 words,  each 80 bits wide

* In load mode,  when it is logically organized as 40960 words,  each 8 bits wide

The mode of operation is determined by the Master Processor.

Microprogramming is horizontal,  in the sense that each bit or group of bits always controls the same part of the hardware.  This organization allows parallelism between microoperations on different parts of LUCAS.

In order to support simultaneous activities,  several buses are used for communication within the Control Unit,  between the Master and the Control Unit and between the Control Unit and the I/O Register area in the Associative Array.


## 2.2.2 Instruction Timing

The Master stores instructions in the Instruction Register with parameters in the Parameter Registers.  When the Master tries to write data into any of these registers, the Bus Control logic senses if the Instruction Register is empty,  in which case data is loaded and the Master gets an acknowledge signal.  If the Instruction Register already contains an instruction whose execution has not yet started,  the Bus Control logic sends a non-acknowledge signal which results in the Master entering a wait state.  As soon as the Instruction Register becomes free,  the new instruction is loaded and an acknowledge signal is sent to the Master.  The Instruction Register together with the Parameter

Registers are referred to as the <u>instruction pipeline</u> .

To protect the contents of the Parameter Registers from being overwritten, the Instruction and Parameter Register area is not released automatically when the execution of a new microprogram starts, but is under microprogram control.

There is one other mode of communication between the Master processor and the Control Unit, namely the "Control Unit Driven Interrupt" mode (CDI mode). In this mode, the programs that are executed in the Master and in the Control Unit can be seen as two asynchronous concurrent processes. They are asynchronous since even though all instructions are located in the Master's memory, the Control Unit reads its own instructions by interrupting the Master and this is transparent to the program in the Master. The two concurrent processes share two common resources: the I/O registers and the Status Register in the Control Unit. To guarantee exclusive access to the common resources, software semaphores must be used.

So far, the possibilities of the CDI mode have not been fully investigated. If it will be more used, more efficient ways of synchronization and protection of common resources should be considered. The reason for including this mode, which seems more difficult to handle and involves more overhead, is that once an efficient solution to the synchronization problem has been found, programs can be written without the need for the instruction scheduling mentioned earlier. As soon as instructions for the Control Unit appears, they are moved to an instruction buffer where they are fetched by the interrupt routine. In a way this instruction buffer would act as a many-leveled instruction pipeline.


## 2.2.3 Microprogram Sequencer

The Microprogram Sequencer, Am2910 [Mick and Brick 80], generates the addresses to microinstructions in the Control Memory. At the beginning of a cycle, the current microinstruction (control word) is loaded into the Pipeline Register. The control word is divided into several fields, each controlling one part of the hardware. The Sequencer itself is controlled by three fields: one field defines the instruction to the Sequencer, one field specifies the address in case of branch instructions and one field selects a test condition to be used for conditional branching. The Testmultiplexer gates different signals to the test input of the Sequencer:

* The current value of the Mask Register output.

* The state of the Busy flag, which indicates if the Instruction Register has been loaded.

* Zero Address Processor status.

* Zero Loopcounter status.

* Some/None status from the PEs.

2.2.4 Address Processor

A 16 bit field of the microinstruction is used to control the activity in the Associative Array: operations performed in the ALU:s, the set-up of the interconnection network, input/output etc. Since all computations are bit-serial, it is important that the Control Unit can generate the bit addresses needed at a high rate.

For example, to add two fields in the Associative Array (cf. Figure 2.4), the following sequence of bit addresses should be generated by the Control Unit:

```
source1 - bit 0        / used to fetch bit 0 of source 1
source2 - bit 0        / used to fetch bit 0 of source 2
destination - bit 0    / used to store the result bit 0
source1 - bit 1
source2 - bit 1
destination - bit 1
        .
        .
        .
```

The part of the Control Unit which handles this is the Address Processor. The Address Processor is a 12-bit processor capable of doing the integer arithmetic needed for address computations. A new address is generated each clock cycle, stored in the Address Register and used to access the Associative Memory while the next address is being calculated. In this way the Address Processor introduces no delay in the execution of microprograms.

The Address Processor is implemented with three 4-bit bit-slice microprocessors (Am2901A) and an external data memory organized as a LIFO stack. It has 16 internal registers and an ALU. The stack holds 32 12-bit values. Operands to the ALU are the internal registers, the LIFO stack, the Parameter Registers, the I/O Buffer Register (see Section 2.2.6) and a field of the control word.

Operations can be performed on:

- any single operand
- any pair of internal registers
- any register and the top element of the stack
- any register and the data presented on the data input

The result of an operation is always stored in the Address Register. It may also be written back into one of the internal registers and it can be pushed on the stack.

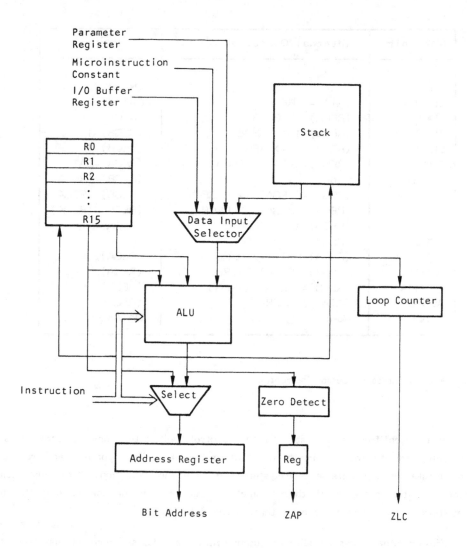

Figure 2.6 The Address Processor.

In order to reduce the number of bits needed to control the Address Processor, a subset of sixteen instructions have been chosen and a PROM is used to code a 4-bit field of the microinstruction into the 10 bits needed to control the Am2901A. In addition to the instruction to the Address Processor, the microinstruction contains two 4-bit fields which independently select two of the internal registers for operands (REGA and REGB).

Table 2.1 summarizes the instruction set of the Address Processor. In the table, REGB stands for the internal register addressed by the REGB field of the microinstruction and (REGB) for the contents of this register. DATA stands for the value of the data inputs.

| Mnemonic | Internal Operation | Output |
|----------|-------------------|--------|
| TBZ | None | (REGB) |
| LDBD | DATA -> REGB | DATA |
| LDBA | (REGA) -> REGB | (REGA) |
| INCB | (REGB)+1 -> REGB | (REGB)+1 |
| DECB | (REGB)-1 -> REGB | (REGB)-1 |
| ADAD | (REGA)+DATA -> REGB | (REGA)+DATA |
| TAEQB | None | (REGB)-(REGA) |
| ADBA | (REGB)+(REGA) -> REGB | (REGB)+(REGA) |
| SUBBA | (REGB)-(REGA) -> REGB | (REGB)-(REGA) |
| AINCB | (REGB)+1 -> REGB | (REGA) |
| ADECB | (REGB)-1 -> REGB | (REGA) |
| AADAD | (REGA)+DATA -> REGB | (REGA) |
| AADBA | (REGB)+(REGA) -> REGB | (REGA) |
| ASUBBA | (REGB)-(REGA) ->REGB | (REGA) |
| ALDBD | DATA -> REGB | (REGA) |
| PLADR | None | DATA |

Table 2.1 Address Processor Instructions

An instruction from the Master to the Control Unit often includes parameters which typically indicate the location of data within the PEs. These parameters are stored by the Master in the Parameter Registers and once the execution of the instruction has started, the contents of the Parameter Registers can be loaded into the internal registers of the Address Processor through the data input.

A zero-indicator senses an all-zero output from the Address Processor and generates the ZAP (Zero Address Processor) signal, which is fed into the Testmultiplexer. This allows the use of the internal registers as loop counters for microprogram looping.

Since the inner loops of bit-serial arithmetic operations tend to keep the Address Processor busy in each clock cycle (recall the example above), an extra loopcounter has been incorporated in the Control Unit. This 12-bit counter is loaded from the same sources as the data input to the Address Processor. In this way it is possible to load it directly from a Parameter Register to be used in unnested loops. In nested loops the initial loopcounter value is held in one of the internal registers of the Address Processor. To set up the innermost loop, this value is pushed on the stack and then popped back into the loopcounter. Loopcounters for the outer loops are handled internally in the Address Processor.

## 2.2.5 Common and Mask Registers

The Control Unit also includes a Common and a Mask Register. They are of the same size as the PE memories, 4096 bits, and are addressed by the contents of the Address Register. Input and output of data is handled through their corresponding I/O Registers which are 8-bit shift registers, also accessible from the Master. When an I/O Register has been loaded from the Master, the data is moved into the Common or Mask Register under microprogram control. The output from the Common Register is sent to the PEs on the COMMON line. The Mask output is connected to the Testmultiplexer.

In operations where one of the operands is a scalar, for example in parallel search operations or when adding a constant to a field in the Associative Array, the Common Register is used to hold this operand. The role of the Mask Register is to mask out certain bits when the operations are performed. In bit-serial operations, the Sequencer can use the mask value to conditionally skip certain addresses by "short-circuiting" the loops.

The need for a Mask Register in the Control Unit is not evident because its task can apparently be handled by the Address Processor. However, the fact that data from the Associative Array can be loaded into the Mask Register during the execution of a microprogram makes it useful in several algorithms, for example:

> Multiplication. If we want to multiply all the elements of a field with the same value, the value is moved to the Mask. Multiplication can now be performed using an algorithm which skips over strings of 0's and 1's, resulting in a significant speed-up over the standard algorithm (adding and shifting in each step), which is used to multiply two fields on LUCAS. (Note that this is particulary important on a bit-serial computer, since addition to the partial product takes much longer time than simply shifting it).

## 2.2.6 I/O Buffer Register

An important communication link in the Control Unit is the I/O Buffer Register. It is used to move data from a selected PE to the Control Unit. First one PE should be selected. This is accomplished by either a complete associative search or by loading the Tag Registers with a bit slice from the Associative Memory, where the result of a previous search may be stored. To complete the operation, the Control Unit activates the Select First chain, in order to make the selection unique, and sends an IORS (I/O Read Selected) signal to the PEs. The selected PE puts the 8 bit contents of its I/O Register on the I/O Data Bus to be loaded into the I/O Buffer Register.

Once the value has been loaded into the I/O Buffer Register it can be used for several purposes:

* The contents of the I/O Buffer Register may be written into the I/O Registers in all the PEs. This possibility permits a very flexible communication pattern between the PEs: one associative search operation selects a data source, a second search selects one or several destinations.

* The I/O Buffer Register may be read by the Master. This implements the data output register of the Associative Memory.

* Its contents can be copied into the I/O Register of the Common or the Mask Register. In this way it is possible to perform linked search operations, where the first associative search selects the key to the next search operation.

* The 8 bits of the I/O Buffer Register, padded with zeroes to the left, may be loaded into the Loopcounter or into the Address Processor, allowing indirect address links and loop values to be stored in the Associative Memory.

## 2.2.7 Status Register

The Master Processor may at any time interrogate a Status Register in the Control Unit. The Master has only read access to this register. The status information given contains the following six bits:

BUSY     Indicates that the instruction pipeline is full.

NONE     When this status bit is TRUE, none of the PEs has its Tag set. After an associative search it is often useful to know whether any word matched the search criterion.

ZAP     This bit indicates Zero Address Processor status.

ZLOOPC     This bit indicates Zero status of the Loopcounter in the Address Processor.

S1/S2     Two general purpose signals from the Control Unit. Their values are defined by a two-bit field of the control word. They can for example be used to indicate the progression in a running microprogram.

# 2.3 PARALLEL PROCESSING ARRAY

## 2.3.1 Processing Elements

A Processing Element (Figure 2.7) consists of four parts:

* A set of one-bit registers: T(tag), R(result), C(carry), and X(auXiliary).

* An Arithmetic Logic Unit (ALU).

* A Data Selector.

* Part of a network that implements the SELECT FIRST and SOME functions.

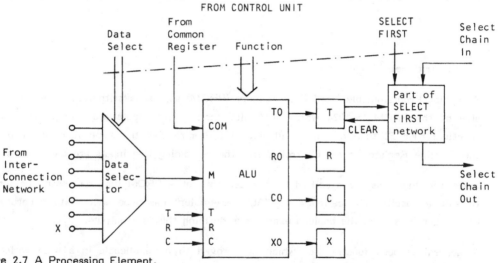

**Figure 2.7** A Processing Element.

## 2.3.1.1 Registers

The four registers, T, R, C, and X, have slightly different features.

The T (Tag) register has its output connected to the write control logic of the corresponding Memory Module. Thus it can be used as activation control, inhibiting change in the memory of those PEs where T equals zero. Furthermore, the Tag register is connected to the SELECT FIRST-network, which on a control signal from the Control Unit resets all Tag registers but one, namely the one with the lowest number in the linear ordering of the PEs. The Tag register is also the input to the SOME-network. This network indicates to the Control Unit whether some or none of the Tags are set. Finally, the Tag register controls the I/O Register of the Memory Module in a way described below.

The R (Result) register is the only register from which data may be written directly into the memory.

The C (Carry) register is a general purpose register. In arithmetic operations it is used to hold the carry bit.

The X (AuXiliary) register is also general purpose. Its output is not directly connected to the ALU. Instead, one of the Data Selector inputs is used, as shown in Figure 2.7.

### 2.3.1.2 Arithmetic Logic Unit

A bipolar Programmable Read Only Memory (PROM) serves as arithmetic logic unit. The size of the PROM is 1024 words of 4 bits each. Five inputs are used to specify the function; thus 32 functions are available. All PEs receive the same function code from the Pipeline Register in the Control Unit. The remaining five inputs are data inputs.

Since the functions are specified by the contents of a PROM they can easily be altered to suit a specific application. An "ALU assembler" has been written to generate the PROM contents from the boolean expressions defining the four outputs.

A general purpose function set which has proved to be applicable in a wide variety of computational areas, including image processing, signal processing and data base processing is listed in Appendix 1.

### 2.3.1.3 The Data Selector

The Data Selector allows a Processing Element to receive data from eight different Memory Modules according to the wiring of the Interconnection Network. One of the eight sources is fixed to be the output of the associated Memory Module (the D input). The remaining seven inputs can be wired to any source. All PEs receive the same Data Select code.

2.3.1.4 The SOME and SELECT FIRST networks

The output of the SOME-network indicates to the Control Unit whether some or none of the Tag registers are set. It has the structure shown in Figure 2.8, giving a depth of 16 gates when the number of PEs is 128.

When the Control Unit issues the SELECT FIRST command, only one (the first) Tag register is to remain set to one, all others are reset. This is done by an iterative combinatorial network with the states of all the Tag registers as inputs and CLEAR signals to the registers as outputs. To reduce the depth of the network, the outputs of the 8-input gates in the SOME-network are used as look-ahead. The structure of the SELECT FIRST network is shown in Figure 2.9.

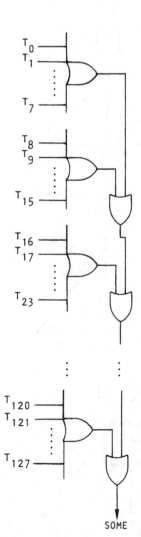

Figure 2.8 The SOME-network.

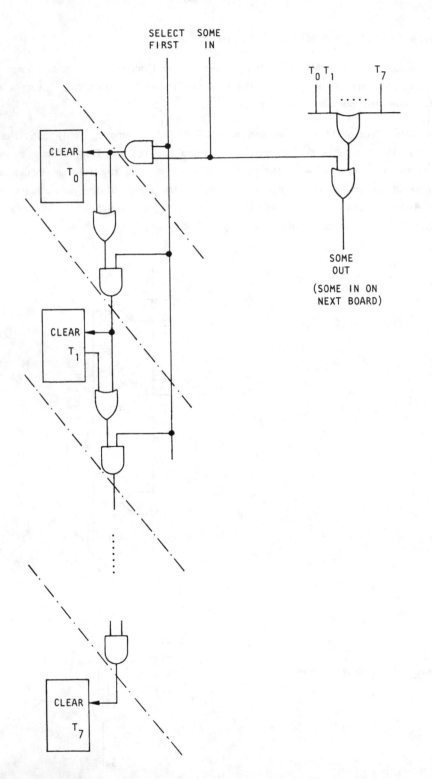

<u>Figure 2.9</u> The SELECT FIRST- and SOME- network of a board of eight consecutive Processing Elements.

## 2.3.2 Memory Modules and input/output structure

With each of the Processing Elements there is a Memory Module of 4096 bits and a
facility for input and output of data. Figure 2.10 shows one of the modules.

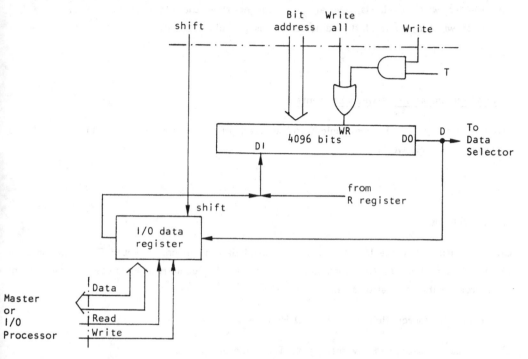

Figure 2.10 A Memory Module with its I/O Register.

The memory, which is an ordinary 4096 x 1 read/write memory chip with 55 ns access
time, receives a 12 bit address from the Control Unit and two different write signals.
When Write-All is activated all Memory Modules are written into, whereas Write gives
writing in a module only if the Tag register of the corresponding Processing Element is
set to one.

The 4096 bit memory will sometimes be referred to as a "word" of the Associative
Memory. PEs with the Tag register set will be referred to as selected PEs, and the
associated words as selected words.

The 8-bit I/O Registers are used for input and output of data. Usually, data in the
Associative Array is in the form of vectors, where each item of the vector is stored in
one memory word. The memory words can only input or output one bit of data at a
time, but this may be done in all the 128 words simultaneously. The 128 I/O Registers
transform the data format between 8 bits in parallel, as seen by the Master, and 128
bits in parallel, in the orthogonal direction.

A data input process can be divided into two phases: one to fill the I/O Registers from the Master processor or the I/O Processor, one to shift the contents into the Associative Array. The first phase needs one write cycle of the Master or the I/O Processor to transfer 8 bits, the second phase transfers 128 bits in one Control Unit clock cycle. The Master write cycle is several times longer than the clock cycle period. The I/O Processor write cycle is of the same length as the clock cycle.

## 2.3.3 Communication Between Elements

Two distinct paths for communication between PEs are present: the I/O Bus and the Interconnection Network.

## 2.3.3.1 I/O Bus

Communication over the I/O Bus is used to send data from one selected PE to all or to a subset of the PEs, to the Common or to the Mask Register. One byte is moved from its source to its destination(s) as follows:

1) Copy the source field into the I/O Registers

2) Select the source PE by setting its Tag register to One

3) Perform a READ-SELECTED operation, which copies the I/O Register of the selected PE to the I/O Buffer Register

4) Perform an IOWRALL operation. The I/O Buffer Register contents is broadcasted to all the I/O Registers, including those of the Common and the Mask Registers.

5) If the destination is Common or Mask then perform a bit-serial input from the corresponding I/O Register. If the destination is one or several PEs then set the corresponding Tags and perform a tag-masked input from the I/O Registers

In applications where LUCAS acts as an associative memory, the I/O Buffer Register is used as a data register for input and output. To retrieve data, the Master reads the I/O Buffer Register after step 3 in the procedure above. Data which should be written into the Associative Memory is first placed in the I/O Buffer Register whereafter steps 4 and 5 are executed.

## 2.3.3.2 Interconnection Network

The interconnection network comprises a 128 bit wide bus and the Data Selector in the PEs. The outputs of the PE memories are connected to the interconnection bus, where one line is reserved for each PE. On the input side, one input of the Data Selector is used to connect each PE with its memory, and a strapping area on the PE boards allows the remaining seven inputs to be connected to any of the 128 lines on the bus (see Figure 2.11).

Conceptually, communication over the interconnection network differs in several aspects from communication over the I/O Bus.

* The source and the destination of all links are fixed and not data dependent.

* Transport of data is done in parallel between different source-destination pairs, resulting in a permutation of the input data.

* Communication between PEs, where no direct link exists, can be obtained by multiple passes through the network.

Interconnection structures suitable for specific applications can be wired on LUCAS. However, there is also a need for a general purpose network, capable of permuting data in a flexible way, hopefully useful in many application areas.

As a general purpose interconnection network for LUCAS, the perfect shuffle+exchange structure has been chosen. The main reasons are: (1) the generality of the network, (2) the few connections needed - only two per PE - and (3) the efficiency of the network for calculation of the Fast Fourier Transform (as shown in [Pease68] and [Stone71]), which is useful in both signal and image processing.

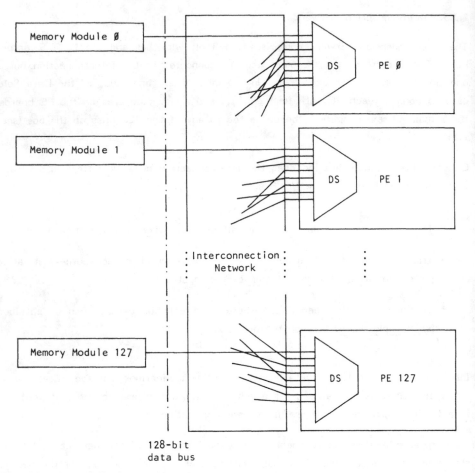

Figure 2.11 Interconnection structure.

The Data Selector of each PE has two inputs from this network - one ´shuffle´ input and one ´shuffle+exchange´ input - as shown in Figure 2.12. If the S input of the Data Selector is used, a perfect shuffle is made. If the N (=Neighbour´s shuffle) input is used, both perfect shuffle and exchange are made. Thus the exchange operation takes no extra time.

Using the Tag registers as a mask, individual box control may be used on LUCAS. This will be described later.

The perfect shuffle+exchange structure with individual box control is generally regarded as the most useful general purpose interconnection scheme for SIMD computers, since it is capable of realizing the most frequently used permutations ([Stone71], [Lawrie76], [Yew and Lawrie 81]). In spite of this, LUCAS is - to our knowledge - the first operational SIMD computer to use this network.

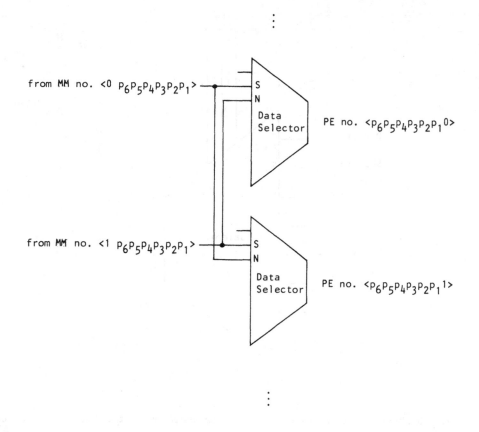

**Figure 2.12** Connections to Data Selectors for the realisation of the Perfect Shuffle+Exchange network.

The Interconnection Network on LUCAS also includes data paths from the neighbours above and below, as shown in Figure 2.13. These are often used in image processing. One input to the Data Selector is the output from the X-register of the PE.

All Data Selectors receive the same Data Select code from the Control Unit. Therefore, there is no direct possibility to implement individual box control, because this requires that some Data Selectors choose the Shuffle input, and some the Shuffle+Exchange input. It has to be done in two steps, using the state of the Tag register to decide the box setting. In the first step, the R registers of all words are loaded from memory via the Shuffle input. In the second step, the R registers are again loaded from memory, but only in selected words, and now using the Shuffle+Exchange input.

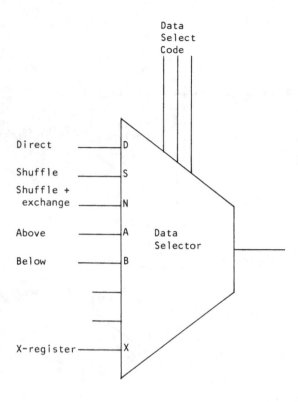

<u>Figure 2.13</u> Implemented connections to the Data Selector of the Processing Element.

From a general point of view, data communication over the interconnection network is useful when the interconnection structure is regular and independent of the data values. It has been used in e.g. matrix operations, image processing and Fast Fourier Transform. Communication over the I/O Bus is used in applications where the associative feature of LUCAS is predominant, which means that the current data values determine which PEs should communicate. It has mainly been used in database processing.

### 2.3.4 I/O Processor

Computing systems using parallel processing often become I/O bound, i.e. the speed of the system is limited by the capacity of the input/output channel. To avoid this, a dedicated I/O Processor [Kordina83] has been attached to LUCAS, increasing the data transfer rate from 0.8 Mbytes/second to 10 Mbytes/second. This allows e.g. fast data transfer from a disk drive or from an A/D converter sampling a video signal.

Often, the data comes from the peripheral device in a format not suitable for direct loading into the Associative Array of LUCAS. For example, an image is usually read line-wise but should in some cases be stored in another format in LUCAS. The I/O Processor is designed to take care of such necessary rearrangements of data. It is equipped with a Buffer Memory and an Address Processor capable of generating various address sequences. For rearrangement of data, the address sequences when writing and reading data to/from the Buffer are different.

The I/O Processor is constructed with Am2901 bit-slice processors as the Address Processor and with an Am2910 microprogram sequencer. Figure 2.14 shows a block diagram of the processor. Multi-level pipelining is used because of the speed requirements.

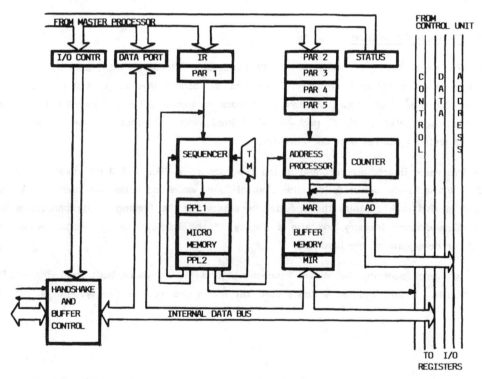

Figure 2.14 The I/O Processor.

The I/O Processor is controlled by the Master Processor through a set of registers mapped into the memory space of the Master. The registers have the following functions:

The Instruction Register (IR) receives the start address of the microprogram to be executed. The register is 8 bits wide.

Parameter Register 1 (PAR1) is used to specify the number of bytes to be read or loaded each time the microprogram is executed. The register is 12 bits wide.

Parameter Register 2...5 (PAR2...5) are general purpose registers and the use of them depends on the task. For example, in one task where data is loaded into the I/O Registers, the parameters would represent: start address of the Buffer Memory where data is read, step size of the buffer address, start address of the I/O Registers to receive the data and, finally, the number of times this microprogram should be executed.

Microprogramming of the I/O Processor is similar to microprogramming of the Control Unit.

### 2.3.5 Physical Description

The Processor Array, consisting of 128 Processing Elements with associated Memory Modules and input/output circuitry, occupies 16 double layered printed circuit boards (Photo 2.1 (a)). Each board of eight processors measures 220 x 230 mm (Photo 2.1 (b)). It contains a total of 70 IC packages - 59 implement the processors and 11 are signal buffers and I/O address decoding circuitry.

The Processor Boards are mounted in the top rack of a 2000 x 800 mm cabinet. (Photo 2.2). Immediately below resides the Control Unit which occupies two boards. A third board in this rack contains the circuitry necessary for the loading of microprograms into the Microprogram Memory and also a display of the microinstruction word, which was used for debugging of the hardware.

The next rack contains the Master Processor. It is a Z80 system built from Prolog STD-bus boards. It also includes a floppy disk unit and a graphical display system.

53

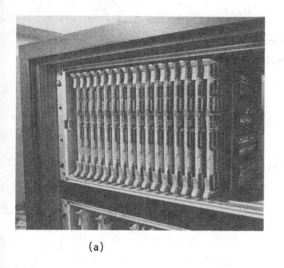 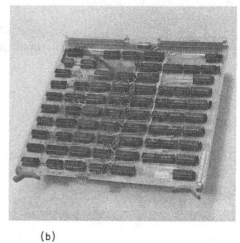

(a)                                    (b)

<u>Photo 2.1</u> (a) The 16 Processor Boards

        (b) A Processor Board comprising eight Processors

<u>Photo 2.2</u> LUCAS

# Chapter 3
## BASIC INSTRUCTIONS

In this chapter we will describe the basic types of instructions that can be performed on data in the Processor Array. Examples of the different instruction types are given and execution times are calculated.

## 3.1 CLASSIFICATION OF INSTRUCTIONS

At each moment one bit from each Memory Module is accessible by the PEs. Taken together these bits form a bit-slice of the total memory. The total memory will often be referred to as the associative memory (AM). A number of consecutive bit-slices form a field of the AM. (Since the memory chips are of random access type, the constraint that the bits must be consecutive is not necessary, but this is normally the case). The contents of the Tag registers may be used to mask out certain words in an operation. We use the term selector to refer to the bit vector describing the contents of these registers. A selector may be stored in a one-bit field of the associative memory.

### 3.1.1 Basic Types of Instructions Operating on the Associative Memory

The instructions used to manipulate data in the associative memory may be classified according to the types of operands and the types of results. An operand may either be a constant, stored in the Common Register, or a vector, stored in a field of the associative memory. (We will use 'field' and 'vector' alternatingly to denote this type of operand). The result of an operation is either a field or a selector, i.e a one-bit field.

A selector can always be used in an operation to mask out some PEs. Thus, it may also be regarded as an operand, present in all operation types. We do not explicitly indicate this when we list the different types below.

This view results in the following six basic instruction classes,   each one illustrated in
Figure 3.1.

(a)   **<field> --> <field>**

Examples:   Increment field
            Copy field
            Permute field (the vector in the destination field is a certain permutation of
                  the vector in the source field)

(b)   **<field> --> <selector>**

Examples:   Maximum value of a field
            Minimum value of a field

(c)   **<field,field> --> <field>**

Examples:   Add fields
            Multiply fields
            Maximum of fields (The  elements  of  the  source  vectors  are  compared
                  pairwise  and  the  maximum  of  them  is  put  in  the
                  destination field)
            AND between fields

(d)   **<field,field> --> <selector>**

Examples:   Field equal to field (The selector will mark those words where the elements
                  of the two fields are identical)
            Field greater than field (The  selector  will  mark  those  words  where  the
                  elements  of  source  field  1  are  greater  than  the
                  corresponding elements of source field 2)

(e)  **&lt;constant,field&gt; --&gt; &lt;field&gt;**


Examples:    Add constant

Multiply by constant

Subtract constant

Subtract from constant

AND with constant


(f)  **&lt;constant,field&gt; --&gt; &lt;selector&gt;**


Examples:    Exact match

Closest match

Greater than constant


These basic instruction types can be combined to get other types.  As an example, consider the merging of two vectors to produce a third vector.  To control the merge, a selector is used.  In those words,  where the selector is 0,  the element of vector 1 will be chosen; in those words where the selector is 1 the elements of vector 2 will be chosen (see Figure 3.2).  If other inputs to the Data Selector than the direct input are used, many different,  useful merges can be obtained.  The merge operation actually is the result of two successive &lt;field&gt;-to-&lt;field&gt; operations,  using different source fields and different selectors,  one selector being the complement of the other.

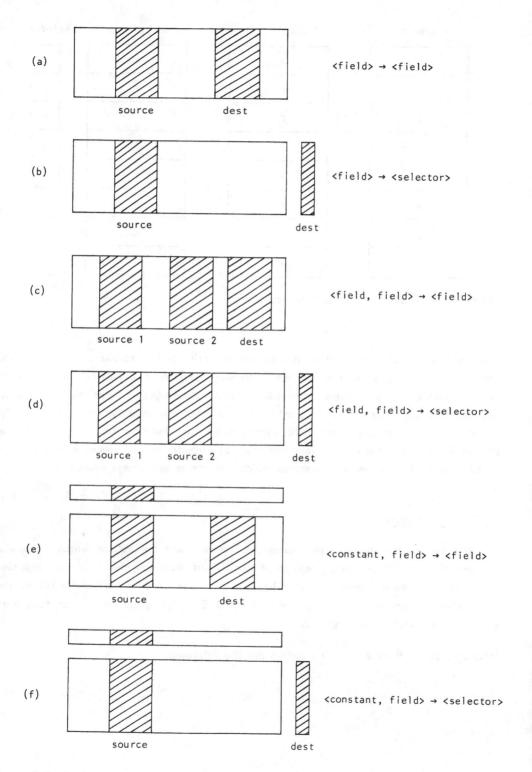

<u>Figure 3.1</u>  Basic types of instructions operating on the associative memory

| source 1 | source 2 | destination | selector |
|:---:|:---:|:---:|:---:|
| 0 | A | A | 1 |
| 1 | B | 1 | 0 |
| 2 | C | 2 | 0 |
| 3 | D | D | 1 |
| 4 | E | E | 1 |
| 5 | F | 5 | 0 |
| 6 | G | 6 | 0 |
| 7 | H | H | 1 |

Figure 3.2 Illustration of a Merge operation

The specification of an instruction includes the operation and up to four parameters. The basic instruction types listed above require between two and four parameters. Types (b) and (f) require two parameters (field address and field length). Types (a), (d) and (e) require three parameters (two field addresses and the field length). Type (c), finally, requires four parameters (three field addresses and the field length). Of course, in special cases, the value of parameters may be implied in the operation - e.g. the destination field being one of the source fields, or the length always being eight bits.

### 3.1.2 I/O Instructions

For transfer of data between the associative memory and the outside world, and also between the associative memory and the Common and Mask Registers, the I/O registers are used. However, these can also be used for data transfer between words of the associative memory. In the latter case the I/O Buffer Register is used as temporary storage, as described in Chapter 2.

Instructions that involve the I/O registers are the following:

(a)     &lt;field&gt; --&gt; &lt;I/O registers&gt;


(b)     &lt;I/O registers&gt; --&gt; &lt;field&gt;
        A selector may be used as a mask.


(c)     &lt;I/O registers,Selector&gt; --&gt; &lt;I/O Buffer Register&gt;


        This instruction puts the contents of the selected I/O register in
        the I/O Buffer Register. The selector must have one single '1'.


(d)     &lt;I/O Buffer Register&gt; --&gt; &lt;I/O registers&gt;
                                 &lt;Common I/O register&gt;
                                 &lt;Mask I/O register&gt;


        This instruction puts the contents of the source register in all
        I/O registers simultaneously.


I/O register instructions can likewise be combined to form instructions with other formats.
As an example,  consider the case of moving the value of the selected word of one field
to all selected words (according to another selector) of another field.  This instruction,
which may be expressed as

        &lt;field,selector,selector&gt; --&gt; &lt;field&gt;

is a concatenation of the following ones:

        &lt;field&gt; --&gt; &lt;I/O registers&gt;

        &lt;I/O registers,selector&gt; --&gt; &lt;I/O Buffer Register&gt;

        &lt;I/O Buffer Register&gt; --&gt; &lt;I/O registers&gt;

        &lt;I/O Registers&gt; --&gt; &lt;field&gt; using the second selector as mask.


In the following sections (3.2 through 3.4) we will give examples of basic,  widely useful,
instructions.  Most of the example instructions have been implemented on LUCAS and
they form part of a general purpose instruction set for the machine.

## 3.2 MOVES, PERMUTATIONS AND MERGES

### 3.2.1 Introduction

In this section we present some basic instructions for moving data in the associative array. Actually, merely moving data, without changing it, is of little use in the associative array. The reason for moving data is to put it in position for operating on it. Since the communication network is between the memories and the PEs, data movement and operation can in many cases be combined. However, there are also situations where pure data movement takes place. One example is input and output to and from the array, another is the case when the data routing preceding an operation must be done in several steps because the possibilities offered by the interconnection network are limited. A context where data movements are common is data base processing. Data items are moved within the array to form new tuples in the tables in a relational data base. However, as is shown in Chapter 8, the need to move data is still relatively small, much less than when the same data structures are stored in a conventional computer.

### 3.2.2 Basic Moves

An example of a pure move instruction is the "Load Outdata All" instruction

    LDOA source

which outputs an 8-bit field to the I/O registers. This takes one clock cycle per bit slice, plus time for parameter loading, etc, in total 11 clock cycles. The microprogram is included in Section 5.4.6.2 as an example of microprogramming.

A pure move between two fields in the associative array is accomplished by the instruction

    MOVE source, destination, length.

Each bit slice takes two clock cycles to move (one read, one write). With parameter loading etc, the total time is 2b+6, where b is the field length.

The instruction

    BROADCAST source, selector, destination, length

takes the contents of the source field in the first selected memory word and broadcasts it to the destination field of all words selected by the 'selector' bit-slice. First, data is moved from the source field to the I/O registers of all words, then from the selected I/O register to the I/O Buffer Register, next to all I/O registers, and finally to the destination field. 24 clock cycles are needed to broadcast an 8-bit word.

### 3.2.3 Use of the Interconnection Network

The perfect shuffle+exchange network of LUCAS is illustrated in Figure 3.3.

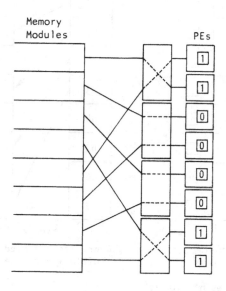

Memory Modules

PEs

**Figure 3.3** The principle of the perfect shuffle + exchange network in LUCAS

In reality - as described in Chapter 2 - the exchange function is controlled by choosing the S (as in Shuffle) or N (as in Neighbour's shuffle) input to the Data Selector of the PE. Since all Data Selectors are controlled by the same signals, the same input must be chosen for all PEs. Thus, if we want to use the straight state in some PEs and the interchange state in others, as shown in Figure 3.3, the transfer must be done in two steps. The state of the Tag register is used to control which input is taken. In Figure 3.3 the Tags are '1' in the PEs that are to use the shuffle+exchange input. First, data are transferred to selected PEs using this input. Then the Tags are complemented and data are transferred to selected PEs using the shuffle input. Alternatively, all PEs first receive data over the shuffle input. In PEs with T=1 these data are then overwritten with the data arriving over the shuffle+exchange input. The latter procedure is slightly faster, since the Tags need not be inverted.

## 3.2.3.1 Merges

Since the transfer described above is a two-step process, data may equally well be fetched from different fields in the two steps. In that case the destination field will contain data from both the source fields, intermixed according to the pattern of ´1´s and ´0´s in the Tags. As an example, Figure 3.4 shows how the upper halves of two fields are merged to form a new field.

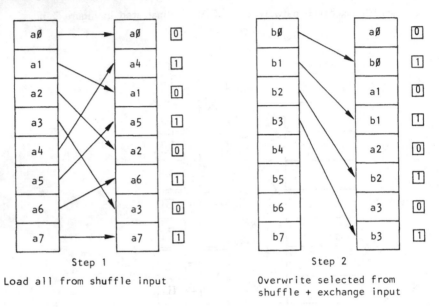

Step 1

Load all from shuffle input

Step 2

Overwrite selected from
shuffle + exchange input

**Figure 3.4** Merging the upper halves of two fields

In a merge operation any of the eight inputs to the Data Selector can of course be used. A merge operation is fully characterized by

* the addresses of the two source fields

* the address of the destination field

* the length of the fields

* the Data Selector input used for data from source field 1 in PEs with T=1

* the Data Selector input used for data from source field 2 in PEs with T=0

* the selector (the contents of the Tags).

All these cannot be specified in the instruction. The Data Selector inputs must be implicitly specified by the operation code. We also assume that the selector is loaded into the Tags in advance. Our example operation using the N and S inputs, respectively, is then expressed

MERGENS source 1, source 2, dest, length.

In words, we express this: Merge (source 1 shuffled+exchanged) with (source 2 shuffled) into dest where T=1/0.

With the same selector, the operation MERGEAD, which uses the Above and Direct inputs instead of N and S, will merge the even-numbered elements of the two sources into the destination field.

The execution time for merge operations on b-bit data is $3b+6$. With $b=8$ this makes 30 clock cycles, or 6.0 microseconds using a 5 MHz clock. Another kind of merging operation is the following: The elements of two vectors are compared pairwise, and the maximum of them is put in the destination field. This merge is not controlled by the Tag contents but by the data itself.


## 3.2.4 Automatic Routing

As has been shown in [Lawrie75] many frequently useful permutations can be done by the Omega network, which in turn can be implemented by n passes through a single-stage perfect shuffle+exchange network connecting $2^n$ memories with $2^n$ processors. Lawrie also gives a very simple algorithm to find the switch settings necessary for performing a certain permutation (see Section 1.4.2).

When choosing the switch setting of a certain exchange element according to this scheme, conflicts may of course arise when many data items are routed in the network simultaneously. Both inputs may, for example, want to use the lower output. Figure 3.5 shows a conflict-free permutation; Figure 3.6 shows one which cannot be implemented in n stages. In the latter figure, the unique path bringing a data item from source 001 to destination 010 has one connection - the last one - in common with the unique path from 011 to 011. Therefore a conflict occurs.

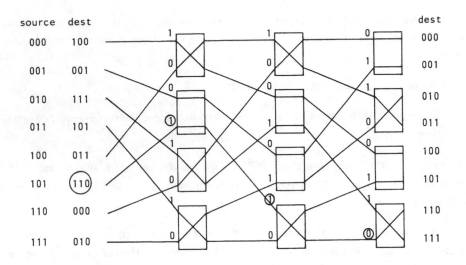

Figure 3.5 A conflict-free permutation. The routing of source 101 to destination 110 is specifically indicated

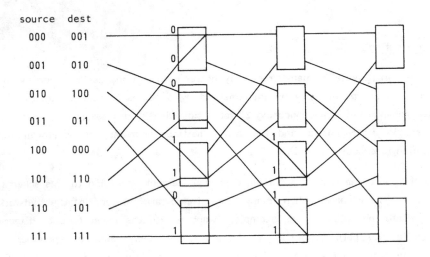

Figure 3.6 A permutation of $2^3$ elements that cannot be performed in 3 passes

Many of the permutations that cannot be performed in n passes can be performed in 2n passes - maybe all can. Yew and Lawrie [Yew and Lawrie81] have suggested an extension of Lawrie's algorithm, which is capable of deciding switch settings for a large class of permutations that can be performed in 2n passes. The algorithm works as follows:

When a conflict occurs in the application of Lawrie's algorithm, the control bit of the upper input is given the privilege to decide. This is the same as only using the control bit of the upper input in all situations.

Unfortunately, Yew's and Lawrie's algorithm does not work for all permutations that can be carried out in 2n passes. The permutation in Figure 3.6 can be realized in 2n passes, as shown in Figure 3.7, but Yew's and Lawrie's algorithm does not find the necessary switch settings. However, used repeatedly, it finds a switch setting for 4n passes.

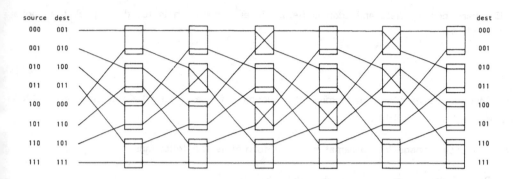

Figure 3.7 Realization of the permutation of Figure 3.6 in 6 passes

The strategy used to find the switch settings in Figure 3.7 can be expressed as follows: When a conflict occurs, let the data item that has earlier been routed correctly be transferred on correctly; if both have been correctly routed earlier, or both wrongly routed, choose the "straight" state.

3.2.4.1 Implementation

Algorithms of the above kind can be used to automatically route data items to the desired destinations. The destination address is simply sent along with the data and is used to set the routing switches. The algorithm of Yew and Lawrie has been implemented on LUCAS in the following way:

Each word of the memory is assumed to contain one item of a data field and one item of a control field. The latter contains the binary address of the destination word. Furthermore, each word is assumed to have a field containing the address of the word.

For i:= n-1 to 0 do

Load the Tag registers with the pattern
1 0 1 0 1 0 . . . 1 0.


Begin

Merge (position i of control field shuffled) with (position i of control field shuffled+exchanged) where T=1/0. Put the result in the Tags. (Now, pairs of PEs have the same Tag contents).

Merge (data+control field shuffled+exchanged) with (data+control field shuffled) where T=1/0.  Put the result back in the same fields.

End

Compare control field and address field.  If any mismatch is found,  repeat the above procedure.

The Master Processor can determine the success of the routing by reading the 'SOME' bit of the Status Register.

The instruction needs four parameters.  The format is the following:

ROUTE data,  control,  address,  data length

## 3.3 SEARCHES,  COMPARISONS AND LOGICAL INSTRUCTIONS

Search operations on a set of data elements look for elements with specific properties, e.g.  the element(s) with the greatest numerical value,  those exactly matching the search argument,  or pairs that consist of identical elements.  These examples represent three different instruction types according to the classification given in part 3.1.1,  namely types (b),  (f),  and (d),  respectively.

### 3.3.1 Type <field> --> <selector>

The instruction "Maximum of field,  tagmasked"

MAXT field address,  length

marks in the Tag registers the word(s) (among the selected ones) with greatest value in the field.  It proceeds from most significant bit to least significant bit discarding candidates with a '0' in the current position if there are candidates with a '1'.  The microprogram is included among the examples in Chapter 5.  The time is 3b+5 clock cycles.  Thus,  the maximum element in a vector of 128 8-bit data items is found in (3*8 + 5)*200 ns = 5.8 microseconds,  using a 5 MHz clock.

### 3.3.2 Type <field,field> --> <selector>

The instruction "Compare fields, tagmasked"

COMPFT source1, source2, length

marks in the Tag registers those words - of the selected ones - where the contents of the two fields are identical. This is accomplished by a series of successive LRMA (load R from M-input, all) and CRMT (Compare R to M-input, tagmasked) instructions to the ALU. The total time is 2b+6 clock cycles. With b=8, 22 cycles are needed, which is 4.4 microseconds, using a 5 MHz clock.

The instruction "Field greater than field, tagmasked"

GREAFT source1, source2, length

marks in the Tag registers those words - of the selected ones - where the contents of field 1 is greater than the contents of field 2. Actually a subtraction is made, but of the result only the sign bit is used. If overflow occurs in the subtraction, the sign is inverted so that a correct result is obtained also in this case. Instruction time is 2b+7 clock cycles, which for b=8 yields 23 clock cycles, or 4.6 microseconds, using a 5 MHz clock.


### 3.3.3 Type <constant,field> --> <selector>

The instruction "Compare field to Common, tagmasked"

COCOT field_address, length

marks in the Tag registers those words - of the selected ones - where the contents of the examined field is identical to the contents of the same field in the Common Register. Since bits from both operands can be input to the PEs simultaneously, this comparison only takes one clock cycle per bit. In total, b+4 clock cycles are needed. Thus, a search for an 8-bit data item in a vector of 128 items is accomplished in 2.4 microseconds.

The instruction "Greater than Common, tagmasked"

GREACOT field_address, length

marks in the Tag registers those words - of the selected ones - where the contents of a certain field is greater than the contents of the same field in the Common Register. The ACIMA function of the ALU (see instruction list in Appendix 1) is used to subtract the Common Register output bit from the Memory output bit, one bit each clock cycle and starting with a ´1´ in the Carry register. The total time is b+4 clock cycles also in this case.

We consider two versions of closest match: minimum arithmetic distance and minimum Hamming distance.

The instruction "Closest match, arithmetically, to Common, tagmasked"

CMACOT field_address, length

computes the difference between the Common Register value and the field value in each word, then forms the absolute values of these differences, and finally searches for the minimum. The time is 7b+constant.

The search for minimum Hamming distance,

CMHCOT field_address, length, counter_length

proceeds by first forming the exclusive OR between the Common Register value and the field value, then counting the number of ones in each of these results, and finally searching for the minimum value among the counts. The first phase takes 2b+constant time, the second takes 2bc+constant, where c is the counter length. (A counter field is used in each word. The time can be reduced because, initially, the full counter length is not needed). The third phase is the search for minimum, which takes 3c+5 clock cycles. In total 2b+3c+2bc+constant time is used for the operation.


## 3.3.4 A More Complex Search

As an example of a more complex search instruction, we consider the following:

The maximum value in a matrix stored one row per memory word is formed by the instruction

MAXMAT matrix start address, no. of columns, data length.

The execution of this instruction proceeds in the following way:

> Find the maximum element of the first column.
>
> Move this value to that field of the Common Register that has the same address as the second column.
>
> Search for a greater element in this column.
>
> If there is one, move its value to that field of the Common Register that has the same address as the third column, else move the old value to this place.
>
> etc.

At the end of this procedure, a field of the Common Register contains the maximum value. A bit slice in the Associative Array and a register in the Address Processor are constantly updated to keep track of where the maximum value so far is to be found.

## 3.4 ARITHMETIC INSTRUCTIONS

In this section we describe how basic instructions for addition, subtraction and multiplication are implemented on LUCAS.

### 3.4.1 Addition and Subtraction

The instruction "Add fields, tagmasked"

ADDFT source1, source2, destination, length

adds the contents of one source field to another, writing the result in the destination field. The implementation is a repetition of the following three ALU instructions (see Appendix 1), constantly incrementing the address pointers.

```
LRMA(source1)
ADMA(source2)
WRRT(destination)
```

Putting the length in the Loopcounter of the Address Processor makes it possible to perform the loop counting and test without overhead. The total time for the instruction is 3b+8. This means that 128 pairs of 8-bit numbers are added in 6.4 microseconds, using a 5 MHz clock. The microprogram can be studied as an example in Chapter 5.

The implementation of the subtract-fields instruction

SUBFT source1, source2, dest, length

which subtracts source field 2 from source field 1, differs from the above only in that, instead of ADMA, the ADMIA function of the ALU is used, and that the carry register is set before starting. This realizes a subtraction according to the two's complement method.

Addition of a constant to a field, with the constant stored in the Common Register, is done with the instruction "Add Common to field, tagmasked"

ADCOFT source, destination, length

This takes shorter time, because bits from both arguments can be input to the ALU simultaneously. The ALU function used is ACMA, and the execution time is 2b+6 cycles.

Subtraction of a constant or subtraction from a constant are made in a similar way, using the ALU functions ACIMA and ACMIA, respectively.


### 3.4.2 Multiplication

### 3.4.2.1 Multiplication of Two Fields

Multiplication of two fields of two's complement numbers

MULFA  source1,  source2,  destination,  length

is implemented using Robertson's algorithm in the following way. (The microprogram is given in Chapter 5). A product field of twice the length of the source fields, minus one, is used. The bits of the multiplier in the source2 field are scanned from right to left and put in the Tags. For each bit, the multiplicand in the source1 field is added to the proper positions of the product field, but only in those words where the Tag = 1. The sign bit in two's complement numbers actually has weight = -1. Therefore, the final step is a subtraction in words with the sign bit equal to one.

The execution time is the following (b is the length of the operands):

Step 1 : Loading the multiplicand, adjusted to the right, into the product field, but only in those words where the rightmost bit of the multiplier is '1'. Double sign bit is used.
Time : 3b+3 cycles.

Step 2 : Clearing of the rest of the product field.
Time : b-2 cycles.

Step 3 : Repeated conditional addition of the multiplicand to the product field.
Time : $(b-2)(3(b+1)+8) = 3b^2+5b-22$ cycles.

Step 4 : Conditional subtraction based on the sign bit of the multiplier.
Time : 3b+12 cycles.

Total time : $3b^2+12b-9$ cycles.

As an example, b=8 gives 279 cycles, or 55.8 microseconds.


### 3.4.2.2 Multiplication of a Field by a Constant

Multiplication of a field by a constant has a shorter execution time. The reason is that the number of additions can be reduced; only when the multiplier contains a '1' at the current position, an addition has to be made.

When multiplying by a constant, the constant may be put either in the Mask Register or in a Memory Module of the Processor Array. Both can be scanned by the Control Unit and the bits tested for zero or non-zero value. When a bit of a constant stored in the array is to be tested, a selector is used to point out the word, the bit is loaded to the Tag register, and the SOME-line is interrogated.

The average time for multiplication by scalar will be half the time for multiplication of fields.

A further reduction of the number of add-type operations can be achieved if the multiplier is recoded into a form that has fewer non-zero bits. The signed-digit (SD) code is such a form [Hwang79]. In an SD number, the allowed digit set is ( 1 ,0,1), where 1 stands for -1. The weights of digits are the usual powers of two.

The SD code of a number is not unique. For example, the decimal number 7 can be coded into a 5-digit SD vector in three different ways: 00111, 0100 1 , and 1 1 00 1 . One of these has a minimal number of non-zero digits, but in general not even the minimal form is unique.

A minimal SD vector that contains no adjacent non-zero digits is called a canonical signed-digit (CSD) vector . Such a vector can be obtained by the following procedure (Figure 3.8):

Starting at the least significant bit, replace sequences of m '1's, where m > 1, by m-1 '0's preceded by a ' 1 ' and succeeded by a '1'.

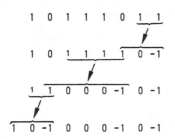

Figure 3.8 Recoding a number to canonical signed digit code

By the following method, we can arrive at a microprogram to convert a vector stored in a field of the associative memory to CSD form :

The procedure described above is realized by an automaton scanning the bits of B from right to left and with the state transition graph shown in Figure 3.9.

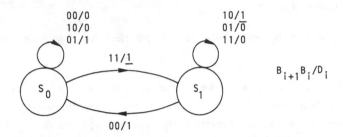

Figure 3.9 State transition graph for bit serial recoder

$s_0$ is the initial state. As long as $B_i=0$ we stay in $s_0$, outputting $D_i=0$. When a single '1' is found, $D_i=1$ is output. When $B_{i+1}=B_i=1$ is encountered, $D_i= \underline{1}$ is output and the state is changed. As long as $B_i=1$ we stay in $s_1$, outputting $D_i=1$. $B_i=0$, $B_{i+1}=1$ will cause us to output $\underline{1}$ , still staying in $s_1$. Only if two consecutive '0's are found will we return to $s_0$, outputting a '1'.

Coding $s_0$ as q=0 and $s_1$ as q=1 gives the following next-state function $q^+$:

$$q^+ = qB_{i+1} \vee qB_i \vee B_{i+1}B_i$$

The output is three-valued. We choose the following code:

|        | $u_1$ | $u_2$ |
|--------|-------|-------|
| 0      | -     | 0     |
| 1      | 0     | 1     |
| $\underline{1}$ | 1 | 1 |

This gives the expressions

$$u_1 = q^+$$

$u_2 = q + B_i$ , where + is add modulus 2

If we equip the ALUs with functions that suit these expressions exactly, the conversion can be made at maximum speed, which is three cycles per bit-slice (one read and two writes). If we want to use the standard ALU function set, 6 cycles per bit-slice will be needed. The state is held in both the R and C registers. The following sequence of functions implements the above functions (j and j+1 are the bits written into when bit no. i is scanned):

Contents of registers

| C | R |
|---|---|

| | | |
|---|---|---|
| | $q$ | $q$ |
| XORRMA, address i | | $q+B_i$ |
| WRRA, address j | | |
| LRMA, address i | | $B_i$ |
| ADMA, address i+1 | $q^+ (=u_1)$ | |
| LRCA | | $q^+ (=u_1)$ |
| WRRA, address j+1, incr j, loop | | |

The relevance of doing the conversion to CSD form in the Processor Array will be seen in Chapter 7, where matrix multiplication is described. During the execution of the algorithm, each element of one of the matrices is to be used as a multiplier once. Therefore it is convenient to do the conversion to CSD form of an entire column simultaneously. This is probably a rule for data produced in the array: if one item is going to serve as a multiplier, many items are.

Using a CSD coded multiplier, the number of add-type operations (additions and subtractions) in a multiplication will on the average be $b/3$, where b is the length of the multiplier [Hwang79]. Therefore, the average time for multiplication by a CSD coded scalar will be one third of the time for multiplication of fields. For example, 8-bit multiplication takes on the average 19 microseconds, with a 5 MHz clock.

In Chapter 10 we will describe the design of a new processing element that includes a multiplier, resulting in a multiplication time that grows only linearly with the data length.

## 3.5 SUMMARY OF EXECUTION TIMES

Table 3.1 gives a summary of execution times of basic operations that we have dealt with in this chapter. To be able to compare the speed of the 128-PE LUCAS with the speed of a sequential computer we have also calculated the time in which a sequential computer is required to perform the same operation on one data item, or on a pair of data items, depending on the instruction type. We call this time the "Equivalent Sequential Time per operation", or EST. It is given in nanoseconds.

For example, if a sequential computer is to have the same performance as LUCAS running with a 5 MHz clock, it must be able to add two 8-bit numbers in 50 ns, including data fetch and storage, addressing and loop counting.

| | 8-bit data | | 16-bit data | |
|---|---|---|---|---|
| | Micro-seconds | EST | Micro-seconds | EST |
| **MOVES AND MERGES** | | | | |
| Load Outdata (8-bit only) | 2.2 | 17 | | |
| Move field | 4.4 | 34 | 7.6 | 59 |
| Broadcast field | 4.8 | 38 | 9.6 | 75 |
| Merge fields | 6.0 | 47 | 10.8 | 84 |
| **SEARCHES AND COMPARES** | | | | |
| Maximum of field | 5.8 | 45 | 10.6 | 83 |
| Compare fields | 4.4 | 34 | 7.6 | 59 |
| Field greater than field | 4.6 | 36 | 7.8 | 61 |
| Compare field to Common | 2.4 | 19 | 4.0 | 31 |
| Field greater than Common | 2.4 | 19 | 4.0 | 31 |
| **ARITHMETIC** | | | | |
| Add (Sub) fields | 6.4 | 50 | 11.2 | 88 |
| Add Common to field | 4.4 | 34 | 7.6 | 59 |
| Multiply fields | 56 | 436 | 190 | 1484 |
| Multiply field by Common (aver.) | 28 | 219 | 95 | 742 |
| Multiply field by CSD-coded Common (average) | 19 | 145 | 63 | 492 |

Table 3.1 Execution times for some basic instructions on LUCAS running with 5 MHz clock frequency. EST is the Equivalent Sequential Time per operation

# Chapter 4

# COMPARISON WITH RELATED DESIGNS

The interest in associative computing started in the fifties and has been steadily increasing. Surveys on the topic can be found in [Thurber75, Thurber76, Yau and Feng 77, Parhami73, and Hwang and Briggs 84]. Numerous proposals for the design of associative computers have been made, yet only a few real machines have been built and actually used. Many application areas for associative computers have been identified, but so far the lack of cost efficiency has limited their use. This situation is now changing, due to the development in semiconductor technology. A few machines with characteristics similar to those of LUCAS have been built. We will briefly review the main features of six such designs and compare them to LUCAS. Two of the machines have been implemented in a university environment (Vastor and CLIP4). Three of them (STARAN, DAP and PROPAL 2) are commercial products, but very few copies of them have been built. MPP finally, is built by industry for dedicated use by NASA. STARAN, DAP, PROPAL 2 and Vastor can be considered as being general purpose processor arrays, whereas CLIP4 and MPP are designed exclusively for image processing.

## 4.1 STARAN

STARAN [Batcher74] from Goodyear Aerospace Corporation was the first bit-serial processor array to be built. The first machine was demonstrated in 1972. It was built from standard off-the-shelf integrated circuits.

An array in STARAN consists of 256 Processing Elements. Several arrays can be used together. Each Processing Element has three flip-flops. Any Boolean function of one bit from the memory and one bit from either of the flip-flops can be performed. The memory words are 256 bits long, in later versions extended up to 9 kbits.

A key element of the STARAN computer is the multidimensional access (MDA) store [Batcher77]. Elements of data are scrambled in a certain way as they are written into memory so that data can be accessed in different directions. For example, a 256 bit word or a 256 bit slice are accessed equally easy. This is achieved by an ingenious scheme that always puts two bits of the same word in different memory chips and at different addresses. Therefore, modifications of the bit-addresses to each memory chip, and passing of data through a so called Flip network, are needed.

The Flip network also accounts for the routing of data between Processing Elements (see Section 1.4.2). It has many characteristics in common with the perfect shuffle/exchange network implemented on LUCAS. The STARAN network is of multistage type, whereas LUCAS uses a single-stage network. Individual box control, as discussed in Section 1.4.2 is difficult to achieve on STARAN but can be programmed on LUCAS as shown in Section 3.2.3.

Input/output takes place over a 32-bit wide data bus. The Flip network allows different subsets of the PEs to be reached in one I/O operation. Also, the MDA store allows the 32 bits to be stored in parallel in one word. A provision is made also for 256 bit parallel input/output, but this requires special purpose peripheral configurations.

In conclusion, STARAN and LUCAS have many features in common. The STARAN architecture had great influence on the design of LUCAS.

## 4.2 DAP

The Distributed Array Processor - DAP - [Reddaway79] was developed by the ICL company in England. The first experimental model was operable in 1976. The first customer model was delivered to London University in 1980.

The pilot DAP has 1024 PEs arranged in a 32 x 32 array. The customer model has 4096 PEs in a 64 x 64 configuration. Each PE can communicate with its nearest neighbours in the North, South, East and West directions.

The PEs comprise three one-bit registers: Activity, Carry and Result registers. Associated with each PE is a 4 kbit memory module. All memory modules receive the same bit address; no address modification and permutation of data, as in STARAN, is done.

For the purpose of input/output and data broadcasting, "highways" in the vertical and horizontal directions are used. The width of a highway is the same as the side of the processor array, thus allowing a PE to send data to all PEs in the same row or in the same column. Thus, DAP allows 32-bit wide I/O transfer in the pilot version and 64-bit wide transfer in the customer version.

A special feature with DAP is that the totality of memory modules forms a standard memory module of the Host computer. This is in a way similar to the LUCAS arrangement in which any 8-bit slice of the memory can be mapped into the address space of the Master computer via the I/O registers. However, data is accessed in entirely different ways. While on LUCAS an 8-bit portion of each memory word is accessed at a time, on DAP a 32-bit slice over a row or column of the PE is available.

The difference lies in the fact that with LUCAS the Host accesses the I/O data registers which are the medium for data format conversion. With DAP the PEs are accessed directly.

## 4.3 PROPAL 2

PROPAL 2 [Cimsa79] is a processor array computer designed and marketed by the French company CIMSA. The number of processors can be between 8 (one board) and 2048 (8 racks of 32 boards), arranged with one-dimensional connectivity. A "condition" flip-flop is included in each PE together with a 16-bit work register. A Boolean one-bit arithmetic/logic unit takes one bit from the work register and the other bit from either the condition flip-flop, the associated 256-bit memory word or a parallel input. An 8-bit shift register is included which speeds up multiplication by holding the partial products.

The work registers play an important role in interprocessor communication. The contents of a register can be transferred in parallel to the neighbouring PE above or below. End-around connectivity can be used between the top and bottom PEs under control of the Host.

Input and output can be performed in two ways: One is through the ensemble of work registers which acts as a 16-bit wide shift register. During the shifting, processing in the PEs is suspended. The other I/O method uses a one-bit input line of each PE. Thus, the parallelism of this path can be extremely large.

PROPAL 2 is controlled by a microprogrammable minicomputer. The microinstruction word is divided into two halves of 48 bits each. One is used to control the minicomputer itself, the other controls the parallel processor.

## 4.4 Vastor

Unlike all other systems surveyed in this section, the Vastor computer [Loucks et al.82] designed at the University of Toronto, uses a standard, off-the-shelf processing element - the Motorola MC14500B, which is marketed as a control unit for industrial applications.

The number of PEs is 256. Each PE has a 1024 bit memory word and all memory words receive the same bit address.

A shift register with one bit per PE is the medium used for interword communication and input/output. Passing data between PEs takes considerable time unless mere shifting is required. The conversion from byte oriented to bit-slice oriented data necessary at input can be done by the shift registers, but only in every 8th word at a time. This makes input/output quite complicated.

The size and cost of Vastor are about the same as of LUCAS. All other machines that we consider represent much larger implementational efforts. In the case of Vastor, 16 boards are used and a component cost of $2000 is reported for a full 256 PE system. (Only 16 PEs have actually been implemented).

Performance results reported for Vastor indicate that LUCAS is about 10 times faster on operations that do not require inter-PE communication and more than a hundred times faster on tasks that require such communication.

## 4.5 CLIP4

CLIP4 [Duff79] is one system in a series of processor arrays which have been constructed at University College, London. It is exclusively aimed at image processing. 9216 PEs are arranged as a 96 x 96 array. Each PE communicates with eight neighbours, four of which are diagonal.

32 bits of memory are associated with each PE, which is much less than any other processor that we consider. The PEs contain three one-bit registers each. Two independent Boolean functions of two inputs each can be performed simultaneously.

## 4.6 MPP

The Goodyear Areospace Corporation, who designed and marketed STARAN, was contracted by NASA in 1979 to build a "massively parallel processor", MPP [Batcher82], for the processing of satellite images. It has an architecture similar to DAP with 128 x 128 processing elements connected in a two-dimensional arrangement.

Each PE has associated a 1 kbit memory word. The PEs are slightly more powerful than the DAP PEs. Each one contains five one-bit registers, a full adder and a two-input Boolean logic unit. Furthermore, a variable-length shift register is included to speed up multiplication.

An additional one-bit register, S, used exclusively for data routing, is included in each PE. When inputing data (i.e. images), 128 bits are input in parallel at one edge of the array and stored in the S-registers. Data is shifted from column to column of S-registers until, finally, the whole image is stored in the S-registers. Then the processing is interrupted and the input data stored in the memories. Input and output can proceed simultaneously so that an input image is shifted in at one edge while at the same time an output image is shifted out at the opposite edge.

The PEs of MPP can be said to be connected in two different ways: For processing a two-dimensional connection is used, whereas for input/output the PEs are connected as 128 separate 128-bit shift registers.

## 4.7 CONCLUSION

The machines surveyed share one important property: they all comprise a large amount of bit-serially working processing elements. It is probably not the case that limited budgets and technological limitations are the main reasons for this, but rather an understanding of the generality of the bit-serial approach. The processing elements of all the designs are in fact rather similar, although some of them are slightly more powerful than the others. The processing elements of LUCAS fall somewhere near the middle of the scale.

The differences between the various designs mainly concern the interconnection arrangement and the input/output structure. This mirrors the fact that the designers have had different application areas in mind for the different machines. Machines primarily intended for image processing typically use a two-dimensional interconnection network and fast input/output, while machines designed for general purpose show other, sometimes more elaborate, schemes for communication.

As for PE interconnection, LUCAS is most similar to STARAN, which is the only design that uses a network akin to the perfect shuffle/exchange network. However, LUCAS does not have the complicated memory storage method that STARAN utilizes. The input/output system is also quite different.

LUCAS is similar to DAP and MPP in the simplicity of data storage but different with regard to interconnection and input/output.

The size and cost of LUCAS are like those of Vastor. All other machines are larger and more expensive.

# Part 2.
# PROGRAMMING

All applications programs on LUCAS are divided into two parts: one part which is executed sequentially in the Master Processor and one part which executes in parallel on data located in the Associative Array. The parallel part consists of microprograms for the Control Unit of LUCAS. The sequential part, which may be written either in assembly language or in high-level language, takes care of scalar processing and external I/O. In addition to this, the Master program is also responsible for providing the instructions to the Control Unit. Input and output of data to and from the Associative Array involves both the Master Processor and the Control Unit: the Master loads or reads the PE I/O Registers and the Control Unit executes microprograms for moving data between the PE memories and the I/O Registers.

LUCAS has four programming levels with different support tools:

| PROGRAMMING LEVEL | BASIC SUPPORT TOOL | ELABORATE SUPPORT TOOL | OTHER TOOL |
|---|---|---|---|
| HIGH-LEVEL LANGUAGE | Procedure Library | Pascal/L | |
| MACHINE CODE | Macro Library | | File Handler |
| MICRO CODE | Micro Program Assembler | LUCAS Micro Programming Language | Microprogram Debugger |
| PICO CODE | Table Generator | | |

The lowest level, "picocode", is used to define the instruction set of the PE ALUs. These are implemented as programmable read-only memories (PROM), which allows a change in the instruction set in order to tune LUCAS to a certain application. A table generator has been developed, which takes Boolean expressions of the inputs to the ALU and produces the PROM contents in the form of a binary hex file. The file format is a standard format accepted by most PROM programmers. The current instruction set, which is of general purpose type and supports both arithmetic and Boolean operations, is listed in Appendix 1.

Microprogramming is supported by several tools:

* Microprogram assembler

* High-level like language for microprogramming

* Microprogram debugger

The microprogram assembler was developed at an early stage of the design phase, when it proved to be an important tool for debugging and testing the hardware. It is implemented in the form of a macro definition library to a commercially available macro processor (MAC from Digital Research) and runs on the Master system.

A high-level like language has been designed for microprogramming LUCAS. It allows microprograms to be written on an "algorithmic level", which means that the programmer does not need to deal with low level hardware control (enabling buffers, waiting for signals to propagate through the system etc.). It uses a control structure which is similar to high-level languages (if-then-else, while etc.). An optimizing compiler produces microcode of approximately the same quality as hand coded microcode.

A Microprogram Debugger allows microprograms to run at full speed on LUCAS with a breakpoint facility. The contents of both the Microprogram Memory and of the Associative Memory may be displayed, changed, loaded from or written to disk. The program has four functional modules:

* Microprogram Memory Monitor. This module allows microprograms to be loaded from disk, the contents of the microprogram memory to be displayed in symbolic form (microprogram disassembler) and the contents of the microprogram memory to be changed using symbolic notation (microprogram line assembler).

* Execution Monitor. This module allows the user to load the Parameter Registers and start a microprogram. A breakpoint may be inserted in which case the microprogram runs at full speed up to this point, where the execution is halted.

* Associative Array Monitor. The contents of the PE memories and of the Common and the Mask Registers may be displayed and updated using several different formats (hexadecimal, ASCII characters, integers or fixed point numbers). The PE registers may be inspected and an area of the Associative Array may be stored on disk or loaded from disk. The PE memory contents may be output to a graphical display processor, resulting in a "pixel mapped" image on the TV screen of the display unit.

* Communication Module. Allows transparent communication with the data communication network at the University of Lund, LUNET. The microprogram compiler runs on a VAX 11/780 which is connected to LUNET. The communication module allows microprograms to be developed on the VAX and transferred directly to the microprogram memory of LUCAS.

For machine level programming a collection of standard microprograms, which can be used to implement the parallel part of most programs, has been developed. These instructions constitute the standard software interface between the Control Unit and the Master Processor. Assembly programs are written in the assembly language for the Master. A macro library defines constants and macros, which are used to communicate with the Control Unit. The instructions to LUCAS have the following general format:

INSTRUCTION, P1, P2,P3, P4

INSTRUCTION is the instruction name and the $P_i$s are the optional parameters, which serve as operand descriptors to the instruction. The meaning of the parameters is standardized as follows:

| | |
|---|---|
| P1 | gives the location of the first source operand |
| P2 | gives the location of the second source operand |
| P3 | gives the location of the destination |
| P4 | specifies the length of the operand(s) |

A File Handler is defined as a collection of subroutines which can be linked to user programs. This provides a file handling capacity for the Associative Array.

In order to use LUCAS in a high-level language environment, a procedure library has been defined which constitutes a high-level software interface to a Pascal system, which runs on the Master. Since the interaction between LUCAS and the Master is extremely simple, the interface, which is written in assembly code, could be kept small (less than 1K bytes).

This approach allows programs written in a high-level language to interact with LUCAS without too much effort needed for the implementation. Once the basic structure, such as the memory allocation scheme for the Associative Array, is decided, new procedures can easily be added when new microprograms are written. However, the approach results in a performance reduction for various reasons. Memory allocation is done at run time instead of at compile time and every instruction which is sent to LUCAS results in Pascal procedures being called. Also, error checking is minimal and operations on field variables can not be described in the form of expressions.

To overcome these deficiencies, a high-level language has been developed for LUCAS. This language, which is an extension to Pascal, is described in Chapter 6.

# Chapter 5

# LUCAS MICROPROGRAMMING LANGUAGE

## 5.1 INTRODUCTION

LUCAS is used in applications where its capabilities of processing structured data in parallel can be utilized to obtain a significant increase in processing speed over a standard minicomputer. The bit-serial nature of the computations performed by LUCAS is both convenient and efficient for processing low-precision data, which is the case in for example image and database processing. However, it is extremely sensitive to inefficiencies in the implementation of the bit-serial algorithms. The innermost loops are often very tight, typically 2-5 machine cycles, and one or two unnecessary instructions in the loops have a tremendous impact on the processing speed. This means that most users will be forced to write some parts of their programs in microcode.

Disadvantages of programming in microcode are well known, and not specific for LUCAS. The programmer must be very well acquaintanced with the underlying architecture of the machine and take into consideration all peculiarities with for example timing and pipelining. If microprogramming is horizontal (as in LUCAS) it is possible to let microoperations, which control different parts of the machine, overlap and be executed simultaneously. Deciding which operations could overlap requires a detailed knowledge of the internal workings of the computer and optimal or near optimal solutions are very hard and time consuming to find. On the other hand, it is important to exploit this possible parallelism.

With an increasing number of microprogrammable computers appearing, the interest in microprogram development tools is growing. The use of high-level like languages for microprogramming is appealing. A language which incorporates typical high-level qualities, such as block structure, procedures and structured control statements of type "if-then-else" for selection and "while" for repetition, will support modern programming methods, which facilitate both development, maintenance and documentation of programs. Another important aspect is that the language compiler could be responsible for the tedious task of forming the complete microinstructions with optimal (or near optimal) overlapping between the microoperations. Such a language is not automatically machine independent but it is obvious that a unified approach to the design of languages of this kind could be adopted.

Current research in the area of microprogramming techniques has two directions: the design of suitable programming languages and the development of methods for optimizing the microcode.

The request for highly efficient microcode influences the definition of languages. Most designers agree that the firm demand for machine independent languages, which prevails in the area of high-level languages, is not applicable to microprogramming. Ramamoorthy and Tsuchiya formulate their point of view in [Ramamoorthy74]:

> "The desirable properties of a high-level microprogramming language must be a compromise between machine dependency, ease of detection and representing explicit and implicit parallelism, and the innate ´naturalness´ required of all programming languages to establish effective man-machine communications."

It deserves to be mentioned that the essential point in the argument for machine independence of high-level languages, is that programs should be transportable between different computers. It is reasonable to assume that the need for this, in the context of microprogramming, is very small. Therefore, it is less important if two microprogramming languages differ in their details. What is important is that they use similar basic constructs and that a unified machine independent methodology for their implementation is developed with machine independent techniques for compilation and optimization.

The MPG system [Baba and Hagiwara 81] is an example of a machine independent approach to high-level microprogramming. A program written in the language (MPGL) has two parts: a machine description (MDS) and an algorithm description (ADS). The MDS is used to initialize the compiler and to prepare it for translation of the ADS part, which consists of machine specific algorithms.

A similar technique has been proposed by DeWitt [DeWitt76]. His language includes "extension statements" and "extension operators" which allow the definition of new data types and operations. The core language includes a high-level like control structure, integers and primitive assignment statements. The result is similar to the MPG system: a program consists of a declaration part where the extensions are defined and an algorithm part which is machine dependent.

According to Dasgupta [Dasgupta80], a microprogramming language could be quite primitive and still be called high-level if it has certain machine- and implementation-independent characteristics, such as structured control constructs and a possibility to "describe and name, arbitrarily, microprogrammable data objects". His approach to machine independent microprogramming takes the form of a generic family of languages, called a schema . The schema includes all the possible constructs and data types that can be used when the schema is instantiated into a language for a particular machine.

This instantiation defines the specific properties of the machine in the form of declarations of the data objects which are available (registers, memories, stacks, flip-flops etc.) and specifications of the possible operations on these data objects. The schema includes several high-level control structures (if-then-else, case, while, repeat), a primitive data type, which is the bit, and five structured data types: sequence of bit, array, stack, record and associative memory.

The LUCAS microprogramming language, which will be presented in this chapter was defined with the following design objectives:

1) It should have a machine independent framework defining a general program structure which resembles that of high-level languages.

2) The machine dependent characteristics which are added should allow a change of the PE instruction set without the need to re-define the language and with minimal changes needed in the compiler.

3) The semantics of the language should be close enough to the machine to allow an efficient implementation, where the code produced is of the same quality as hand written microcode

The language has a structure where microprograms and subroutines they use are grouped together in modules. Variables and constants may be declared either on the module level or locally in the microprograms or the subroutines. The control constructs are of high-level type. The language allows microprograms to be written without dealing with low-level hardware control.

Experience from microprogramming in microprogram assembly code on LUCAS has shown that the part of the system which is the most difficult to program is the Control Unit, and especially the Address Processor will become a bottleneck if not properly handled. The use of local and global variables in the language, arithmetic expressions on variables and automatic handling of parameter passing to subroutines make the Address Processor disappear from the programmer's view.

In fact, no explicit programming of the Control Unit needs to be done at all, which means that the programmer deals with a much less complex architecture. This, together with the high-level like control constructs of the language, have resulted in a very powerful tool for microprogram development. The readability of programs is also very good, which simplifies the documentation.

## 5.2 MICROPROGRAMMER'S VIEW OF LUCAS

This section describes the architecture of LUCAS as seen by the microprogrammer when using the microprogramming language.  According to this view,  LUCAS consists of an array of 128 processing elements (PEs),  128 memory modules (PE memories),  a Common Register,  a Mask Register,  an I/O Buffer Register and an Interconnection Network (see Figure 5.1).  Processing of data is done in a bit-serial fashion by the PEs.

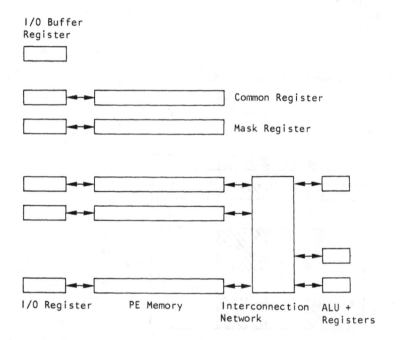

Figure 5.1 The Microprogrammer's view of LUCAS.

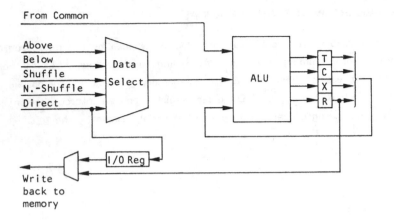

Figure 5.2 Processing Element (PE) in LUCAS.

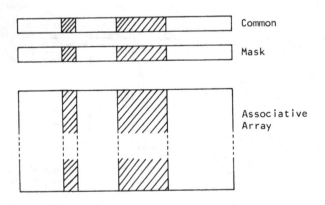

Figure 5.3 Bit-slice and field in the Associative Array.

A PE (see Figure 5.2) comprises an ALU, four one-bit registers, an eight-bit input/output register and a multiplexer for data selection. One of the registers, the Tag (T), is used to select the PE. When the Tag has the value ONE, the PE will execute every instruction it receives. If the Tag has the value ZERO, only instructions which are destinated for all the PEs will be executed and other instructions will be interpreted as no-ops by the PE.

All data paths are one bit wide. This means that only one bit of data is accessible at a time from the PE memories, the Common, the Mask and the I/O Registers. This is commonly referred to as a bit-slice of data. Every operation on data which is more than one bit wide, must be executed as a sequence of operations. Data of this kind, which is composed of a number of bit-slices, is called a field (see Figure 5.3).

Instructions to the PEs are of the following kind:

* Input/Output . (1) Write the I/O Register output value into the PE memory. (2) Shift the memory output value into the I/O Register. (3) Similar instructions for the Common and Mask I/O Registers.

* Register operations with data from PE memory . Instructions are executed in the ALU. Operands are the four one-bit registers and the memory output bit, which is connected to the ALU via the multiplexer (see Figure 5.2). The result of the operation is stored in the four registers.

* Register operations with data from Common . The same type of operations, leaving the result in the registers, but now the output from the Common Register is used as an additional operand.

* Memory write . The value of the R Register is written into the PE memory. The data does not pass through the Interconnection Network, so data is written into the corresponding PE memory.

* I/O Buffer Register operations . (1) Copy the value in the I/O Register of a selected PE into the I/O Buffer Register. (2) Broadcast the I/O Buffer Register contents to all the I/O Registers, including those of Common and Mask.

* Operations on the Tag Registers . Several of the operation types described above are affected by and affect the Tags. In addition to these, there are instructions to set all Tags (to ONE) and to reset all Tags except one.


## 5.3 INTRODUCTION TO THE LANGUAGE

The entire program text presented for compilation constitutes a compilation unit . The syntactical construct that represents the basic compilation unit, is the module . A module starts with a module heading and terminates with the keyword endmod . The body of the module has two parts, a declaration part and a submodule part .

An entity declared in the declaration part of a module is known, or visible within the module and may be referenced from any point following its declaration. Declared entities are of the following types:

    constants

    variables

    subroutines

The submodule part can take two forms. It can consist of one or several new modules, nested within the basic module, which is then called the global module , or it can be composed of a number of microprograms.

The microprograms are the only entities visible outside the compilation unit. A microprogram defines a machine level instruction for LUCAS and is invoked from the Master computer when it sends an instruction to LUCAS. Once a microprogram has started, it runs to completion without being interrupted. It terminates its execution with a microcode branch to a predefined location and LUCAS informs the Master that a new instruction may be sent. The only place inside a compilation unit where a microprogram is visible is in its own body - it can be explicitly aborted.

The concept of a subroutine differs from that of a microprogram in that the subroutine is visible inside the module where it has been declared, but not outside the compilation unit. A subroutine may be invoked from a microprogram, from another subroutine or recursively from itself.

Both microprograms and subroutines can have parameters and may declare local constants and variables. Figure 5.4 gives the syntax diagrams for the general structure of a compilation unit.

The scope of a declaration is defined as the part of the program text over which the declaration has an effect, i.e. where the name of the declared entity is known. Figure 5.5 illustrates the general scope rules of the language.

Compilation Unit

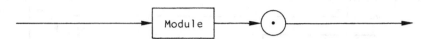

Module

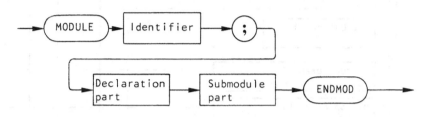

Declaration part

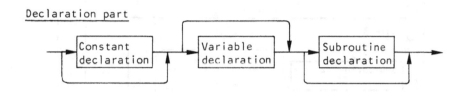

Submodule part

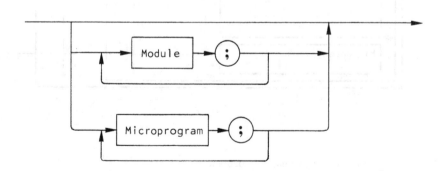

igure 5.4 The general structure of a compilation unit.

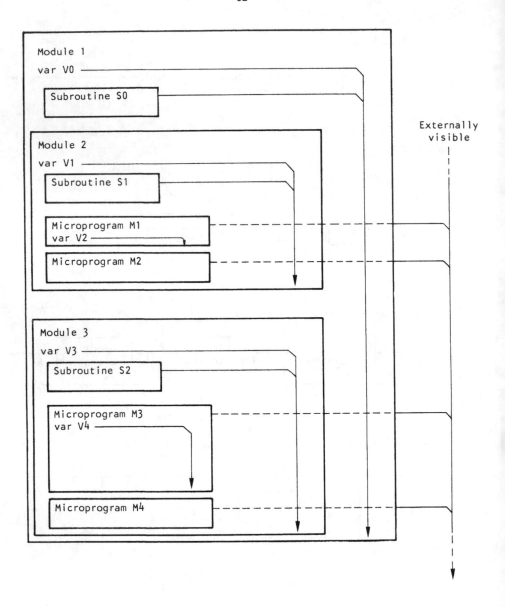

Figure 5.5 Scope rules in nested modules.

A slightly modified form of the Backus-Naur form (BNF) will be used to represent the syntax of the language. This notation has the following metasymbols:

$$< \qquad > \qquad ::= \qquad | \qquad / \qquad /^x$$

´<´ and ´>´ enclose non-terminals, ´::=´ should be interpreted as "means" or "can be rewritten as". ´I´ should be interpreted as "or". A pair of slashes, ´/´, is used to denote repetition of the enclosed symbols zero or more times. When the terminating slash is indexed, such as ´/$^x$´, the meaning is that the enclosed symbols may be repeated at most x times.

´<empty>´ denotes the empty string.

Programs are written in a free format with the "standard" lexical rules for identifiers, numbers, etc (Pascal-like notation). Comments are surrounded by curly brackets or bracket-asterix pairs: ´(*´ ´*)´.

## 5.4 LANGUAGE ELEMENTS

### 5.4.1 Constants

A constant is an identifier which is associated with an integer value at the time of its declaration. This identifier may later be used in the program text in place of the integer value it represents. The constant declaration has the following form:

<constant declaration> ::=
    <u>const</u> <identifier>=<sign><constant> /;<identifier>=<sign><constant>/;

<sign> ::= <empty> I -

<constant> ::= <number> I <constant identifier>

The association between the identifier and the value is valid throughout the module, unless the same identifier is redeclared in a module, subroutine or microprogram which is nested within the module where it was originally declared.

```
const   c1 = 100;
        c2 = 256;
```

### 5.4.2 Variables, Assignments

Declaration of variables is either implicit or explicit. Parameters to subroutines and microprograms (see Sections 5.4.3 and 5.4.4) are treated as locally declared variables within the body of the subroutine/microprogram. The format of the explicit variable declaration is:

<variable declaration> ::=
   var <identifier> /,<identifier>/ ;

A variable may be assigned values in the range 0 to 4095. The same rules of scope apply to variables as to constants.

```
var   v1,v2,v3;
```

A variable is used in the following contexts:

* **Pointer to data in the Associative Array** . The current value of the variable is used to indicate a bit-slice in the Associative Array.

* **Test variable in control constructs** . The value of the variable is tested in the condition part of the control statements.

A value assigned to a variable in one microprogram is valid in any other microprogram in the same module until either the variable is re-assigned or a microprogram of some other module is executed.

In the current implementation of the language, a maximum of sixteen variables may be visible at any point in the compilation unit. (This is due to the allocation scheme for the variables which are located in the registers of the Address Processor.) However, this restriction does not normally cause any problem if local variables are used whenever possible.

The assignment statement has the following general form:

<assignment> ::=
    <variable1> := <sign><constant> |
    <variable1>:=<variable2> |
    <variable1>:=<variable1> <operator> <constant> |
    <variable1>:=<variable1> <operator> <variable2>

<operator> ::= + | -

This means that a variable can be assigned:

* the value of a constant or number,  optionally negated.

* the value of any variable (including itself).

* its current value plus or minus a constant or a number.

* its current value plus or minus the value of any variable (including itself).

Variables can also be pushed onto or popped from a predefined stack by use of the standard procedures SPUSH and SPOP.

```
v1:=256;
v1:=v4;
v1:=v1+256;
v1:=v1+v2;
v1:=v1+v1;
SPUSH(v1);
SPOP(v4);
```

5.4.3 Subroutines

A subroutine declaration consists of a subroutine heading,  local declarations and an executable body.

```
<subroutine declaration> ::=
    <subroutine heading> <local declaration part> <statement part>

<subroutine heading> ::=
    subroutine <identifier>; I
    subroutine <identifier> ( <formal subroutine parameter list> );

<formal subroutine parameter list> ::=
    <identifier> /,<identifier>/

<local declaration part> ::=
    <empty> I <constant declaration> I <variable declaration> I
    <constant declaration> <variable declaration>

<statement part> ::=
    begin <statement list> end

<statement list> ::=
    <statement> /; <statement>/
```

The parameter passing convention is call-by-value. The identifiers which are (implicitly) declared in the formal parameter list of the subroutine heading are conceptually equivalent to local variables of the subroutine. They are initialized from the calling program part, whereas any additional local variables have undefined values when the execution of the subroutine starts.

The subroutine may be invoked from any executable part of the module where it is declared. Actual parameters can be variables, constants or numbers.

```
<subroutine call> ::=
    call <identifier> I call <identifier> ( <actual parameter list> )

<actual parameter list> ::=
    <actual parameter> /,<actual parameter>/

<actual parameter> ::=
    <variable identifier> I <sign><constant>
```

## 5.4.4 Microprograms

The declaration of a microprogram is similar to the subroutine declaration, only the heading is different.


<microprogram heading> ::=
   **microprogram** <identifier>; I
   **microprogram** <identifier> ( <formal microprogram parameter list> );

<formal microprogram parameter list> ::=
   <microprogram parameter> /,<microprogram parameter>/$^3$

<microprogram parameter> ::=
   <empty> I <identifier>

The formal parameter list includes a maximum of four parameters, separated by ´,´. A parameter which occurs in the list is implicitly declared as a local variable to the microprogram.

The difference between a subroutine and a microprogram lies in the invocation procedure. A subroutine is called from inside the module where it is declared, whereas no mechanism is defined in the language for calling a microprogram. Instead, microprograms are invoked from programs at another level: the machine code level of the Master processor.

The parameter passing is of call-by-value type; the Master initializes the parameter variables before the microprogram is started. The hardware interface between LUCAS and the Master allows at most four parameters to be passed through the Parameter Registers of the Control Unit. As seen in the formal definition of the parameter list, a parameter may be left blank, which denotes that no value is passed through the corresponding Parameter Register.

   Microprogram M1(p1,p2);

means that parameters are passed through Parameter Registers 1 and 2.

   Microprogram M2(p1,,,p2);

means that parameters are passed through Parameter Registers 1 and 4.

A microprogram terminates its execution by branching to a predefined routine, OPFETCH, which reads the next instruction coming from the Master and starts the corresponding microprogram.

Communication of values between two microprograms is possible via variables declared on the module level. If a microprogram needs more than four parameters, it is put in a module together with an auxiliary microprogram, which assigns its parameters to variables declared on the module level, as follows:

```
Module M1;
var par1,par2,par3,par4;

    Microprogram Loadparam(p1,p2,p3,p4);
        begin
            par1:=p1; par2:=p2; par3:=p3; par4:=p4
        end;

    Microprogram Mic(par5,par6,par7,par8);
        begin
            ... / If Loadparam has been executed,
            ... / par1 - par8 will be defined when Mic starts
        end;
endmod.
```

## 5.4.5 Statements I - Program Flow Control

### 5.4.5.1 General

The body of a subroutine or a microprogram contains executable statements which are grouped in a statement list. A statement list is a (possibly empty) list of statements separated by semicolons.

Two basic groups of statements are defined: those that specify operations on data in the Associative Array and those that control the execution flow. Statements can be of the form "compound statements" in which case a statement list, preceeded by the keyword begin and followed by the keyword end , replaces a single statement. Statements may also be empty.

In previous sections we have already come upon two kinds of statements: the assignment statement and the subroutine call. These will not be further discussed.

## 5.4.5.2 Conditions

Most of the constructs used for program flow control are conditional in that they specify two possible ways to proceed in the execution depending on the value of the condition part of the construct.  Conditions can take the values "true" or "false".


<condition> ::=
    <variable> <test> <variable> I <variable> <test> 0 I TRUE I FALSE I
    SOME I NONE I ZMASK(<address>) I NZMASK(<address>)


<test> ::= = I <>


<address> ::= <variable> I <constant>

The first two conditions test if two variables have the same value and if a variable has the value zero, respectively.  TRUE and FALSE are predefined conditions with the values "true" and "false".  SOME has the value "true" if at least one PE has its Tag Register set.  NONE is the complement of SOME.  ZMASK(address) is "true" if the Mask Register has the value zero in position address.  NZMASK is the complement of ZMASK.

(When comparing the possible test conditions in the language with the test conditions in the Control Unit,  as described in Chapter 2,  it is noted that the conditions which are generated in the Control Unit do not appear in the language.  However,  these conditons are implicitly tested by the control mechanisms of the language.)



## 5.4.5.3 If-Then-Else

The if-then-else construct is used to select one of two possible paths in the program flow.  In an abbreviated form of the construct,  the if-statement,  the else part is left empty.  It is possible to nest several if-then-else statements,  in which case each else should be associated with the most recently encountered then .

```
<if-then-else statement> ::=
    if <condition> then <statement> else <statement>

<if statement> ::=
    if <condition> then <statement>
```

5.4.5.4 Loop Constructs

The language has three loop constructs for specifying repetition of statements: while , repeat and iterate .

```
<while statement> ::=
    while <condition> do <statement>
```

Before each repetition of the statement part, the condition is evaluated. If it is "true", the statement will be executed. If it is "false", the loop terminates and the execution continues with the statement following the while construct.

```
<repeat statement> ::=
    repeat <statement list> until <condition>
```

The repeat statement is similar to the while statement. The difference is that the condition which is used to control the repetition, is tested at the end of the loop, not at the beginning as in the while statement.

A minor difference is that the construct specifies repetition of a list of statements rather than of one single statement. The keyword-pair repeat - until serves the additional purpose of statement brackets, replacing a begin - end pair.

In many cases, the number of times a loop should be repeated is known in advance. This is especially common in bit-serial processing, where the basic loops have to be executed a fixed number of times, depending on the precision of the operands. Using a while statement, such a loop has the following form:

```
        b:=noofbits;
        while b>0 do
        begin
            ...
            b:=b-1
        end;
```

We note that the loop control variable, b in the example above, is accessible within the loop, where it for example may be used as a pointer to data in the Associative Array. However, very often the loop control variable needs not be accessed in the loop since it is merely used to control the iteration. This kind of loop can be very efficiently implemented on LUCAS (by the use of special-purpose loopcounters).

A loop construct of this kind is defined in the language:


<iterate statement> ::=
    iterate <value> times <statement>

<value> ::= <variable identifier> I <constant>




5.4.5.5 Exit

An exit statement specifies a structured termination of a loop, a subroutine or a microprogram. Within a loop the exit statement will cause an immediate termination of the loop and execution will continue with the first statement following the loop structure. Exit from a subroutine means that the control is transferred to the calling program. The effect of an exit from a microprogram is a branch to the OPFETCH microprogram.


```
    iterate b times
    begin
        CMCT(direct,fielda);
        if NONE then exit;
        fielda:=fielda+1;
    end;
```


The example shows the innermost loop of a parallel search operation, where data from a field in the Associative Array is compared to the contents of the Common Register.

(The CMCT instruction compares the Common Register contents to the contents of the PE memory at bit address "fielda".) Normally the loop is executed b times, where b is the word length, but with the use of the exit statement, the execution of the loop is terminated when all Tags are false.

In the case of nested loops, a simple exit causes termination of the smallest loop enclosing the exit statement. However, any enclosing loop, subroutine or microprogram may be terminated by specifying its name in the exit statement. In the case of subroutines and microprograms, the name used is the name given in the declaration of the subroutine/microprogram. A loop structure may be given a local name by using a label, which preceeds the loop heading.

```
LOOPA: while b<>0 do
        begin
            ...
          repeat
              ...
            if b=0 then exit(LOOPA);
              ...
          until c=0;
            ...
        end;
```

## 5.4.6 Statements II - Array Operations

### 5.4.6.1 PE Instructions

The PE instructions embrace operations performed on the registers and on the memory in the Processing Elements. The instructions are of three kinds:

Without parameters. These instructions use the PE registers both as operands and to store the result.

With one parameter. These instructions use the PE registers as operands but store the result in the PE memory. The parameter specifies the PE memory address.

With two parameters. These are instructions where one of the operands comes from the interconnection network. The first parameter gives the PE memory address of the source bit. The second parameter specifies the permutation of data over the network.

The PE instruction set may be altered by reprogramming the ALU PROMs. The current instruction set is given in Appendix 2. The following are examples of PE instructions:

| | |
|---|---|
| LTRA | Load T from R in All PEs |
| LTRT | Load T from R Tagmasked (in selected PEs) |
| WRRA(adr) | Write R into the PE memories in All PEs at bit address "adr" |
| LRMA(adr,ABOVE) | Load R from Multiplexer in All PEs. ABOVE specifies that the data should come from the memory of the PE immediately above in the Associative Array. |

5.4.6.2 Input and Output

Input and output of data is physically handled by the I/O Registers, which are loaded either from the Master Processor, the I/O Processor or by microcode. The language includes instructions for this purpose.

Output of data is accomplished by shifting the I/O Registers while specifying the bit-slice address of data to be output.

        RSHIFT(address)
Normally one byte of data is output at a time, starting with the least significant bit.

```
Microprogram LDOA(location);
begin
    iterate 8 times
    begin
        RSHIFT(location);
        location:=location+1
    end;
end;
```

Input of data is handled in a similar fashion.

```
WRIA(address)
      or
WRIT(address)
```

WRIA causes the I/O Register output bit to be written into the memory of all PEs. WRIT is the tag-masked correspondence to WRIA. None of these instructions actually shifts the I/O Register. This must be carried out by means of the SHIFT instruction, which causes all the I/O Registers to be shifted right one step.

```
iterate 8 times
begin
    WRIT(location); SHIFT;
    location:=location+1;
end;
```

Note that input and output of data may be performed in one single loop. This will result in a more efficient code than if two separate loops are used.

```
iterate 8 times
begin
    WRIT(inadr);
    RSHIFT(outadr); /send data to the/
                    / I/O Register and shift/
    inadr:=inadr+1; outadr:=outadr+1;
end;
```

5.4.6.3 Common, Mask and I/O Buffer Operations

The Common Register and the Mask Register are both 4096 bit random access memories, similar to the PE memories. They receive the same bit address as the PEs. The output from the Common Register may be used as an operand in certain PE instructions and the Mask output is used in conditions (see Section 5.4.5.2).

Both the Common and the Mask Register communicate with a corresponding I/O Register. These I/O Registers are either loaded from the Master Processor, the I/O Processor or by microcode, exactly as the PE I/O Registers. Data is output to the I/O Registers with the same instruction that outputs data to the PE I/O Registers: RSHIFT(address). However, note that, since the data in the Common and Mask Registers is static, output of data is normally not meaningful.

Input of data is accomplished with the instructions

> WRCOM(address)
>> and
>
> WRMASK(address)

A write instruction does not shift the I/O Registers. This must be specified separately.

> iterate 8 times
> begin
>> WRCOM(location); SHIFT;
>> location:=location+1
>
> end;

The I/O Buffer Register provides a flexible communication link between PEs, between PEs and the Common and the Mask Registers, and also between PEs and the Master. It can be loaded either with the I/O Register contents of a selected PE or from the Master.

LDIOBS          LOAD I/O BUFFER SELECTED. Load the I/O Buffer Register from the I/O Register of a selected PE (must be uniquely selected).

IOBWRALL        Copy the I/O Buffer contents to all the I/O Registers.

Example Move one byte at location 'source' in the tag-selected PE to location 'destination' in every PE where the R Register is ONE.

```
Microprogram BroadcastSelected(source,destination);
begin
    iterate 8 times
    begin
        RSHIFT(source);
        source:=source+1;
    end;
    SELF;      (* Make selection unique *)
    LDIOBS; IOBWRALL;
    LTRA;      (* Load Tags from R *)
    iterate 8 times
    begin
        WRIT(destination); SHIFT;
        destination:=destination+1;
    end;
end;
```

## 5.5 PROGRAM EXAMPLES

The first example shows a microprogram for the operation MAXT - Maximum of Field Tag Masked - see Section 3.3.1.

```
Microprogram MAXT(Field,Length);
(* Parameter Field is address to most significant bit *)
begin
    iterate Length times
    begin
        CMOT(Field,DIRECT); (* old Tags -> X, Select ONEs from remaining *)
        if NONE then (* restore old Tags *)
                LTXA;
        Field:=Field-1;
    end;
end;
```

The next example is the Add Fields Tag Masked - ADDFT - operation from Section 3.4.1:

```
Microprogram ADDFT(Source1,Source2,Dest,Length);
begin
   CCA;  (* Clear the Carries *)
   iterate Length times
   begin
      LRMA(Source1,DIRECT);  (* Load source bit in R *)
      ADMA(Source2,DIRECT);  (* Add second source bit to R *)
      WRRT(Dest);              (* Write Dest Tag-masked *)
      Source1:=Source1+1; Source2:=Source2+1; Dest:=Dest+1;
   end;
end;
```

The next example shows a complete module with routines for 2′s complement multiplication of integer fields. The module contains the microprogram MULFA and two subroutines which implement addition and subtraction of fields of arbitrary length. The algorithm is described in Section 3.4.2. The steps in the description of the algorithm are indicated.

```
(**************************************************************)
(*
(*                 Module for field multiplication
(*
(**************************************************************)

Module FieldMult;

   Subroutine AddFieldsT(S1,S2,D,L);
   begin
      CCA;
      iterate L times
      begin
         LRMA(S1,DIRECT); ADMA(S2,DIRECT); WRRT(D);
         S1:=S1+1; S2:=S2+1; D:=D+1;
      end
   end;

   Subroutine SubFieldsT(S1,S2,D,L);
   begin
      SCA;
      iterate L times
      begin
         LRMA(S1,DIRECT); ADMIA(S2,DIRECT); WRRT(D);
         S1:=S1+1; S2:=S2+1; D:=D+1;
      end
   end;
```

```
Microprogram MULFA(Multiplicand,Multiplier,Destination,Length);
var D,M,K;
begin
                                                              (*STEP 1*)

    LTMA(Multiplier,DIRECT); Multiplier:=Multiplier+1;
    M:=Multiplicand; D:=Destination;
    (* First iteration needs no addition since part. prod.= 0 *)
    iterate Length times
    begin
        LRMA(M,DIRECT); ANDTRA; WRRA(D);
        M:=M+1; D:=D+1;
    end;
    WRRA(D); D:=D+1; (* double sign bits *)


                                                              (*STEP 2*)

    (* Clear rest of part. prod. field *)
    K:=Length-2;
    iterate K times
    begin
        WRRA(D); D:=D+1;
    end;


                                                              (*STEP 3*)

    (* Multiplication loop. Use double sign bits *)
    D:=Destination+1; Length:=Length+1;
    iterate K times
    begin
        LTMA(Multiplier,DIRECT); Multiplier:=Multiplier+1;
        call AddFieldsT(D,Multiplicand,D,Length); D:=D+1;
    end;


                                                              (*STEP 4*)

    LTMA(Multiplier,DIRECT);
    call SubFieldsT(D,Multiplicand,D,Length);
  end;

endmod.
```

## 5.6 MICROPROGRAM COMPILER

### 5.6.1 Introduction

The translation process for a microprogramming language resembles that of an ordinary high level language in many aspects and standard compilation techniques may be employed in several parts of the compiler. The main difference lies in the code generation scheme. The horizontal microinstruction format provides a potential for parallelism between the functional parts of the machine which must be utilized in order to assure maximum performance. A number of strategies for recognizing the parallelism in microprograms and several algorithms have been proposed for microcode optimization. The term compaction is most often used in this context, since the algorithms aim at a reduction in the size of the code without any claims of obtaining an optimal solution.

The compiler which has been developed for the LUCAS microprogramming language uses a compaction algorithm based on the First-Come First-Served algorithm [Dasgupta and Tartar76]. This algorithm has been modified to give a better performance and also to allow microoperations which execute during more than one machine cycle in pipelined operations.

The compiler has five phases: lexical analysis, syntax analysis, generation of intermediate code, code improvement and code assembly. The first three phases constitute the first compilation pass, i.e. when the compiler reads the source code file. The code improvement phase performs several passes over the intermediate code, which is scanned back and forth during this phase. The last phase is basically a two-pass assembler which produces the final microcode.

The presentation given here is a brief outline of the compiler. For further details the reader is referred to [Fernstrom83].

### 5.6.2 Intermediate Code

The first three phases use standard compilation techniques to produce the intermediate code. The intermediate code consists of a list of pseudo-microinstructions (PMIs). A PMI is similar to a microinstruction but with only a limited number of its fields defined. It controls the smallest meaningful activity in some part of the machine and consists of a microoperation (MO) together with its possible parameters (which are also microoperations). For example:

CJP ZAP 100     Conditional jump to address 100 on zero Address Processor status is a PMI which controls the Sequencer of LUCAS. It consists of the MO CJP, which is an instruction to the Sequencer, and its two parameters: the MO ZAP, which controls the Testmultiplexer and 100 which defines the value of the Sequencer's data field.

The following procedures are defined for the generation of intermediate code:

Gen         The single parameter of this procedure is the name of an MO. The procedure generates a new PMI containing this MO.

Join        Join is similar to Gen but places the MO in the last generated PMI.

Datajoin    This procedure has two parameters: the name of a microinstruction field and an integer value (number or variable). The referenced field of the last generated PMI is assigned the integer value.

Insert      This procedure is used to insert a PMI in the list of PMIs already created. It has two parameters: a pointer in the list and the name of an MO which will be put in the generated PMI. Subsequent calls to Join and Datajoin will operate on the inserted PMI.

Chain       Chain is used to "connect" a sequence of MOs when code for pipelined (= multicycle) operations is generated. During the code improvement phase the MOs are moved according to certain rules. Calling Chain assures that the last generated PMI and the next one produced will keep their consecutive order during code improvement.

The PMI in the example above (CJP ZAP 100) is generated by the following calls to the code generating procedures:

```
Gen(CJP);
Join(ZAP);
Datajoin(Sequencerdata,100);
```

All the variables of a compiled program are allocated in the sixteen internal registers of the Address Processor. Allocation is done when a variable is entered in the symbol table and it is thereafter never reallocated. This simple solution is possible since all the registers have exactly the same function.

When a subroutine is called, the compiler checks for overlapping in the allocation of registers between the calling and the called procedure. If such an overlap exists, the Address Processor stack is used to save the overlapping registers of the calling program.

The intermediate code is a symbolic form of the microcode and would, if processed by a microprogram assembler, produce executable but inefficient microcode.

The intermediate code is a doubly linked list of PMIs. This structure has been chosen to allow convenient insertion and deletion of the elements and also to allow scanning of the list in both directions. The final code which is presented to the microcode assembler (the last phase of the compiler) consists of a list of microinstructions (MIs). An MI is formed in the code improvement phase by merging PMIs according to certain rules.

## 5.6.3 Code Improvement

Two methods for improving the code are used. The first one preserves the order of all activities. If operation j preceeds operation k in the PMI list, either j still preceeds k in the resulting code or they are located in the same MI. We refer to this method as packing of the microcode. Packing is useful for debugging microprograms. The order of execution follows the order of operations in the source code and still a fairly efficient code is used as compared to executing the PMI list. A more efficient microcode is obtained if the reorganization of the intermediate code allows a change of the relative order between the PMIs. Such a scheme which guarantees that the resulting MI list is semantically equivalent to the original PMI list is called a code compaction .

The packing process starts with an initially empty MI list. Beginning with the first PMI, subsequent PMIs are merged into one single MI until a conflict occurs. The produced MI is appended to the MI list. Actually, packing can be performed during the first compilation pass, in which case no list of PMIs has to be created. The following is an outline of the packing algorithm:

```
generate empty MI;
EMIT:=false; CONFLICT:=false;
while PMI list not empty do
begin
    get next PMI from list;
    if PMI has label then CONFLICT:=true
    (* PMI is a branch target, so must be in new MI *)
    else
        if resource conflict between MI and PMI then CONFLICT:=true
        else
            if MI must execute before PMI then CONFLICT:=true
            else
                begin
                    add PMI to MI;
                    if PMI is a branch then EMIT:=true;
                    if PMI is part of a pipelined sequence of operations
                        with subsequent operations then EMIT:=true;
                end;
    if EMIT or CONFLICT then
    begin
        append MI to list;
        generate empty MI;
        if CONFLICT then add PMI to MI;
        EMIT:=false; CONFLICT:=false;
    end;
end (*while*)
if MI not empty then append MI to list;
```

MIs and PMIs are implemented as lists of sets. The sets define data dependencies, the resources needed, the fields of the microinstruction that are used, etc. When a new MI is generated its elements are empty sets. Adding new PMIs to the MI consists of forming the union between the sets of the MI and the PMI and to assign the resulting sets to the MI. The meaning of the two Boolean variables EMIT and CONFLICT is as follows: EMIT is set true when the last PMI was added to the MI but when a new MI must be generated for the next PMI. CONFLICT is set true when the last PMI could not be added to the MI.

Local code compaction deals with the compaction of basic blocks , where a basic block is defined as a sequence of consecutive operations (PMIs in our terminology) which may be entered only at the beginning and which is jump-free, except possibly at its end.

It has been shown [Landskov et al.80] that the problem of finding the optimal solution to the local compaction problem is NP complete. However, several non-optimal algorithms with less computational complexity have proved to be very useful in practice.

An important concept in the compaction process is the data dependency relation between the PMIs. Let i and j be two PMIs where i precede j in the original PMI list. If there is a data interaction between i and j, we say that j is data dependent on i. It is clear that the compaction algorithm must assure that the data dependency relations are kept intact when the MI list is produced.

The compaction algoritm in the compiler is based on the First-Come First-Served (FCFS) algorithm [Dasgupta and Tartar 76]. This algorithm is as follows:

1) The PMIs are added to an initially empty list of MIs. Every PMI is moved up as far as it can go in the list using the rule that a PMI can be moved ahead of an MI if it is not data dependent on any of the PMIs in that MI. When a data dependeny occurs, the PMI has reached its rise limit.

2) Search downwards in the list to find an MI where the PMI may be added with respect to resource conflicts (two PMIs need the same resource or occupy the same field in the microinstruction). If no such MI exists, a new MI containing the PMI is appended to the list.

3) If no rise limit was found in 1), the PMI was not data dependent on any PMI in the MI list and it may be added to any list element. If there is no MI to which the PMI can be added without a resource conflict, the PMI is placed in a new MI at the top of the list. Placing it at the top rather than at the bottom of the list will keep it from blocking any subsequent PMI due to a data dependency restriction.

Practical experiments [Davidson et al.81] have shown that the code obtained is of the same quality as the code produced by the other non-optimal algorithms. In addition, the FCFS algorithm has advantages in both speed and simplicity. Implementations of the algorithm are described in [Mezzalama et al.82, Baba and Hagiwara 81].

In the compiler we have extended the FCFS algorithm by introducing an additional pass. In this pass an attempt is made to push PMIs forward in the MI list as far as possible. If during this pass all the PMIs of an MI are removed, the MI is removed from the list.

Using this Extended FCFS (EFCFS) algorithm, the microcode obtained is often more compact than with the original FCFS and never less compact.

In addition to the EFCFS algorithm, other methods of a more heuristic nature are used for code improvement. The improvement techniques used give good results and optimal code is most often obtained.

# Chapter 6
## PASCAL/L - A HIGH-LEVEL
## LANGUAGE FOR LUCAS

## 6.1 INTRODUCTION

Highly parallel machines of type associative array computers are often programmed in assembly like languages. The reason is that machines of this kind tend to be unique and differ in several important aspects. For example:

* Number of processing elements. This reaches from 64 elements on ILLIAC IV [Barnes et al.68] to over 16,000 on the MPP [Batcher80].

* Complexity of the processing elements. On ILLIAC IV, the PEs are powerful pipelined processors, which perform floating point arithmetic in hardware. At the other end of the spectrum we find machines like STARAN [Batcher79], the MPP, DAP [Reddaway79] and LUCAS, which are all bit-serial processors.

* Interconnection Structure. The topology of the processing array is defined by the PE interconnection network. Examples of interconnection networks are the two-dimensional grid on ILLIAC IV, the Staran Flip network and the Perfect Shuffle/Exchange network on LUCAS.

Common to the languages for SIMD machines is the possibility to declare and to operate on distributed data, i.e. multi-element data where the single elements are located in different processing elements or in different words of an associative memory. However, we note that most of the languages, which have been proposed for highly parallel computers, are directed towards a specific machine. This reflects the fact that if a high level language is to be used, it must fit the architecture well to be efficient.

With the introduction of ILLIAC IV, the need for SIMD oriented high level languages arose. Several languages were proposed of which at least three were implemented and used: CFD [Stevens75] - based on FORTRAN, Glypnir [Lawrie74, Lawrie et al.75] - based on Algol 60 and IVTRAN [Millstein and Muntz 75] - based on FORTRAN.

The first language designed for the ILLIAC IV was TRANQUIL [Kuck68], which was specified at the same time as the design of the ILLIAC IV system. TRANQUIL is based on Algol 60, with some minor deletions, and includes extensions for parallel execution of statements and declaration of arrays that are stored over the PEs. Using its data declarations, it is possible to specify the layout of variables in the PE memories (STRAIGHT or SKEWED mapping). A PARTITION declaration is used to partition previously declared arrays in several ways and to form subarrays. Parallel execution of one (e.g. a for-loop) or several statements is specified by means of a SIM statement:

SIM BEGIN (S1; S2; ... Sn) END

The implementation of the language was never completed.

Glypnir was the first implemented language for ILLIAC IV. It is a less ambitious language than TRANQUIL, which supports a more general form of parallelism where arrays can be of any size and the compiler is responsible for "squeezing" them to fit the ILLIAC IV memory.

In contrast to this, all distributed data variables in Glypnir have 64 elements in its parallel dimension (ILLIAC IV has 64 processing elements), and it is the programmer's task to map smaller or larger arrays into this form.

Control statements are extended, as compared to Algol, in that they may also be used to control parallel execution. The statement:

IF <Boolean expression> THEN <Stmt-1> ELSE <Stmt-2>

results in Stmt-1 being executed in PEs where the corresponding elements of the Boolean expression are TRUE and Stmt-2 in the PEs where the elements are FALSE.

The Glypnir compiler is said to generate a relatively efficient code even though no optimization is included. A factor 1.5 to 3 in execution speed is reported as compared to assembly programming.

The ILLIAC IV IVTRAN system [Millstein and Muntz 75, Millstein73] is based on the following assumptions:

* The presumptive user is accustomed to programming in FORTRAN. The new language must be of FORTRAN type.

* It should be possible to use the system for existing programs, written in standard FORTRAN.

This resulted in a new language, defined in terms of parallel extensions to FORTRAN. In order to allow standard FORTRAN programs to be used, a pre-processor was added to the IVTRAN compiler, where parts of the source program, which could have been expressed in IVTRAN, are rewritten. This part of the complier, which is called the "Paralyzer" (Parallelism Analyser and Synthesizer) [Presberg and Johnson 75], produces an IVTRAN program from the FORTRAN source program. The form of the IVTRAN program is either source code (intended for the interested user) or - since the Paralyzer works on an intermediate form of the program which is produced by the parser - in a form suitable for the next compiler phase.

Parallel Pascal [Reeves et al.80, Reeves and Bruner 80, Reeves et al.81] is one of the languages which have been proposed for the MPP. The language is defined in terms of extensions to Pascal. As compared to standard Pascal, the new language is extended in several ways:

* Data can be declared as "parallel", which means that it should be located in the parallel processing array of the MPP.

* Expressions can be formed with parallel arrays.

* Several standard functions, which may be used with parallel arrays are included. These are defined for all sizes and shapes of arrays. Functions include Shift and Rotate of arrays any number of steps along one or several of its dimensions. Reduction functions, based on the primitive reduction functions in APL, are also included.

* To specify that an operation should be performed in a subset of the processing elements of the parallel processing array, Parallel Pascal extends the meaning of the if-then-else construct in a way similar to Glypnir.

As part of the Phoenix Project [Feierbach and Stevenson 78], a language called Actus has been defined [Perrott79]. The language, which is based on Pascal, is in many aspects similar to both Parallel Pascal and to Pascal/L. However it includes constructs, such as independent indexing in the processing elements, which could not be efficiently implemented neither on the MPP nor on LUCAS.

Special purpose languages have also been described for use in important application areas for associative array processors. Pixal [Levialdi et al.80] consists of parallel extensions to Algol 60 and is directed towards image processing. Its FRAME construct is used to specify an environment to each cell in the array upon which operations are performed.

Another language which is suitable for image processing is PascalPL [Uhr79]. It is defined in terms of extensions to Pascal. Parallel operations (instructions which are executed simultaneously by two or more processing elements) can be included inside procedures which are declared as parallel. A STRUCTURE specification, similar to the

FRAME construct in Pixal is defined.

A language which implements a very flexible indexing scheme is APLISP (A Parallel Language for Image and Speech Processing) [Mueller et al.80]. Here the parallel arrays are treated as sets and subsets are chosen by "index sets". Operations on the index sets, such as the Cartesian product, intersection or concatenation, allow a powerful indexing of the operands, including both alignment and "window specification" similar to the ones defined in Pixal and PascalPL.

Several languages for database processing on associative computers have also been proposed [Resnick and Larson 75, Bratsbergseugen et al.79, Love75].

## 6.2 OVERVIEW OF PASCAL/L

There are two different approaches to the design of a high-level language for a parallel computer. Either the parallelism of the computer has a correspondance in the syntax of the language and special constructs are used to express parallel operations on data, or the language does not contain any primitives for parallel processing, in which case the compiler is responsible for detecting inherent parallelism in programs that are written in a sequential language. Both have advantages and disadvantages.

In the second approach the user does not have to learn a new language. Existing programs can directly be moved to the parallel computer. Programs can be developed and tested on an ordinary sequential computer before they are transported to the parallel machine. The language is also independent of the parallel structure of any particular machine.

However, if the parallelism is not apparent in the language, the user will not be motivated to design algorithms which are suitable for parallel computation. A sequential language forces the programmer to transform an inherently parallel algorithm into sequential code. It is also unlikely that a completely sequential algorithm could be transformed to run efficiently on a parallel machine. Thus in the interest both of efficiency and understanding of parallel algorithms we have favoured a language where the parallelism is visible.

For several reasons It is preferable to use an existing sequential language as a base, when defining the new language:

* Sequential operations are indeed necessary and must be included in the language anyway.

* The implementation may be simplified in that existing compilers can be modified to accept the new language.

* The user needs to learn relatively few new concepts.

* The use of the language is not restricted to parallel algorithms and the same language can be used to program the entire system including compilers and operating system.

When designing a high-level language for LUCAS, several different languages were considered for the choice of a suitable sequential language. APL deals with parallel arrays of data in a very general way and many of the ideas in APL are relevant to parallel processing on an SIMD computer. However, the dynamic data structures in APL and the powerful operations on these would make it very difficult to achieve an efficient implementation. FORTRAN is currently the most used language in many of the applications where LUCAS may be used. On the other hand, its poor data structures makes it unsuitable for database processing, which is one of the pilot application areas for LUCAS.

Pascal is a well structured language with powerful control and data structures which makes it suitable for many different applications. It has strong typing of variables, and a large amount of error detection is possible both at compile time and at run time.

Compilers for Pascal are relatively uncomplicated to implement. The syntax has been chosen so that only one symbol lookahead is needed, enabling the use of simple parsing techniques. To facilitate the code generation and to allow compilers to be portable, an implementation scheme with code generation for a stack oriented virtual machine is used. The fact that portable compilers - written in Pascal - exist, simplifies the implementation on different machines.

We decided that the new language, Pascal/L(UCAS) [Fernstrom82], should be defined in terms of extensions to Pascal. The extensions are chosen so that the new language corresponds to the processing capabilities of LUCAS. This means that typical SIMD operations, where one instruction operates on several data items, can be specified. A characteristic property of associative processing is the ability to designate the part of data which will be subject to parallel computations in terms of properties of the data, regardless of where it is stored.

Since the use of LUCAS is restricted to algorithms which are well suited for the architecture, only constructs which can be efficiently implemented have been included. Floating point arithmetic, for example, is not included.

The following extensions to Pascal are defined:

* Declaration of variables that will be allocated to the Associative Array. In the following these will be referred to as "parallel variables", whereas "scalars" or "sequential variables" stand for variables which are located in the memory of the Master Processor.

* An indexing scheme to access parts of parallel variables.

* Expressions and assignments involving parallel variables.

* An extended control structure, allowing the use of parallel variables as control variables.

* Standard functions for data alignment, input and output of parallel variables.


## 6.3 LANGUAGE DESCRIPTION

### 6.3.1 Declaration of Data

The one-dimensional organization of the Associative Array makes it especially suited for operations on one- and two-dimensional arrays. In principle, arrays of any dimension could be represented in LUCAS, but the natural storing scheme where adjacent array elements also are physical neighbours, would be lost. Pascal/L is therefore restricted to arrays of one or two dimensions.

Parallel variables are characterized by their dimension and their range . The number of subscripts in the declaration defines the dimension of the variable. The range can be seen as a measure of parallelism and is given by the size of the first subscript.

There are two kinds of parallel variables: selectors and parallel arrays .


### 6.3.1.1 Selectors

A selector defines a Boolean vector over the Processing Elements and is intended to control the parallelism of operations. (At execution time this is accomplished by setting the Tags in those PEs where the corresponding selector element has the value TRUE.)

<selector type>  ::=
    selector[<range>] |
    selector[<range>] := (<Boolean aggregate>)

```
<range> ::=
    <constant>..<constant>

<Boolean aggregate> ::=
    <choice> => <Boolean value>

<choice> ::=
    <constant> | <constant>..<constant> |
    <constant>..<constant> step <constant>

<Boolean value> ::=
    true | false
```

We use the same form of BNF as in Chapter 5 to represent the syntax.

For example:

    var SEL : selector [0..99];

declares a selector with the range 0..99,  i.e.  a selector with elements in the first 100 PEs.

    var SEL : selector [0..99]:=(0..98 step 2 => true);

declares a selector with the range 0..99 where all the elements with even indices are initiated to the value TRUE and all others to the value FALSE.


6.3.1.2 Parallel Arrays

A parallel array consists of a fixed number of components which are all of the same type and which are located in the Associative Array of LUCAS.  Parallel arrays can be of one or two dimensions.  The size of the first subscript in the declaration is referred to as the range of the array.  It has the property that when the first index is incremented by one in an array reference,  while keeping a possible second index unchanged,  the new array component will be located in the PE whose index is one higher than the PE originally referenced,  but on the same address within the PE memory.  This means that for any fixed value of the second array index,  all components are located in a field of the Associative Array.  The definition implies that in a two-dimensional array all components of a row are located in the same PE,  while the components of a column are located in different PEs.

A component of a parallel array can be of any of the following types: signed integer, unsigned integer, fixed point number, Boolean, character or string. When declaring an array with components of any of the first three types, a precision is specified in the declaration. The precision gives the number of bits used in the computations in the case of integers, and the number of bits on each side of the 'fraction mark' (binary point) in the case of fixed point numbers. The maximum length of a string component (number of characters) is given in the declaration.

\<parallel array type\> ::=

    parallel array[\<range\>] of \<parallel type\> |

    parallel array[\<range\>,\<constant\>..\<constant\>]

                                    of \<parallel type\>

\<parallel type\> ::=

    \<parallel type identifier\> | \<parallel standard type\> |

    record \<parallel field list\> end

\<parallel type identifier\> ::=

    \<identifier\>

\<parallel standard type\> ::=

    integer(\<constant\>) | unsigned integer(\<constant\>) |

    fixed(\<constant\>.\<constant\>) | Boolean | char | string(\<constant\>)

\<parallel field list\> ::=

    \<parallel record section\> /;\<parallel record section\>/

\<parallel record section\> ::=

    \<field identifier\> /,\<field identifier\>/ : \<parallel standard type\>

\<field identifier\> ::=

    \<identifier\>

For example:

    var PARA : parallel array [0..99,0..2] of integer(32);

declares a two dimensional array, where the components are of type signed integer with a precision of 32 bits (including the sign bit). Components of the array are located in the first 100 PEs with 3 components in each PE.

```
var OBSERVATION : parallel array[1..64] of
                 record
                    SITE : string(20);
                    TEMP : fixed(8.4);
                 end;
```

declares a one dimensional array where each PE from 1 to 64 stores a record. Each record has two fields , the first is a string with a maximum of 20 characters, the second a fixed point number where the integer part has a precision of 8 bits (including the sign bit) and the fraction part a precision of 4 bits.

In correspondence with the Pascal terminology, the word 'field' is used to denote components of a record. We have already used the same word when referring to 'fields' in the Associative Array of LUCAS. However, this should cause no confusion since in a parallel array of record, a logical field always is allocated to a physical field in the Associative Array.


## 6.3.2 Indexing of Parallel Variables

Indexing of a variable of array type in Pascal is used to single out one component of the array. When operating on a parallel variable, Pascal/L makes it possible to reference several components along the parallel dimension at the same time. This set of elements is referred to as the referenced range of the variable, as compared to the declared range which is specified in the declaration of the variable.

The indexing scheme allows simultaneous access to a column or a subset of the column components of a two dimensional array, but not to any other part of the array, such as a row or a diagonal. The components of a row are all located in the same PE, which means that they must be sequentially processed. To access a diagonal, or any other part of the array where the components are located in different PEs - except a column - the PEs would have to include an index register to allow different addresses being used in different PEs.

Several ways of specifying the first index exist. If an entire column is referenced, this is denoted by a star '*' in the index position. A part of a column is referenced either by constant indices, in which case the referenced part is known at compile time, or by a selector expression. When a selector expression is used, the array components referenced are identified by the indices where the expression takes the value TRUE. A one-dimensional parallel array may be used without any index at all (and no brackets), in which case all components of the array are referenced.

```
<indexed parallel variable> ::=
    <parallel variable identifier> |
    <parallel variable identifier>[ <first index>] |
    <parallel variable identifier>[ <first index>,<expression>]


<parallel variable identifier> ::=
    <identifier>


<first index> ::=
    * | <constant> | <constant>..<constant> | <selector expression>
```

Examples:

| | |
|---|---|
| P0 | Select all the elements of the one-dimensional variable. |
| P1[*,0] | Select column 0 of P1.  P1 is a two-dimensional parallel variable. |
| P1[S,0] | Where S is a selector: select a subset of column 0 of P1 |
| P1[2..80,0] | Select a subset of column 0 of P1. |

## 6.3.3 Expressions and Assignments

It is possible to combine sequential and parallel variables in expressions as long as no type conflict occurs.  This means for example that it is allowed to form expressions where a scalar integer is combined with a parallel array of integers.

An expression,  which only contains sequential variables and constants results in a sequential value.  An expression,  which includes at least one parallel variable results in a parallel value,  unless the parallel variable(s) is used as a parameter to a function which returns a scalar result.

In the computation of a parallel expression,  all referenced ranges to parallel variables must be identical and any sequential value is parallelized to this range before evaluation of the expression.  This means that

    4+PARA[*]

results in 4 being added to all the components of PARA and

    4+PARA[2..5]

results in 4 being added to components 2,3,4 and 5 of PARA.

There are four kinds of assignment statements:

1) The left hand side and the right hand side are both scalars. This is the normal Pascal assignment statement

2) The left hand side is a parallel variable and the right hand side is a sequential expression. In this case all the components within the referenced range of the parallel variable are assigned the value of the scalar expression.

3) The left hand side is a sequential variable and the right hand side is a parallel expression. The referenced range of the parallel variables must be such that the value of the right hand side expression includes one single component.

4) The left hand side is a parallel variable and the right hand side is a parallel expression. The referenced components of the left hand side variable are assigned the corresponding elements of the right hand side expression. The range of the expression must be equal to, or overlap, the referenced range of the left hand side variable.

The following program exemplifies different kind of assignments.

```
Program Assign;
var ODD :    selector[0..127]:=(1..127 step 2 => true);
    EVEN,
    SEL :    selector[0..127];
    P1,P2 : parallel array[0..127] of integer(16);
    I :      integer;
begin
      ...
    EVEN:=not ODD;  (* Both sides parallel. Same range *)

    P1[EVEN]:=P2*2;  (* Both sides parallel. The range
                     (* of the rigth hand side expression
                     (* overlaps the referenced range of P1 *)

    P1[ODD]:=0;      (* Left hand side parallel, right hand
                     (* side scalar. All the odd elements of
                     (* P1 are assigned the value zero *)

    I:=P2[5];        (* Left hand side scalar, right hand
                     (* side parallel, but the referenced
                     (* range includes one single element *)

    SEL:=P1 > P2;    (* Both sides parallel. Same range *)
```

```
    I:=P2[SEL];          (* Left hand side is scalar, right hand
                         (* side is parallel. SEL must have one
                         (* single component with the value TRUE *)


end.
```

## 6.3.4 Control Structure

Pascal contains five structured constructs which control the sequential program flow: the if , case , while , repeat and for statements. In a sequential Pascal program, all the actions taken can be ordered according to the time interval in which they occur. This ordering defines the program flow and is directed by the control statements and by the order in which statements are written in the program. The execution of programs on LUCAS differs from this in that as many as 128 actions may occur during the same interval, each in a different Processing Element. In the same way as the control constructs in Pascal determine the execution along the time dimension, new concepts are included in Pascal/L to allow the control of selection and repetition along the parallel dimension.

The construct:

```
    if <Boolean expression> then <true-statement>
                            else <false-statement>
```

in Pascal selects one of two different paths in the program flow. In the corresponding parallel statement, the Boolean expression yields a selector. Elements of the selector determine if the true-statement or the false-statement will be executed on the corresponding data elements.

In a global perspective this means that both paths will be followed and that both the true-statement and the false-statement are executed, but on different data and in different PEs. Rather than to extend the meaning of the if-then-else construct, we define a parallel selection with the following form:

```
    where <selector expression> do <true-statement>
                                elsewhere <false-statement>
```

where the elsewhere-part is optional.

Analogous to the Pascal case statement, Pascal/L defines a parallel form of the case-statement. In accordance to the where-do-elsewhere construct, the parallel case does not result in one execution path being followed, but all, each working on different data. The form of the parallel case statement is:

case where <parallel expression> of
                  <constant> : <statement>;
                  <constant> : <statement>;
                  ...
                  <constant> : <statement>;
                  others    : <statement>;
  end;

where the others-part is optional. Like in Pascal, statements may be of the form compound statements, i.e. a list of statements surrounded by a begin - end -pair.

In a similar way an extension to the Pascal

  while <Boolean expression> do <statement>

is defined to control repetition for parallel data:

  while and where <selector expression> do <statement>

Here the statement is repeated as long as the selector expression takes the value TRUE in any element. However, during each repetition of the statement, the selector expression also decides in which PEs the statement should be executed.

The following example shows how V[I] modulus N[I] can be calculated for every element of the two vectors V and N using repeated subtractions:

  var V,N : parallel array[0..127] of integer(16);
          ...
  while and where V >= N do V:=V-N;

## 6.3.5 Standard Functions and Procedures


### 6.3.5.1 Data Alignment

In expressions and assignments where the components of the parallel variables are located in different PEs, the variables must be aligned. The kind of alignment needed is defined by the programmer in terms of standard functions, which correspond to the possible data movements over the interconnection network in LUCAS.

shift(<parallel variable identifier>,I)
rotate(<parallel variable identifier>,I)

The first of these functions shifts a parallel variable I steps along its first dimension, placing component N in position N+I. Zero-elements are shifted in from the edge. The rotate function is similar to the shift function except that the elements that are shifted out at one edge are shifted in at the opposite edge of the parallel variable.

shuffle(<parallel variable identifier>)
exshuffle(<parallel variable identifier>)

The elements of the parallel variable are permuted according to the Perfect Shuffle/Exchange network on LUCAS. These functions are only defined for variables with the declared range 0..127. The first function performs a shuffle of the elements, placing component N with index $n_0n_1n_2...n_k$ in position Shuffle(N) with index $n_1n_2...n_kn_0$ (see Section 1.4.2). The second function performs a shuffle followed by a pairwise exchange of the elements, placing component N with index $n_0n_1n_2...n_k$ in position Exshuffle(N) with index $n_1n_2...n_kn_0'$, where $n_0'$ denotes that the last bit in the index is complemented.


### 6.3.5.2 Selector Operations

first(<selector expression>)

This function is used to find the first component of a selector expression with the value TRUE. It returns a new selector with only this element TRUE.


next(<selector identifier>)

The next-procedure assigns the value FALSE to the first true element of the parameter, which must be a variable.  This is useful when processing selected elements sequentially.


    any


The any-function returns the value FALSE if a previous call to the first-function or the next-procedure returned an all-false selector,  otherwise it returns the value TRUE.


    some(<selector expression>)


A call to the some-function evaluates the selector expression and returns the value TRUE if it contained at least one TRUE element,  otherwise the value FALSE is returned.


Example:

```
var PAR1 : parallel array[0..99] of unsigned integer(12);
    SEL  : selector[0..99];
    SUM  : integer;
begin
    SUM:=0;
    SEL:=PAR1 > 10;
    while some(SEL) do
    begin
        SUM:=SUM+PAR1[first(SEL)];
        next(SEL);
    end;
```

In the example SUM gets the sum of all the elements of PAR1 whose values are greater than 10.


### 6.3.5.3 Input and Output

The Pascal standard procedures read and write are extended to allow input and output of parallel variables.  Details of how this should best be accomplished have not been worked out.  As a preliminary attempt the procedures are extended so that they may take variables denoting parallel arrays as parameters,  meaning that whole parallel arrays may be read or written.

## 6.3.6 Microprograms

It is possible to explicitly invoke a microprogram which has been written in the microprogramming language. This allows a significant speedup for parts of the program that can be expressed in microcode, i.e. parts which only include parallel operations. Examples of such operations are matrix multiplications and image operations.

A microprogram should be declared in the declaration part of the program. The syntax of the declaration is similar to the syntax of microprogram headings in the microprogramming language( see Section 5.4.4):

<microprogram declaration> ::=
    microprogram <identifier> <microprogram parameter list> ; external;

<microprogram parameter list> ::=
    <empty> |
    ( <microprogram parameter> /,<microprogram parameter>/$^3$  )

<microprogram parameter> ::=
    <empty> | <identifier>

A standard function which is used in conjunction with microprograms is the following:

    location(<parallel variable identifier>)

This function results in an integer value, which indicates the bit address to the least significant bit of the parallel variable in the Associative Array.

Invocation of microprograms is similar to procedure calls.

    var   M1,M2,M3 : parallel array[0..127,0..127] of integer(16);
    Microprogram Matmult(A,B,C,precision); external;

    begin
        ....
        Matmult(Location(M1),Location(M2),Location(M3),16);
        ....
    end;

## 6.4 EXECUTION ON LUCAS

In most implementations of Pascal, a virtual stack-oriented "pseudo-machine" is used as the target computer for the generation of intermediate code by the compiler (p-code). In order to execute a compiled program, either a software emulator of the virtual machine interprets the p-code, or a final compilation phase translates the p-code into actual machine code.

In this section we will define some of the extensions to a Pascal pseudo-machine, which are needed to implement Pascal/L. We will present a part of the instruction list for the Pascal/L pseudo-machine, which is adequate to describe the execution of two important constructs in Pascal/L: parallel expressions and the where-do-elsewhere statement.

The use of the Pascal/L pseudo-machine as the target computer for the Pascal/L compiler has the additional advantage that an emulator for the pseudo-machine can be implemented on any standard computer. This means that programs can be tested before they are moved to LUCAS. The tests can include relevant performance estimations and extensive error-checking on the p-code level.

### 6.4.1 Pascal/L Pseudo-machine

The Pascal/L pseudo-machine has several registers and uses three distinct memory areas as shown in Figure 6.1. On LUCAS, two of the memories are located in the memory area of the Master Processor (the Program Memory, the Stack) and the third in the Associative Array (the Parallel Memory).

The Program Memory holds the instructions of the program being executed. A register, PC, points to the instruction that will be executed next.

The Stack contains sequential variables, sequential temporaries and pointers to locations in the Stack, the Program Memory and the Parallel Memory. Two registers point to locations in the Stack: SP, the stack pointer, points to the top-of-stack element and AP, the activation pointer, to the activation record of the currently executing procedure.

The Parallel Memory holds parallel variables and parallel temporaries. Each entry in the Parallel Memory is a 128-element vector and is defined by a descriptor , which is located in the Stack. A descriptor consists of a pointer to the Parallel Memory and a format specification giving the precision of the variable. The Parallel Memory is organized in the form of two stacks: the <u>Parallel Stack</u> and the <u>Range Stack</u> .

The register PSP points to the top element of the Parallel Stack,  which contains <u>parallel</u> <u>variables</u> and <u>parallel temporaries</u> (used during expression evaluation to hold the intermediate results).

Each parallel variable has an associated bit-slice,  the <u>range indicator</u> ,  which indicates the declared range of the variable.    Each temporary on the Parallel Stack has a corresponding range indicator giving its actual range.

The register RP points to the top element of the Range Stack.  This is a bit-slice where the <u>Current (evaluation) Range</u> is stored.    This range is set either when executing a parallel control statement,  e.g.  the where-do-elsewhere statement,  or as the result of an indexing operation.

The Stack is essential for the evaluation of expressions and is used to reference all the operands.   In stack-oriented machines all operands are pushed onto the stack from where they are removed by the arithmetic and logical operators.   Once the operation is completed the result is pushed back onto the stack.  When operating on parallel variables, it is often enough to push a descriptor on the Stack without also pushing the variable itself onto the Parallel Stack.   In many simple expressions (like adding two parallel variables and storing the result in a third) this will result in a considerable reduction of the overhead involved.

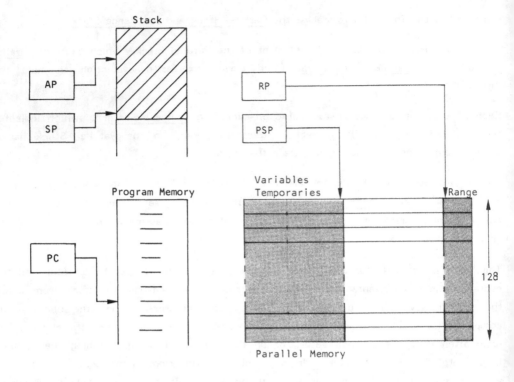

<u>Figure 6.1</u> The Pascal/L pseudo-machine.

The value of an entry in the Stack may have several interpretations:

* a scalar value

* a pointer to another entry in the Stack

* a pointer to a location in the Program Memory

* a descriptor to a variable in the Parallel Memory

* a descriptor to a temporary on the Parallel Stack.

Upon procedure entry, a local data area for the procedure is created both in the Stack and in the Parallel Memory. On the Stack this takes the form of a reserved memory area for scalar variables and for descriptors to the local parallel variables. Bit-slices indicating the declared ranges of the local parallel variables are loaded and selector variables are initiated if needed.

The instructions needed to demonstrate expression evaluation and the where-do-elsewhere construct will now be described. In the following, TOS stands for the entry on top of the Stack and OP for the Stack entry which is addressed by the operand field of an instruction. (TOS) and (OP) stand for entries in the Parallel Stack whose descriptors are TOS and OP respectively.

## LOAD   type,lev,disp

This instruction puts a variable on top of the Stack. The location of the variable depends on the values of 'lev' and 'disp'. Lev indicates the number of static levels to traverse in order to find the activation record and disp is the offset within the activation record to find the variable. Together they define the OP entry in the Stack. Depending on the value of the type-parameter, different actions are taken:

0   Load a scalar. The value of the scalar is pushed on the Stack. (SP is incremented and the value is put in the location indicated by the new value of SP.)

1   Load a parallel variable. The descriptor of the variable is pushed on the Stack, but the variable is not moved to the Parallel Stack.

## LIT   value

This instruction loads the literal specified in the parameter on the Stack.

## COPY   type

Push TOS onto the Stack, i.e. make a duplicate of the element on top of the Stack. Depending on the type-parameter the following actions may be taken:

0   Copy a scalar. The value of TOS is pushed on the Stack.

1   Copy a parallel variable. The descriptor which is in TOS is pushed on the Stack, but the variable is not moved to the Parallel Stack.

2   Copy a parallel temporary. The descriptor which is in TOS is pushed on the Stack, a copy of the temporary is pushed on the Parallel Stack.

STORE    type,lev,disp

This instruction stores TOS in the OP location. Depending on the value of the type-parameter, the following actions may be taken:

0    TOS and OP are both scalars. Copy TOS into location OP and pop TOS.

1    TOS and OP are both parallel variables. They are both represented on the Stack by descriptors to entries in the Parallel Stack. First compute a selector by performing the operation AND between the declared range of OP and the Current Range - as indicated by register RP. Then use this selector while performing a field copy operation in the Parallel Stack. Check that the declared range of TOS overlaps the selector, i.e. that TOS is defined in every component which has been copied, and if not, raise a run time error. Pop the TOS descriptor off the Stack.

2    TOS is a parallel temporary and OP is a parallel variable. They are both represented on the Stack by descriptors to entries in the Parallel Stack. Perform the same actions as in 1), then pop (TOS) off the Parallel Stack by adjusting PSP.

3    TOS is scalar and OP is a parallel variable. Compute a selector as above and use it while performing a field load in the Parallel Stack. Pop TOS.

4    TOS is a parallel variable and OP is a scalar. Compute a selector as above. Check that this selector has one single TRUE element, and if not, raise a run time error. Use the selector to read out the variable element and store it in the OP location. Pop the TOS descriptor off the Stack.

5    TOS is a parallel temporary and OP is a scalar. Perform the same actions as in 4), then pop (TOS) off the Parallel Stack.

STIN    type

This store-indirect instruction is similar to STORE, but the target address is in the second element of the Stack (TOS-1), and not specified in the instruction. The type-parameter has the same meaning as in the STORE instruction.

## NOT/NEG type

These are unary instructions for forming the Boolean complement and the arithmetic negation. They operate on TOS, pop the Stack and push the result back on the Stack. Depending on the value of the type-parameter we have:

0   TOS is a scalar. Perform the operation and replace TOS with the result.

1   TOS is a parallel variable. It is represented on the Stack by a descriptor to an entry in the Parallel Stack. Execute the instruction on the entry in the Parallel Stack which is described by TOS. Push the result on the Parallel Stack with the declared range of TOS stored as range indicator and replace TOS by a descriptor to the new element.

2   TOS is a parallel temporary. It is represented on the Stack by a descriptor to an entry in the Parallel Stack. Execute the instruction on this value in the Parallel Stack. Leave the result in the same location of the Parallel Stack without changing the range indicator.

## ADD/SUB/MULT/DIV/MOD type

These instructions represent binary operations which operate on the two top elements of the Stack. Similar to the previous instructions, the type-parameter indicates if both operands are scalars or if one or both operands are parallel. In the case where both are scalars, the result is pushed onto the Stack after the two operands have been popped. If at least one of the operands is parallel, then the operation is performed in the Associative Array, leaving the result on the Parallel Stack after the operands have been popped.

The type-parameter can take any of the values 0 to 8, as seen in Table 6.1.

TOS-1 is
========

|  | scalar | parallel variable | parallel temporary |
|---|---|---|---|
| TOS is ====== | | | |
| scalar | 0 | 1 | 2 |
| parallel variable | 3 | 4 | 5 |
| parallel temporary | 6 | 7 | 8 |

Table 6.1 The value of the type-parameter in binary operations

SETRANGE    type

Compute a new value of Current Range by performing a Boolean AND between the Current Range and the selector in (TOS). Push the old value of the Current Range onto the Range Stack. Depending on the value of the type-parameter, the following actions are also taken:

0    TOS is a parallel variable.  Pop the TOS descriptor off the Stack.

1    TOS is a parallel temporary.  Pop (TOS) off the Parallel Stack and pop the TOS descriptor off the Stack.

POPRANGE

Restore Current Range to a previous value by popping the Range Stack.

SWAPRANGE

Exchange the Current Range with the top element of the Range Stack.


## 6.4.2 Parallel Expressions

In order to use the pseudo-machine for evaluation of a parallel expression in a Pascal/L program, the expression is translated by the compiler to a form of postfix notation. This form is ideal when a stack is used to compute the expression, since the following simple rule may be used, while scanning the expression from left to right:

> If the next symbol is an operand then push its value on the stack, else (it is an operation) use the element(s) on top of the stack as operand(s) to the operation, pop the operand(s) off the stack and push the result.


When starting the computation, the stack is empty and when the end of the expression is reached, the result is the only element left on the stack. Since we deal with variables as well as constants, the notation is extended so that an operand no longer is represented by its value but by an instruction which should be executed in order to put the value on top of the stack.

This describes a commonly used technique for the intermediate code in language compilers and is the philosophy behind the Pascal p-code [Wirth71]. The code generated from the Pascal/L compiler consists of instructions similar to those described in Section 6.4.1.

Without dealing with how the transformation process works, we will look at an example of a parallel assignment statement in Pascal/L:


```
var P1,P2 : parallel array[0..127] of integer(32);
    ODD    : selector[0..127];
    I      : integer;
begin
      ...

    P1[ODD]:=P2-P1*(2+I);
```


The statement P1[ODD]:=P2-P1*(2+I) has been translated into parallel p-code and will be executed on the Pascal/L pseudo-machine. In the p-code program, which is shown in Figure 6.2, we have replaced the lev/disp-parameters with the name of the variable they refer to.

| | Instr. | Parameter | TOS becomes |
|---|---|---|---|
| 1 | LOAD | 1,P1 | descriptor to par. var. P1 |
| 2 | LOAD | 1,ODD | descriptor to selector ODD |
| 3 | SETRANGE | 0 | descriptor to par. var. P1 |
| 4 | LOAD | 1,P2 | descriptor to par. var. P2 |
| 5 | LOAD | 1,P1 | descriptor to par. var. P1 |
| 6 | LIT | 2 | scalar (the value 2) |
| 7 | LOAD | 0,I | scalar (value of I) |
| 8 | ADD | 0 | scalar (value of 2+I) |
| 9 | MULT | 1 | descriptor to par. temp. |
| 10 | SUB | 7 | descriptor to par. temp. |
| 11 | STIN | 2 | <empty> |
| 12 | POPRANGE | | <empty> |

Figure 6.2 Parallel p-code for the statement P1[ODD]:= P2-P1*(2+I).

### 6.4.3 Where Statement

The general idea for executing a control statement of the form:

where selector expression do statement-a
elsewhere statement-b

on the Pascal/L pseudo-machine is that the selector expression is used to calculate two new values of Current Range which are used when executing statement-a and statement-b respectively. By using the Range Stack to save the old value of Current Range, the problem of how to handle nested where-statements (and similar constructs) is solved. Upon entry of a where-statement, Current Range is pushed on the stack and restored after the statement has been executed.

A first attempt to translate the where-do-elsewhere construct results in the p-code given in Figure 6.3. In the figure the Current Range (CR) and the contents of the Range Stack (RS), with the top element to the left, are shown.

| | Instr. | Parameter | CR | RS |
|---|---|---|---|---|
| 0 | selector expression | | R0 | - |
| 1 | COPY | 1 or 2 | R0 | - |
| 2 | NOT | 1 or 2 | R0 | - |
| 3 | SETRANGE | 1 | Rb | R0 |
| 4 | SWAPRANGE | | R0 | Rb |
| 5 | SETRANGE | 0 or 1 | Ra | R0,Rb |
| 6 | statement-a | | Ra | R0,Rb |
| 7 | POPRANGE | | R0 | Rb |
| 8 | SWAPRANGE | | Rb | R0 |
| 9 | statement-b | | Rb | R0 |
| 10 | POPRANGE | | R0 | - |

Figure 6.3 Preliminary translation of the where-construct.

Before executing the instruction on line 1, we assume that the selector expression is in (TOS). Depending on the type of expression, this is either a parallel variable or a parallel temporary. The first instruction produces a copy of this value on the Parallel Stack. Instructions 2 and 3 invert the value and calculate a new range, by masking with the Current Range. This range will be used during the execution of statement-b. The following SWAPRANGE and SETRANGE operations calculate the Current Range for statement-a. After execution of statement-a, the Range Stack is popped, and SWAPRANGE sets the Current Range to the previous calculated value for statement-b. Execution of the where-statement terminates with restoring Current Range to its initial value.

In Section 6.3.4 where the control statements of Pascal/L were introduced, we did not discuss the semantic aspects of executing them on an SIMD computer. Intuitively, we feel that the execution of the do-part and the elsewhere-part of a where-statement ought to be independent and that no order should exist between statement-a and statement-b. However, when executed on LUCAS as described above, the two statements are processed one after the other. The following example illustrates why the scheme presented is insufficient to assure that the result corresponds to the desired semantics of the construct.

```
var   P1,P2 : parallel array[0..3] of integer(32);
      ODD    : selector[0..3]:=(1,3 => true);
begin
      ...
      where ODD do P1:=rotate(P2,1)
                elsewhere P2:=rotate(P1,1);
```

Assume that the initial values are as shown in Figure 6.4 (a). Depending on the order of execution of the statements, the result will be different as seen in the figure. If we decide that the result of executing one statement, say statement-b, should be independent of whether statement-a has been executed or not, we must require that statement-a does not change any variables until statement-b has been executed. And similarly the other way around.

Figure 6.4 (b) shows the result in the case where both statements calculate their results and update the variables when both are terminated. Note that these updates are independent of the order of execution since they use different values on the Current Range. Figure 6.4 (c) shows the result when statement-a is executed before statement-b and Figure 6.4 (d) when statement-b is executed before statement-a.

| index | P1 | P2 | P1 | P2 | P1 | P2 | P1 | P2 |
|-------|----|----|----|----|----|----|----|----|
| 0 | a | A | a | d | a | C | a | d |
| 1 | b | B | A | B | A | B | d | B |
| 2 | c | C | c | b | c | A | c | b |
| 3 | d | D | C | D | C | D | b | D |
|   | a ) |   | b ) |   | c ) |   | d ) |   |

Figure 6.4 Result depends on the order of execution. (a) initial values. (b) independent excution. (c) statement-a executed before statement-b. (d) statement-b executed before statement-a.

In order to obtain independence between the two statements, temporary locations must be used to store the new values of assigned parallel variables, resulting in the p-code shown in Figure 6.5.

```
     Instr.            Parameter      CR      RS
-----------------------------------------------------
 0   selector                         R0      -
     expression
 1   COPY              1 or 2         R0      -
 2   NOT               1 or 2         R0      -
 3   SETRANGE          1              Rb      R0
 4   SWAPRANGE                        R0      Rb
 5   SETRANGE          0 or 1         Ra      R0,Rb
 6   statement-a                      Ra      R0,Rb
     (modified)
 7   POPRANGE                         R0      Rb
 8   SWAPRANGE                        Rb      R0
 9   statement-b                      Rb      R0
10   POPRANGE                         R0      -
11   copy temporaries to
     parallel variables
```

<u>Figure 6.5</u> Translation of the where-construct.

While executing statement-a, all parallel variables which appear on the left hand side of an assignment (statement-a may be a compound statement) are copied to a temporary area. For each variable copied, there is also an "modify-selector", which will later be used when updating the variable. This selector is initiated to an all-false value.

Statement-a is now executed, but the following modifications have been made in the code:

* All assignments are to the temporary locations of the variables. The corresponding modify-selector is updated to reflect which elements have been changed in the temporary location.

* When using a variable which have been copied to a temporary location, its value is taken from this location, not from the variable.

Statement-b is executed with no changes. Finally variables are updated from their temporary locations, using the corresponding modify-selectors as indices in the updates.

A similar technique is employed for the parallel case-statement.

## 6.5 PROGRAMMING EXAMPLES

Examples of programs written in Pascal/L can be found in the following chapters, and only two examples will be presented here. They are both related to the application studies in the chapters 8 and 9.

### Example 1. Outer Perimeter of Objects

An algorithm for finding the outer perimeter of objects in a binary image works as follows (see Example 14 of Section 9.4.4):

1) Mark one picture element at the edge which belongs to the background
2) Propagate the marker to neighbours in the edge column which belong to the backgound
3) Copy markers to elements in the next column which belong to the background
4) Propagate the markers to neighbours in the column which belong to the background
5) Scan back and forth over the entire image until no new markers are produced


This algorithm can be expressed in Pascal/L as follows:


```
Program Perimeter;
(* Find outer perimeter of objects in Boolean image I *)
var I,M : parallel array[0..127,0..127] of Boolean;
    finished : Boolean;
    k : integer;              (*used to indicate columns*)

begin
    (* edge column *)
    while and where not(M[*,0]) and not(I[*,0]) and
            (shift(M[*,0],1) or shift(M[*,0],-1)) do
        M[*,0]:=true;
    finished:=false;
    while not finished do
    begin
        finished:=true;
        (* scan left *)
        for k:=1 to 127 do
        begin
            M[*,k]:=not(I[*,k]) and M[*,k-1];
```

```
            while and where not(M[*,k]) and not(I[*,k]) and
                       (shift(M[*,k],1) or shift(M[*,k],-1)) do
            begin
                M[*,k]:=true; finished:=false;
            end;
        end;


    (* scan right *)
    if not finished then
        for k:=126 downto 0 do
        begin
            M[*,k]:=not(I[*,k]) and M[*,k+1];
            while and where not(M[*,k]) and not(I[*,k]) and
                       (shift(M[*,k],1) or shift(M[*,k],-1)) do
            begin
                M[*,k]:=true; finished:=false;
            end;
        end;
    end;
end.
```

## Example 2.  Project

One commonly used operation in the relational data base model is the PROJECT operation:

PROJECT R1 OVER A GIVING R2

where R1 and R2 are relations and A an attribute of R1.  This operation creates a new relation, R2, from R1 by discarding attributes other than A.  After that, all redundant tuples are removed from R2.

Each relation has a corresponding mark selector which indicates where tuples are defined. A description of the operation can be found in [Kruzela83].

```
Program Project;
var
      R1MARK : selector[0..127]; (* shows where R1 defined *)
      R2MARK : selector[0..127]; (* shows where R2 defined *)
      TEMP1  : selector[0..127]; (* marks remaining tuples in R1 *)
      TEMP2  : selector[0..127]; (* marks all duplicates of the
                                   (* tuple that is under comparison *)
      R1     : parallel array[0..127] of record
                                   A,B,C : string(20);
                                 end;
      INSTANCE : string(20);
```

```
begin
        ..... (* relation R1 is input and R1MARK is initiated *)
        TEMP1:=R1MARK;
        INSTANCE:=R1[first(R1MARK)].A;  (* select first instance of
                                        (* attribute A *)
        while any do
        begin
            TEMP2:=(INSTANCE=R1[TEMP1].A); (* select duplicates *)
            TEMP1[TEMP2]:=not TEMP1;        (* mark as analylzed *)
            R2MARK[first(TEMP2)]:=true;    (* the first is included in R2 *)
            INSTANCE:=R1[first(TEMP1)].A;  (* get the next distinct instance
            end;                           (* of attribute A *)
end.
```

# Part 3
# APPLICATION STUDIES

# Chapter 7
# SOME WELL-KNOWN PROBLEMS
# IMPLEMENTED ON LUCAS

## 7.1 INTRODUCTION

It is often seen that computations performed in separate application areas rely on common mathematical tools and computational techniques. If it can be shown that a particular computer design is well suited for the application of one or several widely used tools, it means that the computer may be useful in many application areas.

In this chapter we study the implementation on LUCAS of three important classes of computations, namely matrix multiplication, computation of the discrete Fourier transform (DFT) by means of the fast Fourier transform (FFT) algorithm, and solution of graph theoretic problems. They all represent tools and techniques that are not limited to any specific realm of computation.

Studies of matrix multiplication on parallel computers have been made in connection with the DAP project [Flanders et al.77] and in [Pease77]. The DAP interconnection scheme is very different from the one used on LUCAS, which results in different solutions to the data routing problem. The approach taken by Pease on a proposed cube-connected processor array also differs widely from the methods reported here.

The FFT algorithm for the calculation of the DFT has been known since 1965 [Cooley and Tukey65]. It is well known that it can be mapped efficiently onto a perfect shuffle-connected processor array [Pease68, Stone71]. However, the implementation on LUCAS is probably the first one in practice.

Graph theoretic problems are relevant in many application areas. Very often they are open to efficient solution on parallel computers [Quinn and Deo 84]. An algorithm for solving the shortest path problem on LUCAS is given. On other graph theoretic problems we also demonstrate how algorithms designed to be efficient on conventional computers can be adapted to a parallel computer like LUCAS.

The three computational areas dealt with in this chapter put rather diverse demands on LUCAS. Matrix multiplication and Fourier transformation utilize the parallel interconnection network to a high degree and require that it be effective, so that full parallelism can be maintained all the time, which means that communication must be carried out without conflicts. The graph theoretic problems require that searches be performed efficiently, and also that some quite unconventional data passing be performed. LUCAS turns out to meet these diverse demands fairly well.

## 7.2 MATRIX MULTIPLICATION

The multiplication of two n by n element matrices consists of the formation of $n^2$ inner products of pairs of n-element vectors. An inner product of two vectors is defined as

$$\langle a_1, a_2, ..., a_n \rangle * \langle b_1, b_2, ..., b_n \rangle = a_1 b_1 + a_2 b_2 + ... + a_n b_n.$$

When multiplying two matrices, A and B, the element of the i:th row of column no. j is formed as the inner product of the vectors comprising row no. i of A and column no. j of B.

The traditional method for multiplication of two matrices computes the inner products sequentially, one after the other. Each inner product is likewise computed sequentially, as a sequence of multiplications and additions.

Parallelizing the computation can be made in many various ways. Depending on the number of processors available compared to the size of the matrices, different approaches may be favourable.

### 7.2.1 n x n Matrices, n Processors

We first consider the case when n processors are available. The most obvious way of using the parallelism is to calculate the n multiplications of an inner product computation simultaneously. This is known as the "inner-product method" [Hockney and Jesshope 81]. The remaining addition of the terms of each inner product can be made by n processors in $O(\log n)$ time using a suitable communication network, e.g the perfect shuffle+exchange network. Since, on a bit-serial computer, the execution time for addition is small compared to the multiplication time, the reduced parallelism in the addition step is not very severe. However, there are other problems with this approach:

The two vectors that we multiply in order to compute an inner-product must be aligned with each other, so that corresponding elements are available to the same processor. If the A-matrix is stored one <u>column</u> in each processor's memory, the B-matrix must be stored one <u>row</u> in each memory. This will align the rows of A with the columns of B.

If the matrices are loaded into the memory for multiplication only, this need not cause any problem. However, if the matrices are created in the parallel array or are subject to other operations that perhaps demand the same storage method for both, the alignment problem has to be solved in the array. STARAN has this possibility through its Multidimensional Access Memory [Batcher77], where both rows and columns are accessible. This is not possible on LUCAS.

Instead of computing each inner product with the largest possible parallelism, many inner products can be computed simultaneously. ( A total of $n^2$ inner products are to be computed).

Referring to Figure 7.1, in order to form the first column of the result matrix, the following n inner products must be computed:

$$\langle A_{00} A_{01} A_{02} \ldots A_{0,n-1} \rangle * \langle B_{00} B_{10} B_{20} \ldots B_{n-1,0} \rangle$$
$$\langle A_{10} A_{11} A_{12} \ldots A_{1,n-1} \rangle * \langle B_{00} B_{10} B_{20} \ldots B_{n-1,0} \rangle$$

.
.
.

$$\langle A_{n-1,0} A_{n-1,1} \ldots A_{n-1,n-1} \rangle * \langle B_{00} B_{10} B_{20} \ldots B_{n-1,0} \rangle$$

These expressions show that the first **column** of A is to be multiplied by $B_{00}$, the second column by $B_{10}$, the third by $B_{20}$, etc. The results of these multiplications are accumulated, and the final results will appear at the correct positions.

$$
\begin{array}{|llll|}
\hline
A_{00} & A_{01} & A_{02} \ldots A_{0,n-1} \\
A_{10} & A_{11} & A_{12} \ldots \\
A_{20} & A_{21} & A_{22} \ldots \\
 & & \\
A_{n-1,0} & \ldots & A_{n-1,n-1} \\
\hline
\end{array}
\qquad
\begin{array}{|llll|}
\hline
B_{00} & B_{01} & B_{02} \ldots B_{0,n-1} \\
B_{10} & B_{11} & B_{12} \ldots \\
B_{20} & B_{21} & B_{22} \ldots \\
 & & \\
B_{n-1,0} & \ldots & B_{n-1,n-1} \\
\hline
\end{array}
$$

<u>Figure 7.1</u> Two matrices.

Thus, the k:th column of the product is formed by successively multiplying each column of A by the elements of the k:th column of B, constantly accumulating the results. The multiplications are made as multiplications by a scalar, which frees us from the problem of vector alignment. Figure 7.2 illustrates the algorithm, called the "middle-product method".

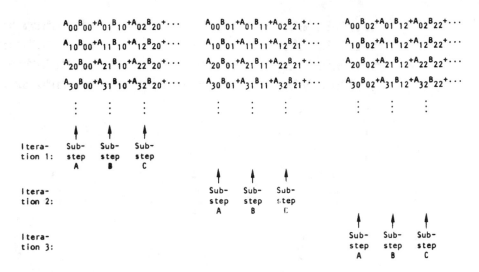

**Figure 7.2** Matrix multiplication algorithm that produces the result column by column (middle-product method).

We arrived at the new scheme by stating that we wanted the result to come out one column at a time, then analyzing which data and which computations were needed to produce the result in this form. Continuing this line of reasoning, we may ask if we can find a method to produce the whole result matrix simultaneously, i.e. proceed in n iterations, where each iteration produces an n x n matrix, and the last one produced is the result matrix. We want all inner products to "grow" simultaneously, as illustrated in Figure 7.3.

As can be seen from the figure, this can be done without problems. In fact this is just doing things in a different order compared to the method described above. The access problems (or, rather, lack of problems) are exactly the same. This is what is called the "outer-product method".

The two methods described work equally well if the matrices are not square. The only constraints on the size are that the number of rows must be smaller than or equal to the number of processors, and that the memory space horizontally is large enough. The middle-product method which produces the result column by column is more space conservative, since the B matrix can be successively overwritten if desired.

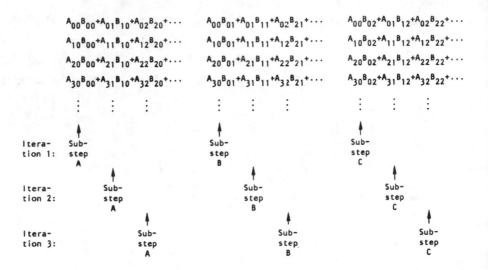

$$A_{00}B_{00}+A_{01}B_{10}+A_{02}B_{20}+\cdots \qquad A_{00}B_{01}+A_{01}B_{11}+A_{02}B_{21}+\cdots \qquad A_{00}B_{02}+A_{01}B_{12}+A_{02}B_{22}+\cdots$$
$$A_{10}B_{00}+A_{11}B_{10}+A_{12}B_{20}+\cdots \qquad A_{10}B_{01}+A_{11}B_{11}+A_{12}B_{21}+\cdots \qquad A_{10}B_{02}+A_{11}B_{12}+A_{12}B_{22}+\cdots$$
$$A_{20}B_{00}+A_{21}B_{10}+A_{22}B_{20}+\cdots \qquad A_{20}B_{01}+A_{21}B_{11}+A_{22}B_{21}+\cdots \qquad A_{20}B_{02}+A_{21}B_{12}+A_{22}B_{22}+\cdots$$
$$A_{30}B_{00}+A_{31}B_{10}+A_{32}B_{20}+\cdots \qquad A_{30}B_{01}+A_{31}B_{11}+A_{32}B_{21}+\cdots \qquad A_{30}B_{02}+A_{31}B_{12}+A_{32}B_{22}+\cdots$$

Iteration 1: Sub-step A     Sub-step B     Sub-step C

Iteration 2: Sub-step A     Sub-step B     Sub-step C

Iteration 3: Sub-step A     Sub-step B     Sub-step C

Figure 7.3 Matrix multiplication algorithm that computes all inner-products "simultaneously" (outer-product method).

Written in Pascal/L the middle-product method looks as follows:

```
Program MATRIXMULT;
var A,B,C: parallel array[0..127,0..127] of integer(8);
row: selector[0..127]:=(0=>True);
acol,bcol: integer;

begin
   for bcol:=0 to 127 do C[*,bcol]:=0;        (*clear C *)
   for bcol:=0 to 127 do                      (* for each B-column *)
     for acol:=0 to 127 do                    (* multiply all columns of A *)
       begin
         C[*,bcol]:=C[*,bcol] + A[*,acol]*B[row,bcol];
         row:= rotate(row,1);                 (* with each element of B-column *)
       end;
end.
```

An estimation of the time required to multiply two 128 x 128 element matrices of b-bit data can be made as follows:

The number of multiplications by scalar are $128^2 = 2^{14}$. If recoding of the multiplier using canonical signed-digit code is done (see Chapter 3), a multiplication will - on the average - consist of b/3 additions [Hwang79]. Each addition takes a time close to 3b cycles. Each multiplication is preceded by a transfer of the multiplier to the Mask Register, which takes approximately 4b cycles. It is followed by an addition over 2b bits. Thus, the multiplication time is approximately

$$2^{14} * (b/3 * 3b + 4b + 6b) = 2^{14}(b^2+10b) \text{ cycles.}$$

For b=8 this is approximately $2.4*10^6$ cycles. With 200 ns clock cycles the time is approximately 0.5 seconds, overhead time not included. The time for recoding is negligible.


## 7.2.2 n x n Matrices, $n^2$ Processors

We next consider the case when we have $n^2$ processors available for the multiplication of two n x n matrices. Since there are $n^2$ inner products to be computed independently of each other, the $n^2$ parallelism can always be fully utilized. However, data alignment before multiplication may cause some overhead. We have studied two alternative methods of doing the computation on a perfect shuffle-connected processor array. The first method is a computation in place method, i.e. each inner product is computed in its final place. This requires a significant amount of shuffling before each multiplication. The other method computes the different terms of an inner product in different processing elements. The final rearrangement of the result is done in the summation phase.

The first method is an outer-product method, i.e. a further parallelization of the one illustrated in Figure 7.3. All inner-products are computed simultaneously in a total of n iterations. In each iteration, all substeps are done in parallel. The method is described in detail in [Svensson83a].

The second method, which appears to be favourable, is a further parallelization of the middle-product method described in Figure 7.2. Here, the entire computation of one inner product is finished before the next one is started. A further parallelization of this method will finish the computation of n different inner products before starting the computation of n new ones.

In order to perform all substeps of an iteration in parallel, the alignment depicted in Figure 7.4 is needed. In iteration no. k the matrix $B^{(k)}$ with n identical rows is formed. Each row is column no. k of B. This can be done in $\log_2 n$ broadcast-shuffles, as shown in Figure 7.5. In the first step in the figure, the operation "Broadcast Upper" (BU) is performed. In the second step, the operation "Broadcast Lower" (BL) is performed. In the general case, row no. $k = \langle k_{p-1}k_{p-2}...k_1k_0 \rangle$ of B is spread to all columns to form $B^{(k)}$ by the following procedure:

```
for j:=p-1 downto 0 do
    if kⱼ=0 then BU else BL;
```

Example : Row no.   <1011> of a 16-row matrix is broadcast to all columns by the sequence BL,BU,BL,BL.

The formal proof (which is simple) is given in [Ohlsson and Svensson 83].

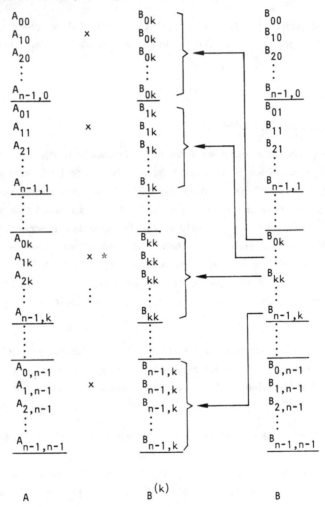

Figure 7.4 Alignment required for computation of column k according to the middle-product method. "x" mark rows where products contributing to element $R_{1,k}$ of the result matrix are computed. "*" marks the row where the element $R_{1,k}$ is to be stored.

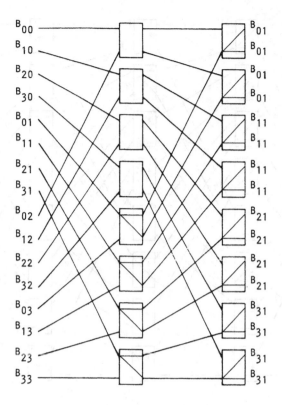

Figure 7.5 Formation of $B^{(1)}$ from B.

The n products contributing to element no. i of a column are situated n words apart, starting in word i. The summation process needed to form the element can be done in parallel with those summations that form the other elements in the column. It is done using the perfect shuffle/exchange network in $\log_2 n$ steps, as depicted in Figure 7.6a. Putting the result at the final destination requires $\log_2 n$ additional shuffles, which is shown in part b of the same figure. As can be seen however, these can be done in parallel for all columns. (For a more formal treatment, see [Ohlsson and Svensson 83]).

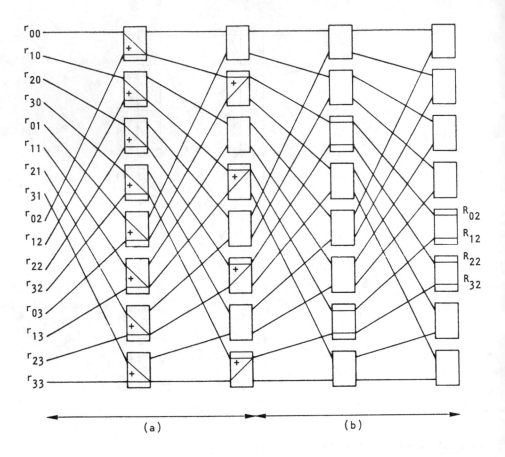

(a)                                    (b)

<u>Figure 7.6</u> a) Computation of $R_0 = r_{00} + r_{01} + r_{02} + r_{03}$
$$R_1 = r_{10} + r_{11} + r_{12} + r_{13}$$
$$R_3 = r_{20} + r_{21} + r_{22} + r_{23}$$
$$R_4 = r_{30} + r_{31} + r_{32} + r_{33}$$

b) Putting the result at the final destination (column 2 assumed)


To sum up the amount of shuffling needed, we note that neither the pre-alignment procedure nor the addition procedure utilize the full parallelism if only one column is treated at a time. However, the columns can be treated partly simultaneously. This reduces the number of stages for each of the procedures. The total number of passes of a bit-slice through the shuffle/exchange network of LUCAS in order to align arguments for multiplication, add the contributions and rearrange the result is the following (b is the data length):

Pre-alignment:            $2(n-1)*3b$

Summation:              $(n-1)*5b$

Post-alignment:         $\log_2 n*2b$

Each pass takes one clock cycle. The multiplication time is approximately $3b^2$ cycles.


## 7.2.3 n x n Matrices, More Than n But Fewer Than $n^2$ Processors

LUCAS with its 128 PEs does not fit into the scheme of Section 7.2.2, since 128 is not an even square. In this section we study the usefulness of the interconnection network when the number of PEs is e.g. $n^2/2$, or more general $n^2/m$, where m is a power of 2.

In such a case, the $n^2$ elements of a matrix are distributed over m fields in the associative memory. Figure 7.7 illustrates the case when n=4 and m=2.

We adopt the middle-product method. To align elements for the computation of column k, the matrix $B^{(k)}$ is formed through broadcasts of column k. The total time to form all such matrices amounts to $m*2(n-1)$ broadcasts if the procedure is parallelized maximally.

In each PE, m multiplications are made and the products added. The sums produced are added over the interconnection network in $\log_2(n/m)$ steps. This procedure of shuffling and adding can again be parallelized, to yield a total of $2n(m-1)$ addition steps. Finally, $\log_2 n$ shuffles of each of the m fields are made.

We see that the middle-product algorithm of Section 7.2.2 is well adopted to the case of fewer PEs. The full parallelism is used throughout the entire algorithm. This gives a processing time m times longer than if $n^2$ processors were available.

$$
\begin{array}{cc}
A_{00} & A_{02} \\
A_{10} & A_{12} \\
A_{20} & A_{22} \\
A_{30} & A_{32} \\
\hline
A_{01} & A_{03} \\
A_{11} & A_{13} \\
A_{21} & A_{23} \\
A_{31} & A_{33} \\
\hline
\end{array}
\qquad
\begin{array}{c}
B_{00} \\
B_{10} \\
B_{20} \\
B_{30} \\
\hline
B_{01} \\
B_{11} \\
B_{21} \\
B_{31} \\
\hline
\end{array}
\qquad
\begin{array}{cc}
B_{01} & B_{21} \\
B_{01} & B_{21} \\
B_{01} & B_{21} \\
B_{01} & B_{21} \\
\hline
B_{11} & B_{31} \\
B_{11} & B_{31} \\
B_{11} & B_{31} \\
B_{11} & B_{31} \\
\hline
\end{array}
$$

| Matrix A | Part of matrix B | After broadcasting column 1 |
|----------|------------------|-----------------------------|

$$
\begin{array}{c}
A_{00}B_{01}+A_{02}B_{21} \\
A_{10}B_{01}+A_{12}B_{21} \\
A_{20}B_{01}+A_{22}B_{21} \\
A_{30}B_{01}+A_{32}B_{21} \\
A_{01}B_{11}+A_{03}B_{31} \\
A_{11}B_{11}+A_{13}B_{31} \\
A_{21}B_{11}+A_{23}B_{31} \\
A_{31}B_{11}+A_{33}B_{31}
\end{array}
\qquad
\begin{array}{c}
\\
C_{01} \\
\\
C_{11} \\
\\
C_{21} \\
\\
C_{31}
\end{array}
\qquad
\begin{array}{c}
C_{00} \\
C_{01} \\
C_{10} \\
C_{11} \\
C_{20} \\
C_{21} \\
C_{30} \\
C_{31}
\end{array}
\qquad
\begin{array}{c}
C_{00} \\
C_{10} \\
C_{20} \\
C_{30} \\
C_{01} \\
C_{11} \\
C_{21} \\
C_{31}
\end{array}
$$

| Computations made in PEs | After addition over interconnection network | Results from column 0 and 1 merged | After 2 shuffles |
|--------------------------|---------------------------------------------|------------------------------------|------------------|

Figure 7.7 Illustration of part of the computations when two 4x4 matrices are multiplied on an 8 PE array.

## 7.2.4 n x n Matrices, More Than $n^2$ Processors

We also briefly consider the case when there are more PEs available than there are elements of a matrix. For example, this is the case when 128 PEs are used for multiplication of 8x8 matrices.

Let there be $m*n^2$ PEs available, where m is a power of 2. The A- and B-matrices now each fill the upper $n^2$ words of a field. If full $m*n^2$ parallelism is to be utilized the matrix elements must be broadcast in a way that aligns them properly for multiplication.

If we spread column k of B as in Figure 7.5, we will automatically, with $m*n^2$ PEs, also spread columns k+1,k+2,...,k+m-1 to the rest of the field,  provided that k is a multiple of m or k=0.  After spreading A by means of $\log_2 n$ broadcasts and a sequence of shuffles,  elements are aligned so that all multiplications needed for columns k, k+1,...,k+m-1 of the result matrix can be done simultaneously.  After addition over the interconnection network,  rearrangement of the result is needed in order to have the result matrix stored in the same order as the input matrices.  This process is more complicated than in the earlier described cases.  However,  since it is done only once for the whole result matrix in parallel,  the extra time caused by this is negligible.

A more detailed description of the $m*n^2$ case is given in [Ohlsson and Svensson83].  The number of cycles required to multiply two n x n matrices of b-bit data with $m*n^2$ processors is the following:

Pre-alignment:    $2*\log_2 m*3b + 2(n/m-1)*3b + \log_2 m(n/m)*2b$
Multiplication:   $(n/m)*3b^2$
Summation:        $(n/m-1)*5b + \log_2 m*3b$
Post-alignment:   $2*(2\log_2 n + \log_2 m)*2b$

To give a sense of the amount of inevitable overhead time in an implementation,  the algorithm has been programmed and tested on LUCAS.  The measured execution times exceed the absolute lower bounds for this type of processor (the formulas given above) with typically 20 - 30%.  The amount of pure data alignment compared to total computation time is for 16-bit data 18% and for 8-bit data 26%.  Table 7.1 gives the execution times in microseconds for multiplication on LUCAS of 8 by 8 matrices with b-bit data.  For comparison,  the same task has been programmed in assembly language on a conventional VAX 11/780 computer.  The execution time obtained was approximately 3600 microseconds,  regardless of the number of bits.

|                  | b=8  | b=12 | b=16 |
|------------------|------|------|------|
| Pre-alignment:   | 55   | 81   | 106  |
| Multiplication:  | 255  | 489  | 799  |
| Summation:       | 34   | 48   | 63   |
| Post-alignment:  | 48   | 70   | 93   |
| TOTAL:           | 392  | 688  | 1061 |

Table 7.1 Execution times.

## 7.3 FAST FOURIER TRANSFORM

The fast Fourier transform (FFT) is a method for efficiently computing the discrete Fourier transform (DFT) of a time series (discrete data samples). The DFT has properties that are analogous to those of the Fourier integral transform, which can be used to determine the frequency spectrum of a continuous, time varying signal. The publication of the FFT method [Cooley and Tukey 65] meant a revolution in signal processing, since the time needed to compute the DFT on a digital computer is reduced by orders of magnitude. A straightforward calculation of the DFT (according to the definition) on a sequential computer takes $O(N^2)$ time, where N is the number of samples, whereas only $O(Nlog_2N)$ time is needed when the FFT method is used. The algorithm is well suited for parallel processing. Using N processing elements, the processing time will be $O(log_2N)$.

First, we will give a short description of the DFT and the FFT algorithm. It is based on the description given in [IEEE G-AE 67]. Then we will show how the FFT is implemented on LUCAS. The interconnection structure plays an important role in the computation.

### 7.3.1 The Discrete Fourier Transform

If a digital computer is to be used for analysing a continuous waveform then it is necessary that the data be sampled. The minimal sampling rate needed in order to obtain a true representation of the waveform is twice the highest frequency present in the waveform.

Assume the time series obtained has length N. Denote by $X_k$ the kth sample of the time series. The DFT of the time series consists of N complex coefficients, $A_r$, r=0,1,...,N-1. Each $A_r$ is obtained by the formula

$$A_r = \sum_{k=0}^{N-1} X_k e^{-2\pi j r k /N} \qquad (7.3.1)$$

Using the shorthand notation $W = e^{-2\pi j/N}$ the expression for $A_r$ becomes

$$A_r = \sum_{k=0}^{N-1} X_k W^{r k} \qquad r=0,1,\ldots,N-1 \qquad (7.3.2)$$

The inverse of (7.3.2) is

$$X_k = (1/N) \sum_{r=0}^{N-1} A_r W^{-rk} \quad k=0,1,\ldots,N-1 \quad (7.3.3)$$

This relationship is called the inverse discrete Fourier transform (IDFT).

The DFT and the IDFT are of similar form, implying that a parallel machine suitable for computing one can be used for computing the other by simply exchanging the roles of $X_k$ and $A_r$, and making appropriate scale-factor and sign changes. In fact, IDFT($A_r$) = $(DFT(A_r)^*)^*$, where $^*$ denotes the complex conjugate.


## 7.3.2 The Fast Fourier Transform

The FFT is a clever computational technique to compute the DFT coefficients. The DFT of a time series is here obtained as a weighted combination of the DFTs of two shorter time series. These, in turn, are computed in the same way, until the DFT of a single point is needed. This is the point value itself, according to expression (7.3.2).

Suppose that the time series $X_k$, $k=0,1,\ldots,N-1$, is divided into two functions, $Y_k$ and $Z_k$, each of which has only half as many points. The function $Y_k$ is composed of the even-numbered points $(X_0, X_2, X_4, \ldots)$ and $Z_k$ is composed of the odd-numbered points $(X_1, X_3, X_5, \ldots)$, see Figure 7.8.

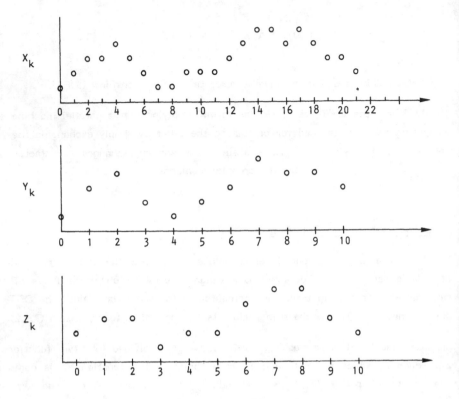

<u>Figure 7.8</u> Decomposition of the time series $X_k$ into two, half as long, series $Y_k$ and $Z_k$.

Now, if $B_r$ and $C_r$ denote the discrete Fourier transforms of $Y_k$ and $Z_k$ respectively, it is easily shown that the discrete Fourier transform, $A_r$, of $X_k$ can be written

$$A_r = B_r + W^r C_r \qquad 0 \leq r < N/2 \qquad (7.3.4)$$
$$A_{r+N/2} = B_r - W^r C_r \qquad 0 \leq r < N/2 \qquad (7.3.5)$$

From (7.3.4) and (7.3.5) the first N/2 and last N/2 points of the discrete Fourier transform of $X_k$ (a sequence having N samples) can be easily obtained from the DFT of $Y_k$ and $Z_k$, both sequences of N/2 samples. Figure 7.9 illustrates this for the case N=8.

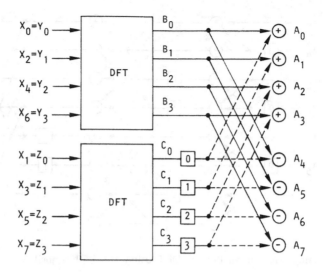

<u>Figure 7.9</u> Signal flow graph illustrating how calculation of an 8-point DFT can be reduced to the calculation of two 4-point DFTs. A number within a square represents multiplication by W raised to the number. In the lower half, the value arriving by the dotted line is subtracted from the value arriving by the solid line. In the upper half the two values are added.

We can use this technique repeatedly, i.e. we can in turn divide $X_k$ and $Y_k$ into half as long sequences. Accordingly, the computation of $B_k$ (or $C_k$) can be reduced to the computation of sequences of $N/4$ samples. These reductions can be carried out as long as each function has a number of samples that is divisible by 2. Normally, $N$ is chosen to be a power of two. We will limit the discussion to that case.

The computation is illustrated by the signal flow graph in Figure 7.10.

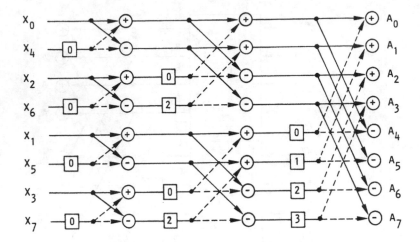

<u>Figure 7.10</u> Calculation of an 8-point DFT using the FFT algorithm.

The graph shows that the computation consists of $\log_2 N$ iterations. In each iteration, $N/2$ multiplications, $N/2$ additions and $N/2$ subtractions are made. Thus, a total of $(3/2)N\log_2 N$ operations are needed, one third of which are multiplications.

### 7.3.3 Implementation on LUCAS

In Figure 7.10, the coefficient values $A_k$ are in conventional order, with increasing indices. The $X_k$ samples, however, are in "bit-reversed" order, meaning that the indices are in natural order if their binary representations are read backwards. If all the nodes on the same horizontal level as $A_1$ are interchanged with all the nodes on the same horizontal level as $A_4$, and all the nodes on the same level as $A_3$ are interchanged with all the nodes on the same level as $A_6$, with the arrows carried along with the nodes, the flow graph depicted in Figure 7.11 is obtained. In this graph, $X_k$ is in the original order, whereas $A_k$ is bit-reversed.

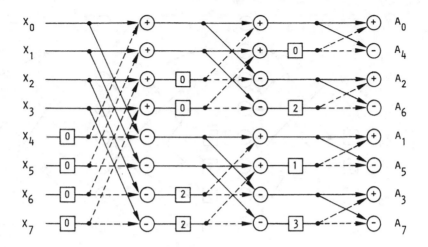

Figure 7.11 Rearrangement of the signal flow graph of Figure 7.10. $X_k$ in natural order, $A_k$ in bit-reversed order.

The interesting feature of this graph is that it has the same structure as the flip network of STARAN, run backwards, which can be shown to be equivalent to a shuffle/exchange network (see Chapter 1). Thus, the flow graph can again be re-drawn, using a shuffle+exchange structure in each iteration (Figure 7.12). This shows that a 128 point FFT calculation can be efficiently mapped onto LUCAS if the input data is placed one sample in each memory word.

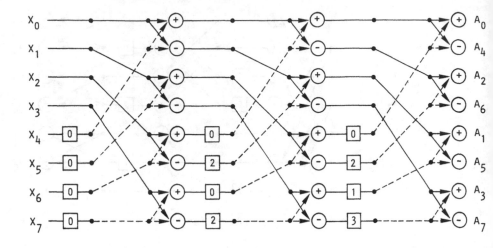

Figure 7.12 Adaptation of the FFT algorithm to the shuffle/exchange interconnection structure.


The multiplications by the W-constants are the most time consuming calculations in the computations. It is unsatisfactory that only half of the PEs (the lower half) participate in these calculations, according to Figure 7.12. However, the quantities to be multiplied are complex numbers. Therefore a multiplication actually consists of four multiplications, plus one addition and one subtraction. The real and imaginary parts of the quantities to be multiplied can be merged before multiplication in such a way that all the PEs participate in the multiplications. This reduces the number of multiplications from four to two.

Figure 7.13 helps to illustrate the detailed execution of one iteration. The starting point is a vector of complex X-values, in Figure 7.13 denoted "OldX", and a vector containing the complex W-values, each W-value appearing twice. The desired result is a vector of "NewX" values, appearing in perfectly shuffled order. The first step is to spread the lower half of "OldX" to all PEs in a way that is suitable for multiplication by the W-values. This is done through MERGE operations (see Chapter 3) resulting in the fields MERG1 and MERG2. The complex multiplication is done as two multiply-fields followed by addition in some words (giving the imaginary-valued part of the product) and subtraction in some (giving the real-valued part). This completes the multiplication phase of the iteration. The products thus obtained (the MUL field) are now to be added to and subtracted from the upper half of "OldX" in order to produce the new X-values. To this end, the upper half of "OldX" is spread out to match the MUL field. Addition and subtraction are performed and a final MERGE is needed to separate the real and imaginary parts of "NewX". "NewX" is obtained in perfectly shuffled order, as desired.

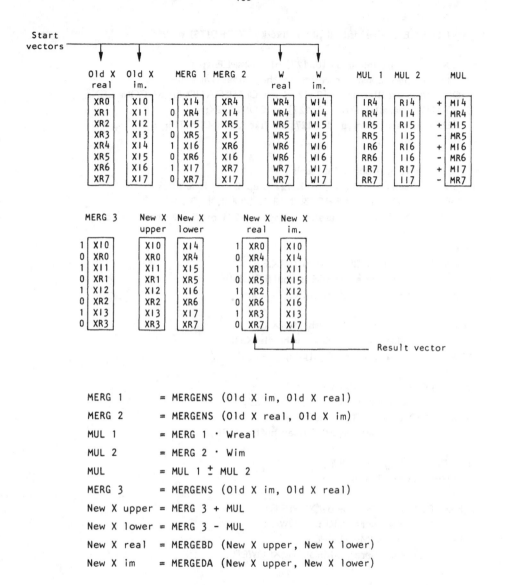

Figure 7.13 Illustration of the execution on LUCAS of one iteration of the FFT.

Expressed in Pascal/L, the FFT algorithm becomes:

Procedure FFT;

```
const NOOFITERATIONS = 7;
      NOOFBITS        = 8;
```

```
type  COMPLEX = record RE,IM : fixed(1.NOOFBITS) end;

var   X      : parallel array [0..127] of COMPLEX;
  (* The complex constants reside in the global variable:
    OMEGA : parallel array [0..127,1..NOOFITERATIONS] of COMPLEX; *)
    SQUARE: parallel array [0..127] of COMPLEX;
    RESULT: parallel array [0..127] of fixed(1.NOOFBITS);
    I      : integer;

Procedure FFTiteration(I : integer);
var ODD    : selector [0..127] :=(1..127 step 2 => True);
    MERGE1, MERGE2, MERGE3, MUL1, MUL2, MUL,
    XUPPER,XLOWER  : parallel array [0..127] of fixed(1.NOOFBITS);

begin
  where ODD do MERGE1:=exshuffle(X.RE)
            elsewhere MERGE1:=shuffle(X.IM);
  MUL1 := MERGE1*OMEGA[*,I].RE;

  where ODD do MERGE2:=exshuffle(X.IM)
            elsewhere MERGE2:=shuffle(X.RE);
  MUL2 := MERGE2*OMEGA[*,I].IM;

  where ODD do MUL:=MUL1-MUL2
            elsewhere MUL:=MUL1+MUL2;
  where ODD do MERGE3:=shuffle(X.IM)
            elsewhere MERGE3:=exshuffle(X.RE);

  XUPPER := MERGE3+MUL;
  XLOWER := MERGE3-MUL;

  where ODD do X.RE:=below(XUPPER)
            elsewhere X.RE:=XLOWER;
  where ODD do X.IM:=XUPPER
            elsewhere X.IM:=above(XLOWER);

end; (*FFTiteration*)

begin
    ...         (*sample values are input to X.RE*)
  X.IM := 0;
  for I := 1 to NOOFITERATIONS do FFTiteration(I);
  SQUARE.RE := X.RE * X.RE;
  SQUARE.IM := X.IM * X.IM;
  RESULT := SQUARE.RE+SQUARE.IM;
  (*power spectrum is now in array RESULT*)

end; (*FFT*)
```

The entire algorithm has also been written as a microprogram. The execution time for a 128 samples FFT when all data are 8-bit is 0.2 ms per iteration, making a total of 1.4 ms. The multiplications take 70% of the total execution time. Since the multiplication executes in a time proportional to the square of the data length, the ratio grows with increased data length. Noting that the real and imaginary parts of the coefficients in the first two iterations have the values zero and plus and minus one only, the multiplications in these iterations can be omitted. This reduces the execution time from 1.4 to 1.1 ms.

LUCAS can be used for computation of the FFT with full parallelism also when the number of samples does not match the size of the array. When the number is larger, e.g. 1024, samples that are 128 units apart are put in the same memory word. This makes it possible to compute the first iterations of the algorithm entirely within the PEs. Assuming $2^n*128$ sample points, LUCAS will need $2^n(\log_2 128 + n)$ iterations of the kind described above to compute the FFT. The following table shows how this number and the execution time grows with the number of samples. (Reduction for the two initial iterations is made).

| n | no. of samples | no. of iterations | time (ms) |
|---|---|---|---|
| 0 | 128 | 7 | 1.1 |
| 1 | 256 | 16 | 2.6 |
| 2 | 512 | 36 | 6.0 |
| 3 | 1024 | 80 | 13.6 |
| 4 | 2048 | 176 | 30.4 |
| 5 | 4096 | 384 | 67.2 |

Table 7.2 Execution times

When the number of samples is smaller than the number of PEs, more than one FFT calculation can be performed at a time. For example, when the number of samples is 32, one sequence of 32 samples is put in memory words 0,4,8,..., another sequence in words 1,5,9,..., still another in 2,6,10,...,etc. The FFT of all four sequences can be calculated simultaneously.

As noted above, the result data from the FFT algorithm appears in bit-reversed order. To get the data out to the host computer in natural order in a simple manner, we have equipped LUCAS with an "address bit reversal" facility. The Master Processor can choose any of two buffers to pass the address to the I/O data registers of the processor array. One of the buffers transfers the address without any changes, the other buffer reverses the bits of the address. Thus data can be brought in or out in bit-reversed order by ordinary block moves.

LUCAS has been used for spectral analysis of speech in real time [Ohlsson82, Fernstrom et al. 83]. The sampling frequency needed in order to cover the significant frequencies of speech is 10 kHz. Real time analysis based on 128 samples requires that the computation be performed in 12.8 ms, which is the time to gather 128 samples. The 1.1 ms needed by LUCAS is well within this limit.

Ohlsson has suggested [Ohlsson84a, Ohlsson84b] an improvement of the processing elements of LUCAS in order to make multiplications faster and thereby make the processor even more attractive for signal processing. In Chapter 10 the suggested improvements will be presented.

## 7.4 THREE GRAPH-THEORETIC PROBLEMS

Problems that can be identified as graph-theoretic show up in diverse areas, e.g. traffic planning and network analysis. A common task is to find the shortest path between two vertices of a graph. The connection between two vertices may be uni-directional or bi-directional. In the first case the graph is called a directed graph . Also, a cost (or path length) may be associated with each path. Such graphs are called weighted .

Solutions of problems of this kind often take the form of searching large trees or updating matrices. Opportunities to exploit the kind of parallelism offered by LUCAS are rich. As examples we will consider algorithms for the solution of two different shortest path problems on LUCAS. In the first problem, paths between vertices are all bi-directional and all have the length 1 (if they exist). The task is to determine the length of the shortest path between two specified vertices. In the second problem the paths are uni-directional and an individual length is associated with each path. The task is to produce a distance matrix showing the lengths of the shortest path between all pairs of nodes. We will also consider an algorithm for finding the minimal spanning tree of a graph, i.e. that subset of edges of the graph that connects all vertices with minimal total edge weight.

### 7.4.1 Shortest Path Between Two Given Vertices. Unit Path Length

Figure 7.14 shows a graph that we will use as an example to illustrate the proposed algorithm. From each vertex, lines are drawn to vertices that can be reached directly, i.e. with path length 1. A compact way of representing the graph on LUCAS is by means of an 'adjacency matrix' shown in Figure 7.15. A '1' in the matrix indicates that there is a direct connection between the vertices in the row and column. Since all paths are bi-directional, the matrix is symmetrical around the main diagonal. In LUCAS the matrix is stored one row per memory word, one column per bit-slice.

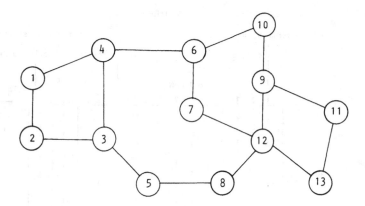

**Figure 7.14** A bi-directional graph.

As an example, we want to find the length of the shortest path between vertex no. 2 and vertex no. 11. We do this by successively building the tree of vertices reachable from 2 in one, two, three,... steps. To start with, the vertices that can be reached in one step are marked in the Tags. OR-ing the contents of those rows that now are tagmarked, gives a row, a "mark word", indicating vertices reachable in exactly two steps. In the next step the logical OR of all bit-slices marked in the mark word is formed and the result is stored in the Tags. The tags now indicate which vertices can be reached in three steps. This procedure is continued, alternating between horizontal and vertical OR-ing of marked bit-slices and rows, respectively, until finally, the destination vertex is reached. In this case we arrive at the destination vertex after six steps.

In each iteration the entire matrix has to be traversed bit-slice by bit-slice. Thus, the time to perform one iteration is proportional to the number of vertices, n. The number of iterations is the same as the length of the shortest path, l.

Execution time = constant * l * n

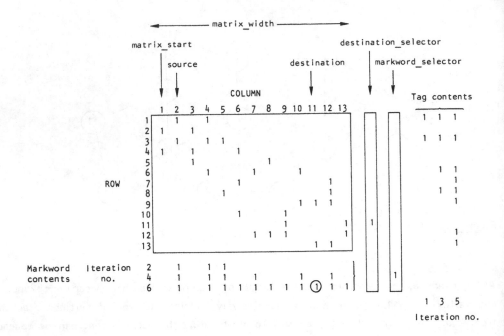

**Figure 7.15** Adjacency matrix of the graph in Figure 7.14. Pointers administrated by the Address Processor are shown, and also the changing contents of the Tags and Mark word as the algorithm proceeds.

We will now make the description more precise by giving it in the high level microprogramming language. The number of parameters needed in the instruction is 6. Thus, the parameters must be loaded to the Control Unit in two passes. One extra register of the Address Processor is needed to count the number of iterations.

```
Microprogram SHORTPATH (*matrix_start,  matrix_width,  source,
                          destination,   destination_selector,   markword_selector*)

Begin
    counter:=1;                                (* Clear iteration counter *)
    LTMA(source,direct);                       (* Mark in Tags, vertices reachable
                                                  in one step *)
    ANDTMA(destination_selector,direct);       (* See if destination reached *)
    If SOME then exit(SHORTPATH);

    LOOP:
    While TRUE do
    Begin
        counter:= counter+1; x:=0;
        Iterate matrix_width times                (* For each bit-slice, form
```

```
                                           logical OR of marked words *)
Begin
  LTMT(matrix_start+x,direct); CRA;
  if SOME then CORA;
  LTMA(markword_selector,direct);
  WRRT(matrix_start+x);                    (* Write result in markword *)
  x:= x+1;

End;

  LTMT(destination,direct);                (* Check if destination reached *)
  if SOME then exit(LOOP);

  counter:= counter+1; x:= 0;
  CRA;

  Iterate matrix_width times               (* Each bit-slice marked in mark word
                                           contributes to horizontal OR *)
  Begin
    LTMA(markword_tag,direct);
    LTMT(matrix_start+x,direct);
    if SOME then ORRMA(matrix_start+x,direct);
  End;

  LTRA;
  ANDTMA(destination_selector,direct);     (* Check if destination reached *)
  if SOME then exit(LOOP);
  LTRA;
  End;
End;
```

From the information in Figure 7.15, gathered during the computation, it is possible to trace back which route or routes that give the shortest path length. Logical AND between bit-slice no. 11 and the Tag contents from iteration no.5 gives '1's at rows 9 and 13. Thus, there are two paths to 11, one via 9 and the other via 13. Now, ANDing row 9 and the mark word from iteration no. 4 gives that the path that passed 9 goes via 10 or 12, etc. To be able to perform this back-tracking we see that successive mark words and Tag contents must be saved. This is easily done and adds very little to the total execution time.

## 7.4.2 Shortest Path Between All Pairs of Vertices in a Weighted, Directed Graph

In a weighted, directed graph the paths between vertices are uni-directional and there is a length associated with each path. Figure 7.16 shows an example of such a graph. We will consider the problem of finding the shortest path between all pairs of vertices. The graph is given in the form of a matrix. The matrix corresponding to the graph in Figure 7.16 is given in Figure 7.17. Note that the absence of a direct path between a pair of vertices is marked "infinite" (if) in the matrix.

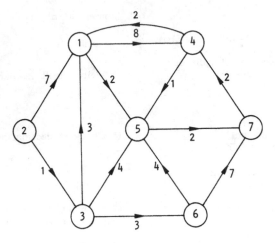

Figure 7.16 A weighted, directed graph.

|   | 1  | 2  | 3  | 4  | 5  | 6  | 7  |
|---|----|----|----|----|----|----|----|
| 1 | 0  | if | if | 8  | 2  | if | if |
| 2 | 7  | 0  | 1  | if | if | if | if |
| 3 | 3  | if | 0  | if | 4  | 3  | if |
| 4 | 2  | if | if | 0  | 1  | if | if |
| 5 | if | if | if | if | 0  | if | 2  |
| 6 | if | if | if | if | 4  | 0  | 7  |
| 7 | if | if | if | 2  | if | if | 0  |

Figure 7.17 The distance matrix of the graph in Figure 7.16.

To solve the problem on LUCAS we will follow an algorithm due to Floyd [Floyd62], which is considered as one of the two most efficient algorithms for sequential computers. It is well suited for parallel implementation. On sequential computers a computation time proportional to $n^3$ is required, where n is the number of vertices. On a parallel computer with n PEs it should be possible to perform the algorithm in a time proportional to $n^2$.

The algorithm works as follows. Starting with the original n by n matrix D of direct distances, n different matrices $D_1$, $D_2$,..., $D_n$ are constructed sequentially. Matrix $D_k$ is obtained from matrix $D_{k-1}$ by inserting vertex k in a path wherever this results in a shorter path.

On a parallel computer with n PEs, an entire column of the matrix can be updated simultaneously. In the k:th iteration, column p of $D_k$ is obtained in the following way (using Pascal/L notation for matrix elements):

$$D_k(,p) := \min [ \; D_{k-1}(,p) \; , \quad D_{k-1}(,k) + D_{k-1}(k,p)]$$

A Pascal/L program for the entire algorithm reads as follows:

```
Program FLOYD;

const noofvertices = 128;
var Dmatrix: parallel array [1..noofvertices,1..noofvertices] of integer(8);
k,p: integer;

begin
   for k:=1 to noofvertices do
     for p:=1 to noofvertices do
       where (Dmatrix[*,k]+Dmatrix[k,p]) < Dmatrix[*,p] do
         Dmatrix[*,p]:= Dmatrix[*,k]+Dmatrix[k,p];
end.
```

It is easily seen that the execution time of this program is proportional to $n^2$. The task that is performed $n^2$ times is an 'add fields' instruction followed by 'field larger than field' instruction and a tagmasked 'move field'. These are all proportional to the field length.

The algorithm requires a representation for an infinite value. We choose a number that is a little smaller than half the largest value that is possible to represent in the given field length. In the worst case, two such numbers are added. This will give no overflow.

7.4.3 Minimal Spanning Tree

The minimal spanning tree (MST) of a weighted, bi-directional graph is defined as that subset of the vertices of the graph that connects all vertices with minimal total edge weight. As an example of a context where the problem of finding the MST arises, consider a telecommunications system. The problem of connecting a set of cities to each other using minimal wire length is exactly the problem of finding the MST (provided that only wires from one city to another are allowed).

An efficient algorithm for finding the MST of a graph is due to Prim [Prim57]. It was improved and implemented on computer by Dijkstra [Dijkstra59] and is normally called the Prim-Dijkstra algorithm. On sequential computers it requires a processing time proportional to $n^2$ on an n-vertex graph.

The algorithm works by successively expanding a subtree (called a _fragment_ ) until, eventually, a spanning tree is obtained. The initial fragment consists of a single vertex, which may be chosen arbitrarily. The fragment is then expanded at each stage by adding to it the nearest neighbour of the fragment, i.e. that vertex not in the fragment with minimal distance to the fragment. Ties are resolved arbitrarily. After n-1 stages the MST has been constructed.

As an example, consider the graph shown in Figure 7.18. Starting with vertex B in the fragment, edges are added to the subtree in the following order: B-D, D-A, B-C, C-E, E-F.

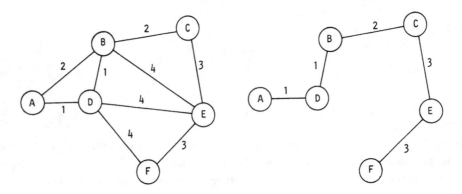

Figure 7.18 Weighted, bi-directional graph (left) and its minimal spanning tree (right).

To implement the algorithm on an n-processor array, we use the same representation of the graph in the associative memory as in the all-to-all shortest path problem above, i.e. a distance matrix. The distance matrix of our example graph is shown in Figure 7.19.

|   | A | B | C | D | E | F |
|---|---|---|---|---|---|---|
| A | 0 | 2 | if | 1 | if | if |
| B | 2 | 0 | 2 | 1 | 4 | if |
| C | if | 2 | 0 | if | 3 | if |
| D | 1 | 1 | if | 0 | 4 | 4 |
| E | if | 4 | 3 | 4 | 0 | 3 |
| F | if | if | if | 4 | 3 | 0 |

**Figure 7.19** Distance matrix of the graph shown in Figure 7.18.

In order to determine which vertex to add to the fragment, Prim's original algorithm is keeping track of the "nearest nonfragment neighbour" of every fragment vertex. The algorithm then requires a running time proportional to $n^3$. Dijkstra's improvement resulted from using another strategy: keeping track of the "nearest fragment neighbour" of each nonfragment vertex. This gives $O(n^2)$ processing time.

Dijkstra's startegy turns out to be the most favourable also on a parallel processor like LUCAS. A distance table is needed in each stage. It contains, for each nonfragment vertex, the name of its nearest neighbour in the fragment and the distance to it. For example, after stage 2, when the fragment consists of vertices B, D and A, the distance table has the following contents:

|  | Nearest neighbour in fragment | Distance |
|---|---|---|
| C | B | 2 |
| E | B | 4 |
| F | D | 4 |

nonfragment vertex

C is chosen as the new fragment member and the table gets the following contents:

| | Nearest neighbour in fragment | Distance |
|---|---|---|
| E | C | 3 |
| F | D | 4 |

When implementing the algorithm on LUCAS we must make sure that all required information passing can be done. Figure 7.20 shows the contents of the distance table after each stage. After the search for minimum value of the distance column (D), and a SELECT FIRST to resolve ties, information about which vertex was chosen must be passed to the Address Processor. This information is used by the Address Processor to address that column of the distance matrix that should be merged into the D column of the distance table on the basis of "smallest value wins".

After interation no:

| Vertex label | | 0 | | | 1 | | | 2 | | | 3 | | | 4 | |
|---|---|---|---|---|---|---|---|---|---|---|---|---|---|---|---|
| | NN | D | T | NN | D | T | NN | D | T | NN | D | T | NN | D | T |
| A | B | 2 | 1 | D | ① | 1 | A | 0 | 0 | A | 0 | 0 | A | 0 | 0 |
| B | B | 0 | 0 | B | 0 | 0 | B | 0 | 0 | B | 0 | 0 | B | 0 | 0 |
| C | B | 2 | 1 | B | 2 | 1 | B | ② | 1 | C | 0 | 0 | C | 0 | 0 |
| D | B | ① | 1 | D | 0 | 0 | D | 0 | 0 | D | 0 | 0 | D | 0 | 0 |
| E | B | 4 | 1 | B | 4 | 1 | B | 4 | 1 | C | ③ | 1 | E | 0 | 0 |
| F | B | if | 1 | D | 4 | 1 | D | 4 | 1 | D | 4 | 1 | E | 3 | 1 |

| To fragment: | B | D | A | C | E | F |
|---|---|---|---|---|---|---|
| Output: | B | B-D | D-A | B-C | C-E | E-F |

**Figure 7.20** The successive contents of distance table and Tags.

The 'Vertex label' field is necessary for this passing of addresses. It contains, for each vertex, the address of its column in the distance matrix. (Actually the field may contain only the binary representation of the word number. This number is then passed to the Address Processor where it is shifted left a few positions and added to an offset address to get the actual column address). The transfer of a data value from the associative memory to the Address Processor is made via the I/O register and the I/O Buffer Register.

At each stage of the algorithm the following is done:

* A search for the minimum value of the D-column in selected words.

* Output of the pair <NN,Vertex label> of the selected word.

* Transfer of the contents in the 'Vertex label' field of the selected word to the Address Processor, and spreading this label to a scratch pad field.

* Merging a new column from the distance matrix into the D-column on the basis of "smallest value wins".

* Merging the scratch pad field into the NN-field using the merging mask determined above.

All these tasks take a time that is independent of the number of vertices, but proportional to the lengths of the fields they work on, in most cases the number of bits in the distance values.

The number of stages in the algorithm is n-1. Thus, we conclude that the task of finding the minimum spanning tree on LUCAS grows only linearly with the number of vertices, provided that this number is smaller than or equal to the number of processing elements. In fact, linear time is optimal if the list of edges is to be output in series. This is because each new edge means adding a new vertex to the subtree, and the number of vertices to be added is n-1. We have shown that the decision which new vertex to choose can be taken in constant time.


7.4.4 Discussion

We have demonstrated how three frequently encountered graph theoretic problems can be solved efficiently on LUCAS. The latter two show an improvement with a factor n compared to sequential execution. As for the first one, an algorithm due to Dijkstra [Dijkstra59] solves the problem in a time proportional to $n^2$ on a sequential computer. The time on LUCAS - using an entirely different algorithm - is proportional to n*l, where l is the length of the shortest path. Preliminary studies give at hand that Dijkstra's algorithm can be followed also in implementation on LUCAS. It would have some characteristics in common with the MST algorithm. The algorithm presented here in part 7.4.1 is simpler to follow and program but probably less efficient if the number of vertices is large and the shortest path between the specified vertices is long.

The parallel implementation of Floyd's shortest path algorithm is very straightforward. The MST algorithm, however, is more tricky. We have not seen any reports on the solution of the MST problem on an n-processor computer. Bentley [Bentley79] describes an implementation of the Prim-Dijkstra algorithm on an $n/\log_2 n$-processor tree-structured system. The execution time is $O(n\log_2 n)$, which means that he too is able to use the full parallelism. In [Deo and Yoo 81] implementation of the same algorithm on a $n^{0.5}$-processor with an execution time that is $O(n^{1.5})$ is reported.

Graph theory is an area with many problems open for parallel solution. With the examples given we have indicated that parallel processors with architectures similar to LUCAS bear good promise to be useful for these purposes.

# Chapter 8

# LUCAS AS A BACKEND PROCESSOR FOR RELATIONAL DATABASE PROCESSING

## 8.1 INTRODUCTION

Though today it is familiar to most people, in some intuitive but mostly correct interpretation, the term database appeared in the literature on information processing for the first time as late as in 1964 [McGee81]. A database is stored in the memory of a computer, and to handle it a new type of software, a database management system, DBMS, evolved. The practical need for more efficient systems for managing the information in the database soon gave rise to new methodologies, new programming languages, new algorithms and also new hardware techniques. A new field of human enterprise, database technology, emerged and its importance is still growing.

The software of present database management systems is very complex and and its efficiency is not always adequate to the needs of its users. The reason is that a DBMS is usually implemented on a conventional general-purpose computer which was designed for other kinds of applications.

The von Neumann computer model, developed in the mid 1940s, was intended to be employed in numerical applications, where basic operations are addition, subtraction, multiplication, etc, and basic data types are numbers stored in a memory and addressed by locations. The proper use of this type of computer is sequential calculations in loops.

The purpose of a DBMS is not calculation but rather manipulation of large volumes of data. Basic operations required are retrieval and updating of data, basic data types are records which are identified by contents rather than by locations. None of those features are supported by the hardware of general-purpose computers. Furthermore, the DBMS offers a great natural potential for parallel execution which is impossible to exploit in a conventional computer.

This disharmony between means and goals became more and more apparent in the late 1960s as databases grew larger, and more sophisticated functions were being incorporated into DBMSs to satisfy growing user demands. In the early 1970s, people at a number of universities in the USA initiated pioneering research projects in the area of special purpose computers for data base management. Since then, this area has become one of the most dynamic research fields in the domain of computer architecture. In an ever increasing stream, numerous papers are published each year, dealing with description, analysis and discussion of new designs and new concepts of database computers.

There are a number of ways to organize the information in a database. One particularly important approach is the logical organization of the data in the form of tables called relations . This approach has many advantages and many advocates [Codd82].

Its main disadvantage is commonly taken to be the fact that a table is a two-dimensional structure and therefore must be translated into a one dimensional string of data if it is to be sequentially processed in a conventional computer. This implies a need for an elaborate software interface between the logical data model seen by the user and the physical storage structure. Even if the relational database management system can be implemented efficiently this necessary interface is responsible for a costly overhead and for the large complexity of the system.

This disadvantage, however, can be turned into an advantage since the simplicity of the two-dimensional table gives an opportunity to exploit new forms of hardware organizations. The most natural way to store and to process tables would be in a computer structure which also looks like a table and where a one-to-one correspondence between the logical and the physical data organization can be achieved. Furthermore, a table containing data is a unity, and the natural way to process it in this table-like hardware structure would be in parallel, by operations having tables as operands. An Associative Array is such a structure and we believe that it can make the management of a relational database simple and efficient. The research presented in this chapter deals with exploring its possibilities. For further details see [Kruzela83, Lindh at al.84].

This chapter is organized as follows:

Section 8.2 gives a brief description of the implementation of relational algebra operations on LUCAS, when it is assumed that the size of the operand relations are such that they can be stored in the Associative Array. Furthermore, this section contains a discussion of the performance of very large Associative Arrays.

Section 8.3 goes a step beyond the material in Section 8.2. A simple but powerful method of evaluating queries to a database stored in the Associative Array is demonstrated.

Section 8.4 is a discussion of the performance of a database computer built with an Associative Array.

Section 8.5 studies the usefulness of an Associative Array for evaluation of the Join operation on very large relations.

Section 8.6 is a discussion of results. Some topics for further research are also suggested.

## 8.2 RELATIONAL ALGEBRA ON LUCAS

### 8.2.1 Introduction

This section presents the implementation of relational algebra operations on LUCAS. Some of the results of this section may be found in [Kruzela and Svensson 81].

We will demonstrate algorithms and give their approximate timing equations. The timing equations are helpful in analyzing the performance of the Associative Array.

The equations will express the total execution time in terms of number of clock cycles consumed by the execution. Parameters in the timing equations will be the sizes of tuples or attributes and the cardinality of involved relations. We assume that the size of each relation is less than the size of the Associative Array.

The operations are implemented by microprograms which are initiated by the Master Processor. Prior to any operation, the Master Processor must send all the necessary parameters e.g. the addresses of attributes or the sizes of tuples, to the Control Unit of the Associative Array. The parameters are stored in the registers of the Address Processor.

To facilitate the understanding of some of the operations, we will give simple diagrams showing the state of the Associative Array before and after the operation and in some cases also during execution of the operation. The diagrams are based on the schematic picture of the Associative Array shown in Figure 8.1. Only the particular section of the Associative Array which is relevant for the operation will be displayed.

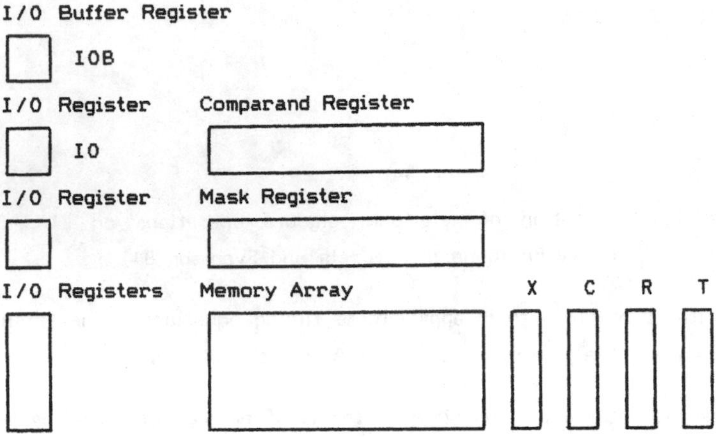

I/O Buffer Register

☐   IOB

I/O Register          Comparand Register

☐   IO          ☐

I/O Register          Mask Register

☐          ☐

I/O Registers          Memory Array          X    C    R    T

☐          ☐          ☐ ☐ ☐ ☐

Figure 8.1 Schematic picture of the Associative Array.


In the diagrams we will use the letters S and D above a box representing the Memory Array to indicate the source and destination of data; 0 and 1 denote a value of a bit; x is an unspecified value of a bit; A,B,E stand for a value of a byte; and X (in the Memory Array) is an unspecified value of a byte.


## 8.2.2 Representation of a relation in the Associative Array

There is an obvious mapping between the logical structure of a relation and its physical representation in the Memory Array.    The relation is a table,    and the most straightforward way to store it in the Memory Array,    which is also a table,    is to allocate each tuple to one memory word,    so that the attributes occupy vertical fields in the array.

Figure 8.2 shows as an example,    a relation consisting of four attributes stored in the Memory Array.


MA

```
        S1  SMITH      20  LONDON
        S2  JONES      10  PARIS
        S3  BLAKE      30  PARIS
        S4  CLARK      20  LONDON
        S5  ADAMS      30  ATHENS
```

Figure 8.2 Relation in the Memory Array.

A relation in the Memory Array is identified by two sets of parameters:

* Information about which memory words hold its tuples.

* The sizes and addresses of its attributes.

The information about which memory words hold tuples of the relation is stored in the Memory Array together with the relation. With each relation in the array there is a unique byteslice called a <u>Workfield</u> at an address assigned by the Master Processor. One particular bitslice in the Workfield indicates by a 1 in its bit pattern that the corresponding memory word holds a tuple of the relation. This bitslice is called a <u>Markbitslice</u> of the relation. The other bitslices of the Workfield are used as a scratch pad during the execution. The content of the Workfield is invisible to the Master Processor. Since all operations on data in the Memory Array are always performed in parallel and data are accessed associatively there is no reason why the outside world should know in which memory words the relation is stored. Before operating on the relation the Markbitslice is usually loaded into the Tags.

The address of an attribute of the relation in the Memory Array is a 12-bit bitaddress (0 . . . 4095) to its rightmost bitslice. The addresses of relations currently in the Memory array are maintained by the Master Processor. They are assigned to the relation when it is loaded into the Memory Array or when it is created as a result of some operation on relations already in the Memory Array. The Master Processor keeps track of a pool of free space in the Memory Array. Before a new relation is to be loaded into the array, or before a new relation is created from relations already existing in the array, the Master Processor checks the size of the attributes (number of bytes) and assigns proper addresses to them. It also assigns an address to the Workfield.

Since addressing of bitslices in the Memory Array is made by random access, any two bitslices may be logical neighbours. The attributes of the relation do not need to occupy a contiguous field in a memory word. The order between the attributes is arbitrary. Furthermore, the attributes of different relations may be freely intermingled in one memory word.

Figure 8.3 shows two relations, S and J, residing simultaneously in the Memory Array. The relation S has three attributes with addresses SA1, SA2, SA3 and a Workfield at address SWF. J has four attributes with addresses JA1, JA2, JA3, JA4 and a Workfield at address JWF. The figure displays only the content of the Markbitslices.

| | SA1 | JA1 | JA3 | SA3 | SA4 | | JA2 | SA2 | SWF | JWF |
|---|---|---|---|---|---|---|---|---|---|---|
| MA | S1 | J1 | PARIS | 20 | LONDON | SORTER | | SMITH | 1 | 1 |
| | | | | | | | | | 0 | 0 |
| | S2 | | | 10 | PARIS | | | JONES | 1 | 0 |
| | | | | | | | | | 0 | 0 |
| | S3 | J2 | ROME | 30 | PARIS | PUNCH | | BLAKE | 1 | 1 |
| | | J3 | ATHENS | | | READER | | | 0 | 1 |
| | S4 | J4 | ATHENS | 20 | LONDON | CONSOLE | | CLARK | 1 | 1 |
| | S5 | | | 30 | ATHENS | | | ADAMS | 1 | 0 |
| | | J5 | LONDON | | | COLLATOR | | | 0 | 1 |

<u>Figure 8.3</u> Interleaved relations in the Memory Array.

One item of data physically represented in the Memory Array can belong to many different relations. This is frequently the case when a query to a database is evaluated inside the Memory Array, as we will see in Section 8.3. In Figure 8.4, we can see four different relations S, T, Q and R. S is the original relation loaded into the Memory Array , T is the same as S with the only difference that the values of the fourth attribute of T consist of only three letters, Q consists of the tuples of S whose fourth attribute has value Paris, R is the result of the Projection on S over the fourth attribute.

| | | | | | | | | | | |
|---|---|---|---|---|---|---|---|---|---|---|
| S: | SA1 | SA2 | SA3 | SA4 | SWF | | | | | |
| T: | TA1 | TA2 | TA3 | TA4 | | TWF | | | | |
| Q: | QA1 | QA2 | QA3 | QA4 | | | QWF | | | |
| R: | | | | RA1 | | | | RWF | | |

| MA | | | | | | | | | |
|---|---|---|---|---|---|---|---|---|
| | S1 | SMITH | 20 | LONDON | 1 | 1 | 0 | 1 |
| | S2 | JONES | 10 | PARIS | 1 | 1 | 1 | 1 |
| | S3 | BLAKE | 30 | PARIS | 1 | 1 | 1 | 0 |
| | S4 | CLARK | 20 | LONDON | 1 | 1 | 0 | 0 |
| | S5 | ADAMS | 30 | ATHENS | 1 | 1 | 0 | 1 |

<u>Figure 8.4</u> Subsets of a relation in the Memory Array.

## 8.2.3 Some basic operations in the Associative Array

Algorithms operating on relations in the Associative Array can be naturally decomposed in a repeating sequence of basic operations. In this section, we will give examples of implementation of some of the basic operations and we will also give their timings.

Load bitslice operation, see Fig 8.5.

One bitslice from the Memory Array, at an address supplied by the Address Processor, is loaded into the R Registers. The state of the T Registers (Tags) is used for selective control of the execution of the operation. The execution will be performed only in those processors in the Associative Array where the Tags are set to one.

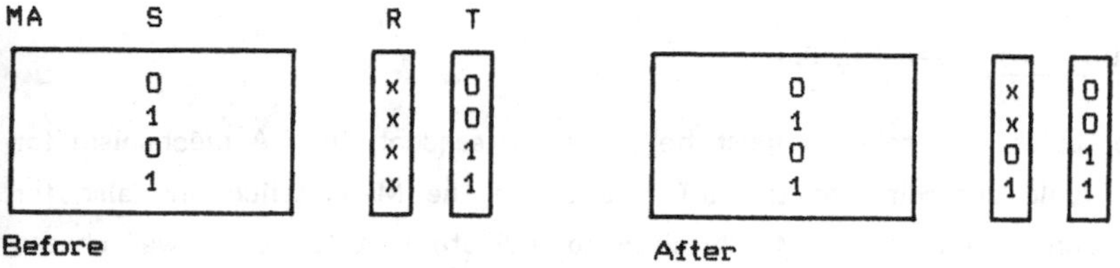

MA          S                    R     T

| 0 | | x | 0 |
| 1 | | x | 0 |
| 0 | | x | 1 |
| 1 | | x | 1 |

Before

| 0 | | x | 0 |
| 1 | | x | 0 |
| 0 | | 0 | 1 |
| 1 | | 1 | 1 |

After

Figure 8.5 Load R Register.

This operation is executed in one clock cycle.

Store bitslice operation, see Fig 8.6.

The contents of the R Registers are stored in the Memory Array at an address supplied by the Address Processor. The values of the R Registers are stored only in the memory words where the Tag is set to one.

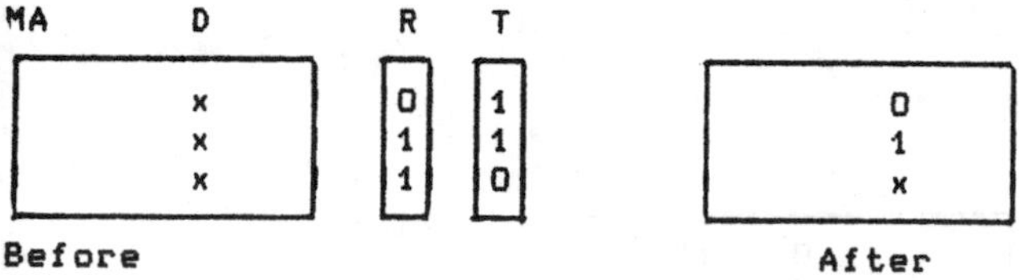

MA          D                    R     T

| x | | 0 | 1 |
| x | | 1 | 1 |
| x | | 1 | 0 |

Before

| 0 |
| 1 |
| x |

After

Figure 8.6 Store R Register operation.

Logical AND operation on bitslices , see Fig 8.7.

The AND is executed in 3 clock cycles. In the first clock cycle, a bitslice (S1) is loaded into the R Registers from the Memory Array, in the second clock cycle, AND is performed between the R Registers and another bitslice (S2) from the Memory Array, with the result loaded into the R Registers. In the third clock cycle, the contents of the R Registers are stored into the Memory Array (D). Addresses to bitslices are supplied by the Address Processor.

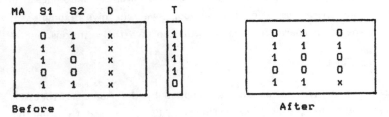

Before                                             After

Figure 8.7 Logical AND operation.

Select the next valid word , see Fig 8.8.

In some algorithms tuples of a relation must be processed sequentially. A mechanism for selecting the first tuple according to the information in the Markbitslice and also for resetting the corresponding bit in the Markbitslice to indicate that the tuple was chosen (removed from the list) is Select first and remove operation.

The execution proceeds in the following way: in the first clock cycle the Markbitslice is loaded into the Tags. In the second clock cycle, the operation Select first is performed on the Tags, resetting all Tags except the first. In the third clock cycle, the NONE signal, indicating whether any of the Tags are set to one, is tested by the Control Unit. If none of the Tags are set to one the operation is aborted, otherwise the contents of the Tags are copied into the R Registers. In the fourth clock cycle the logical operation XOR is performed between the R Registers and the Markbitslice in the Memory Array with the result saved in the R Registers. Finally, in the fifth clock cycle, the R Registers are stored in the Memory Array. The effect of this operation is that the first Tag according to the Markbitslice is set to one and the Markbitslice is updated.

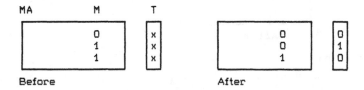

Before                                             After

Figure 8.8 Select first and remove operation.

Spread byte operation,  see Fig 8.9.

This operation transfers one byte from an address in a selected memory word to a
byteslice at another address in all the memory words.   The execution proceeds in three
steps.   First,  the byteslice including the byte to be spread,  is copied into the I/O
Registers in 9 clock cycles.   Then,  the selected byte is spread to all I/O Registers in 2
clock cycles.   Finally,   the contents of the I/O Registers are stored into the Memory
Array in 8 clock cycles.

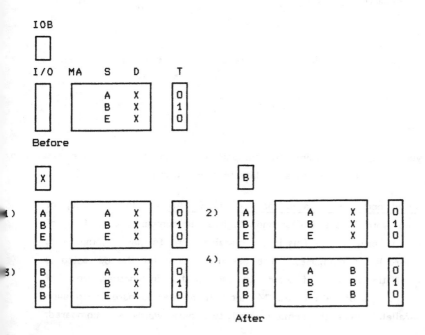

Figure 8.9 Spread byte operation.

The execution of the Spread byte operation takes 19 clock cycles.

Store Comparand operation,  see Fig 8.10

This operation transfers a word in the Comparand Register into all selected memory
words.

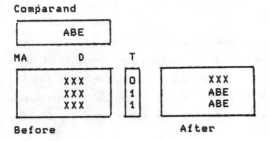

Figure 8.10 Store Comparand operation.

The execution of this operation takes 18*b clock cycles, where b is the length of the word.

Compare operations.

Many different types of basic operations for comparing data in the Associative Array can be implemented. We can classify them according to two criteria:

* The location of compared data in the Associative Array. In one group of operations, a word in the Comparand Register is compared to a field of words in the Memory Array. This is the classical 'one to many' comparison, typical for associative memories. The execution time for the operation is independent of the number of words in the field. In another group of operations two fields of data in the Memory Array are compared with each other in parallel. In each memory word two data words are compared.

* The type of comparison. There are many properties of data that can be used for comparison. The simplest type of comparison is the exact match. In an operation executing the exact match, all corresponding bits are tested for equality in all pairs of words. More complex comparisons are common in cases where the data are interpreted as numbers. Comparisons can then be of the type: greater than, less than etc.

Sometimes, only part of a field of data in the Memory Array is to be interrogated during a compare operation. This feature can be implemented in two ways:

* Using the Mask Register. The content of the Mask Register at the current bitaddress indicates to the Control Unit that the execution of an operation must be disabled in those bitslices.

* Using the Address Processor. The Address Processor, when generating the sequence of bitaddresses to the field, skips the parts of the field that should

not be compared.

For use in algorithms implementing the relational algebra the most important compare operation is <u>Exact match to comparand</u> , shown in Figure 8.11.

In this operation, each bit of a word in the Comparand Register is compared to the corresponding bit in all memory words and the Tags are reset to zero if the bits are not equal.

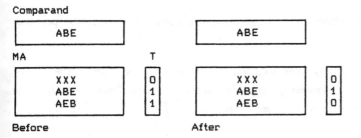

Comparand

Figure 8.11 Exact match to comparand operation.

The execution time for this operation is 10*b clock cycles. b is the length of a word.

## 8.2.4 Internal algorithms for algebraic operations

The result of an algebraic operation, taking one or two relations as its arguments, is a new relation. Depending on where the resulting relation is located, relative to the argument relations, the algorithms for operations can be divided into two groups:

* Algorithms where the result relation is a physical subset, c.f.Fig. 8.4 of one of the argument relations. The algorithms determine which pieces of data in the Memory Array belong to the result by creating the Markbitslice of the result relation. In this group we find the algorithms for: Selection, Intersection, Difference, Semi-join, Projection and Division.

* Algorithms which assemble the result relation in some new area in the Memory Array from pieces of data of the argument relations. In this group are the algorithms for: Union, Product and Join.

To simplify our exposition, we limit ourselves to relations having only one or two attributes.

## Selection

The result of the Selection operation is a relation whose tuples are a subset of those of the argument relation. During execution of the operation a datum in the Comparand Register is compared in parallel with values of an attribute in all tuples of the relation in the Memory Array. The result consists of tuples satisfying the criterion for comparison. As there can be many different conditions for comparison, there can be many different Selection operations. We will show the implementation when the criterion for comparison is equality.

Figure 8.12 illustrates the algorithm for the Selection operation. The execution proceeds in the following steps:

First, the Markbitslice of the argument relation is loaded into the Tags. Then, the Exact Match To Comparand is performed, with the outcome in the Tags. Finally, the Tags are stored in the Markbitslice of the result relation.

Comparand

| LONDON |
|--------|

```
           A   AWF
                   RWF
MA         I   I   I
```

| | | A | AWF/RWF | | | | A | AWF | RWF |
|---|---|---|---|---|---|---|---|---|---|
| XXXXX | XXXXXX | 0 | x | | XXXXX | XXXXXX | 0 | 0 |
| SMITH | LONDON | 1 | x | | SMITH | LONDON | 1 | 1 |
| JONES | PARIS | 1 | x | | JONES | PARIS | 1 | 0 |
| BLAKE | PARIS | 1 | x | | BLAKE | PARIS | 1 | 0 |
| CLARK | LONDON | 1 | x | | CLARK | LONDON | 1 | 1 |
| ADAMS | ATHENS | 1 | x | | ADAMS | ATHENS | 1 | 0 |

Before                          After

Figure 8.12 Selection operation.

The execution of this operation takes

$$T_{Selection} = 10*b \quad \text{clock cycles.}$$

b is the size of the attribute.

## Intersection

The Intersection operation takes two relations as its arguments. The result relation is a subset of one of the argument relations consisting of tuples which belong to both relations.

The principle behind the implementation of the Intersection is that the result relation is determined by a successive identification of its tuples in its 'mother' relation. The tuples from one relation are transferred into the Comparand Register above the other relation, and compared with it in parallel for an exact match. If the tuple in the Comparand Register is identical with some tuple in the relation below, its original in the first relation is added to the result relation by updating its Markbitslice.

Figure 8.13 illustrates the implementation of the Intersection operation.

```
         A          AWF
               B        BWF
         R1                  RWF
MA       |        |    |    |    |

   LONDON  PARIS    1  1  x      LONDON  PARIS    1  1  1
   ATHENS  XXXXXX   1  0  x      ATHENS  XXXXXX   1  0  0
   PARIS   ROME     1  1  x      PARIS   ROME     1  1  1
   XXXXXX  LONDON   0  1  x      XXXXXX  LONDON   0  1  0
   MADRID  BERLIN   1  1  x      MADRID  BERLIN   1  1  0
   ROME    HAAG     1  1  x      ROME    HAAG     1  1  1

Before                          After
```

Figure 8.13 Intersection.

The execution time of the Intersection operation is

$$T_{Intersection} = 30*b*N1 \text{ clock cycles.}$$

N1 is the cardinality of the first argument relation and b is the size of the tuple.

## Difference

The Difference operation has two relations as its arguments. The result relation is a subset of one of the argument relations, consisting of tuples which do not belong to the second relation.

At the start it is assumed that the result relation is equal to the first argument relation. Then, using the Comparand Register, it is successively tested whether the tuples of this relation belong to the second relation or not. If they do, they are eliminated from the result by resetting the result Markbitslice.

Figure 8.14 illustrates the implementation of the Difference operation.

```
        A           AWF
               B    BWF
        R             RWF
MA      I        I  I  I   I

| LONDON  PARIS   1  1  x |    | LONDON  PARIS   1  1  0 |
| ATHENS  XXXXXX  1  0  x |    | ATHENS  XXXXXX  1  0  1 |
| PARIS   ROME    1  1  x |    | PARIS   ROME    1  1  0 |
| XXXXXX  LONDON  0  1  x |    | XXXXXX  LONDON  0  1  0 |
| MADRID  BERLIN  1  1  x |    | MADRID  BERLIN  1  1  1 |
| ROME    HAAG    1  1  x |    | ROME    HAAG    1  1  0 |

Before                        After
```

Figure 8.14 Difference.

The execution time of the Difference operation is

$$T_{Difference} = 30*b*N1 \text{ clock cycles.}$$

N1 is the cardinality of the first argument relation and b is the size of the tuple.

Semi-join

The Semi-join operation has two relations as its arguments. The first argument relation has two attributes, A1 and A2, and the second has one attribute, B. Values of A2 and B are drawn from the same domain. The result relation is a subset of the first argument relation, consisting of tuples where the value of the attribute A2 is the same as some value of the attribute B of the second relation. The implementation is similar to the implementation of the Intersection operation in that the tuples of the result are successively identified and added to the result relation.

Figure 8.15 illustrates the implementation of the Semi-join operation.

```
        A1          A2         AWF
                             B  BWF
        R1          R2              RWF
MA      |           |         |  |  |  |

 SMITH LONDON XXXXXX 1 0 x      SMITH LONDON XXXXXX 1 0 0
 JONES PARIS  ATHENS 1 1 x      JONES PARIS  ATHENS 1 1 1
 BLAKE PARIS  PARIS  1 1 x      BLAKE PARIS  PARIS  1 1 1
 XXXXX XXXXXX BERLIN 0 1 x      XXXXX XXXXXX BERLIN 0 1 0
 CLARK LONDON XXXXXX 1 0 x      CLARK LONDON XXXXXX 1 0 0
 ADAMS ATHENS XXXXXX 1 0 x      ADAMS ATHENS XXXXXX 1 0 1

Before                         After
```

Figure 8.15 Semi-join.

The execution time of the Semi-join operation is

$$T_{Semi-join} = 30*b*N2 \text{ clock cycles.}$$

N2 is the cardinality of the second relation and b is the size of the tuple of the second relation.

## Projection

The result of the Projection operation is a relation which is both a 'vertical' and a 'horizontal' subset of the argument relation. Producing the vertical subset is simple, the Master Processor just records which attributes of the argument relation belong to the result relation in the directory with information about relations loaded in the Associative Array. Producing the horizontal subset is computationally more difficult. After an attribute is eliminated from the argument relation, the tuples with remaining data must be compared with each other. If there are some identical tuples, only one must be chosen to belong to the result relation.

There are two variants of the Projection operation, called Projection1 and Projection2, both illustrated in 8.16.

Projection1: If a key attribute in the argument relation, uniquely identifying each tuple, is still present in the result relation, then there is no need for checking the redundancy in the result. The existence of the key guarantees that there are no identical tuples in the relation. The execution of Projection1 in the Associative Array consists of copying the Markbitslice of the argument relation into the Markbitslice of the result relation.

Projection2: If none of the attributes of the argument relation going over to the result relation (or their combination) is a key, the candidates for tuples of the result must be checked for redundancy. The idea behind the implementation is that the nonredundant tuples of the argument relation are successively selected and added into the result relation.

```
         A1          A2 AWF
         R1                 R1WF
                 R2              R2WF
MA       I          I    I     I     I

  XXXXX  XXXXXX   0   x   x        XXXXX  XXXXX   0   0   0
  SMITH  LONDON   1   x   x        SMITH  LONDON  1   1   1
  JONES  PARIS    1   x   x        JONES  PARIS   1   1   1
  BLAKE  PARIS    1   x   x        BLAKE  PARIS   1   1   0
  CLARK  LONDON   1   x   x        CLARK  LONDON  1   1   0
  ADAMS  ATHENS   1   x   x        ADAMS  ATHENS  1   1   1

Before                            After
```

Figure 8.16 Projection.

The execution time of the Projection1 operation is

$$T_{Projection1} = 2 \quad \text{clock cycles}$$

and the execution of the Projection2 takes

$$T_{Projection2} = 30*b*NR2 \quad \text{clock cycles.}$$

b is the size of the attribute on which the argument relation is projected and NR2 is the cardinality of the result relation.

Division

The result of the Division operation is a 'horizontal' and 'vertical' subset of the dividend relation. We assume that the dividend has two attributes, A1 and A2, and that the divisor has one, B. Values of A2 and B must be drawn from the same domain. The implementation of the Division operation is rather complicated. Basically it proceeds in two phases. In the first phase, tuples from the divisor are successively compared to the attribute A2 of the dividend and a field with a partial result consisting of bitslices with the results of each comparison is created. In the second phase, the information from the partial result field is used in identifying those values of the attribute A1 of the dividend that will become the tuples of the result relation.

Figure 8.17 illustrates the implementation of the Division operation. We give the state of the Memory Array before the computation, after its first phase, and when it is completed.

```
      A1 A2                  AWF
                      B            BWF
      R1                                 RWF
MA     |   |           |      |      |    |
 ┌─────────────────────────────────────────┐
 │ LONDON P1          XX     1      0    x  │
 │ ATHENS P3          P1     1      1    x  │
 │ PARIS  P2          P2     1      1    x  │
 │ XXXXXX XX          XX     0      0    x  │
 │ LONDON P2          XX     1      0    x  │
 │ PARIS  P1          XX     1      0    x  │
 │ BERLIN P2          XX     1      0    x  │
 └─────────────────────────────────────────┘
```

Before

```
                    I  II
                    |   |
 ┌─────────────────────────────────────────┐
 │ LONDON P1    1  0   XX     1      0    0 │
 │ ATHENS P3    0  0   P1     1      1    0 │
 │ PARIS  P2    0  1   P2     1      1    0 │
 │ XXXXXX XX    0  0   XX     0      0    0 │
 │ LONDON P2    0  1   XX     1      0    0 │
 │ PARIS  P1    1  0   XX     1      0    0 │
 │ BERLIN P2    0  1   XX     1      0    0 │
 └─────────────────────────────────────────┘
```

After Phase 1

```
 ┌─────────────────────────────────────────┐
 │ LONDON P1          XX     1      0    1  │
 │ ATHENS P3          P1     1      1    0  │
 │ PARIS  P2          P2     1      1    1  │
 │ XXXXXX XX          XX     0      0    0  │
 │ LONDON P2          XX     1      0    0  │
 │ PARIS  P1          XX     1      0    0  │
 │ BERLIN P2          XX     1      0    0  │
 └─────────────────────────────────────────┘
```

After

Figure 8.17 Division.

The approximate execution time of the Division operation is

$$T_{Division} = 30*b(NA1+*N2) + 4*N2*NA1 \quad clock\ cycles.$$

b is the size of the attributes, N2 is the cardinality of the divisor and NA1 is the number of different values of the first attribute of the dividend.

Union

The Union of two argument relations gives as a result a relation assembled from all tuples of the first relation and those tuples of the second relation which are not already in the first one.

Figure 8.18 illustrates the implementation of the Union operation.

```
        A       AWF
            B       BWF
        R               RWF
MA      I       I   I   I   I

┌─────────────────────────────┐   ┌─────────────────────────────┐
│ LONDON   PARIS    1   1   x  │   │ LONDON   PARIS    1   1   1  │
│ ATHENS   XXXXXX   1   0   x  │   │ ATHENS   XXXXXX   1   0   1  │
│ PARIS    ROME     1   1   x  │   │ PARIS    ROME     1   1   1  │
│ XXXXXX   LONDON   0   1   x  │   │ BERLIN   LONDON   0   1   1  │
│ MADRID   BERLIN   1   1   x  │   │ MADRID   BERLIN   1   1   1  │
│ ROME     HAAG     1   1   x  │   │ ROME     HAAG     1   1   1  │
│ XXXXXX   XXXXXX   0   0   x  │   │ HAAG     XXXXXX   0   0   1  │
│ XXXXXX   XXXXXX   0   0   x  │   │ XXXXXX   XXXXXX   0   0   0  │
└─────────────────────────────┘   └─────────────────────────────┘
Before                             After
```

Figure 8.18 Union.


The execution time for the Union operation is

$$T_{Union} = 30*b*N2 + 18*b*p*N2 \text{ clock cycles.}$$

b is the size of the tuple, N2 is the cardinality of the second argument relation, and p is the ratio between the number of tuples of the second relation added to the result relation and N2.


Product

The Product operation has two relations as its arguments. The result is the concatenation of all combinations of tuples of the argument relations.

Figure 8.19 illustrates the implementation of the Product operation.

```
          A                        AWF
                   B                       BWF
                           R1        R2          RWF
MA      I          I        I        I    I   I   I

 ┌─────────────────────────────────────────────────┐
 │  XXXXX  XXXXXX   XXXXX XXXXXX  0  0  x           │
 │  XXXXX  LONDON   XXXXX XXXXXX  0  1  x           │
 │  SMITH  XXXXXX   XXXXX XXXXXX  1  0  x           │
 │  CLARK  PARIS    XXXXX XXXXXX  1  1  x           │
 │  BLAKE  XXXXXX   XXXXX XXXXXX  1  0  x           │
 │  XXXXX  XXXXXX   XXXXX XXXXXX  0  0  x           │
 └─────────────────────────────────────────────────┘
Before

 ┌─────────────────────────────────────────────────┐
 │  XXXXX  XXXXXX   SMITH LONDON  0  0  1           │
 │  XXXXX  LONDON   SMITH PARIS   0  1  1           │
 │  SMITH  XXXXXX   CLARK LONDON  1  0  1           │
 │  CLARK  PARIS    CLARK PARIS   1  1  1           │
 │  BLAKE  XXXXXX   BLAKE LONDON  1  0  1           │
 │  XXXXX  XXXXXX   BLAKE PARIS   0  0  1           │
 └─────────────────────────────────────────────────┘
After
```

Figure 8.19 Product.

The execution time of the Product operation is

$$T_{Projection} = 22*b*N1*N2 \text{ clock cycles.}$$

b is the size of a tuple N1 is the cardinality of the first and N2 of the second relation.

Join

Among different variants of Join operations we will demonstrate the Join where the result, obtained by concatenating tuples of two argument relations satisfying some specified condition, does not contain the joining attributes.

We assume that both the first and the second argument relation have two attributes, called A1 and A2, and B1 and B2, respectively. The joining attributes are A2 and B2, the condition for joining is their equality. The idea behind the implementation is that values from the attribute A2 of the first relation are successively transferred to the Comparand Register and compared with A2 and B2. Thus selected tuples from the first and the second relation are subsequently concatenated by the Product operation into the tuples of the result relation.

Figure 8.20 illustrates the execution.

The execution time of the Join operation is

$$T_{Join2} = 48*b*NA2 + NA2*(1-p)*TP \text{ clock cycles.}$$

b is the size of the join attribute, NA2 is the number of different values in the join attribute of the first relation, p is the number of values of the join attribute of the first relation which do not match any value in the second relation, TP is the average time for the Product operation.

| MA | A1 | A2 | B1 | B2 | R1 | R2 | AWF | BWF | RWF |
|---|---|---|---|---|---|---|---|---|---|
| LONDON | P1 | PARIS | P1 | XXXXXX | XXXXXX | | 1 | 1 | x |
| XXXXXX | XX | OSLO | P1 | XXXXXX | XXXXXX | | 0 | 1 | x |
| ATHENS | P1 | PARIS | P2 | XXXXXX | XXXXXX | | 1 | 1 | x |
| BERLIN | P2 | XXXXXX | XX | XXXXXX | XXXXXX | | 1 | 0 | x |
| XXXXXX | XX | XXXXXX | XX | XXXXXX | XXXXXX | | 0 | 0 | x |
| XXXXXX | XX | XXXXXX | XX | XXXXXX | XXXXXX | | 0 | 0 | x |

Before

| MA | A1 | A2 | B1 | B2 | R1 | R2 | AWF | BWF | RWF |
|---|---|---|---|---|---|---|---|---|---|
| LONDON | P1 | PARIS | P1 | LONDON | PARIS | | 1 | 1 | 1 |
| XXXXXX | XX | OSLO | P1 | LONDON | OSLO | | 0 | 1 | 1 |
| ATHENS | P1 | PARIS | P2 | ATHENS | PARIS | | 1 | 1 | 1 |
| BERLIN | P2 | XXXXXX | XX | ATHENS | OSLO | | 1 | 0 | 1 |
| XXXXXX | XX | XXXXXX | XX | BERLIN | PARIS | | 0 | 0 | 1 |
| XXXXXX | XX | XXXXXX | XX | XXXXXX | XXXXXX | | 0 | 0 | 0 |

After

Figure 8.20 Join.

## 8.2.5 Performance analysis

One of the fundamental results of Computer Science is the insight that any hardware structure (with some necessary minimal capabilities) can, in principle, compute any computable function. Consequently, the sole fact that operations of relational algebra can be implemented on LUCAS is hardly surprising. Rather more interesting is the question whether they can be implemented efficiently or not.

The Associative Array of LUCAS may serve as a model of a special hardware component of a database computer, maybe larger than LUCAS but with similar properties, and the timing equations can be used in a quantitative analysis of the feasibility of using this component.

The analysis of the timing equations is complicated by the fact that the execution time is dependent not only on the size of argument relations but also on their contents. For example, the execution time of the Projection operation is proportional to the cardinality of the result relation. In order to be able to determine the very important average behaviour of the algorithms, it is in some cases necessary to know the statistical properties of a database, e.g. the expected number of matching tuples.

We assume a clock frequency of 5 MHz. The size of the Associative Array will vary from 128 processors (the size of LUCAS today) to 32k processors (the size of the Associative Array which we believe can be built in the future).

Table 8.1 summarizes the approximate timing equations which give the number of clock cycles for each operation.

The size of the Associative Array is not a parameter in the timing equations. This means that the execution time for an operation on data loaded in an Associative Array with a given size is the same as the execution time on any larger Associative Array. Hence, the relations will always be assumed to be of the largest possible cardinality for the given size of the Associative Array.

| Selection | 10*b |
|---|---|
| Intersection | 30*b*N1 |
| Difference | 30*b*N1 |
| Semi-join | 30*b*N2 |
| Projection1 | 2 |
| Projection2 | 30*b*NR2 |
| Division | 30*b*(N/N2 + N2) + 4*N |
| Union | 30*b*N2 + 18*b*p*N2 |
| Product | 22*b*N1*N2 |
| Join2 | 48*b*NA2 + NA2*(1-p)*TP |

Table 8.1 Approximate execution times of algebraic operations on LUCAS

We will compare the performance of the Associative Array with the performance of a conventional sequential computer. To make this comparison meaningful it is very important to carefully determine what performance measure is to be used. The problem is that we want to compare the execution time of a well defined system with the performance of a computer about which only one general property, its sequential mode of operation, is assumed.

We will base our comparison method on the following observation: The implementation of algebraic operations on a sequential computer is typically based on sorting and merging of tuples of operand relations. For example the Join consists of sorting the operands and merging the sorted relations. Sorting and merging methods are essentially based on comparisons [Knuth73]. Thus, we assume that the primitive operation of a sequential evaluation of algebraic operations is the comparison of two tuples. We will estimate the number of necessary comparisons for an operation, assuming a ´good´ sequential algorithm. (By ´good´ we mean an algorithm using a minimum number of comparisons, even though this is not the only way of measuring the effectiveness of sorting and merging.) Then, if we divide the (known) execution time for an operation in the Associative Array by the number of comparisons and by the number of bytes in a tuple (to compensate for get rid different word-lengths) we obtain a measure which we call an Equivalent Sequential Compare time , ESC. (The influence of the length of a tuple in defining ESC could be eliminated because all execution times, cf. Table 8.1, are linear in b.)

ESC is a rather crude measure, but it is useful for drawing some general conclusions. For example, given an Associative Array, if we know the value of ESC for some algebraic operation then we can conclude that e.g. a 16 bit computer must be able to perform fetch and comparison on two 16 bit words in a time less than twice this value, a 32 bit computer in less than four times this value, etc, in order to be able to achieve the same total execution time for this operation as the Array.

ESC will be quite unfavourable to the Associative Array. ESC reflects only comparisons in the CPU, but sorting or merging involve time consuming data movements, housekeeping operations, etc, as well.

Table 8.2 summarizes the number of necessary comparisons in a sequential implementation of algebraic operations. We are using results from Knuth: to sort n elements at most (n*log n) comparisons are required, to sort n elements having m different values (n*log m) comparisons are required, and that two sorted tables with n elements each can be merged using at most 2*n comparisons.

| Selection | N |
|---|---|
| Intersection | 2*N*logN + 2*N |
| | 2 x sort + merge |
| Difference | 2*N*logN + 2*N |
| | 2 x sort + merge |
| Semi-join | 2*N*log*N + 2*N |
| | 2 x sort + merge |
| Projection2 | N*logNR2 |
| | sort |
| Division | N2*logN2 + 2*N*logN + 2*N |
| | 3 x sort + merge |
| Union | N*log(N/2) + N |
| | 2 x sort (of N/2) + merge |
| Product | 22*b*N1*N2 |
| Join2 | 2*N1*logN1 + 2*N1 |
| | 2 x sort + merge |

<u>Table 8.2</u> Number of comparisons in a sequential implementation

## Intersection Difference, Semi-join

The timing equations for the Intersection, Difference and Semi-join are identical (cf. Table 8.1). For the Intersection and Difference operations, the parameter b is the size of a tuple, and for the Semi-join it is the size of a joining attribute.

Figure 8.21 shows the execution time for two typical sizes (16 and 64) of b.

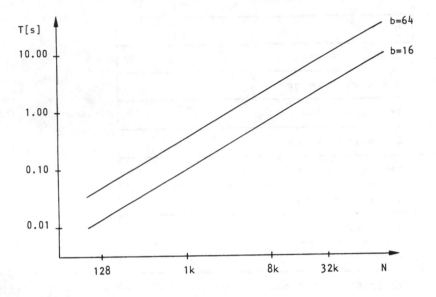

Figure 8.21 Execution times for Intersection, Difference and Semi-join.

For example, computing intersection of two relations with the cardinality of 1 k and a tuple size of 64 bytes takes 0.3 seconds. On twice as large relations it takes 0.6 seconds etc. The maximum possible performance increases linearly with the size (cost), of the Associative Array. This seems to be a very good result, but because we live in the world of sequential computers we must also look at the ESC.

Figure 8.22 shows ESC (in nanoseconds).

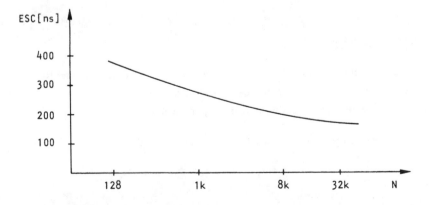

Figure 8.22 ESC for Intersection, Difference, Semi-join.

By examining Figure 8.22, two observations can be made.

The first is that if a sequential computer is to outperform LUCAS (128 processors), it must make a comparison of two bytes in at most 375 nanoseconds, which is very fast even for minicomputers.

The second observation is the following. If we increase the size of the Associative Array e. g. from 128 to 32k, it will be possible to process 256 times larger relations (in 256 times longer time). But, the same execution time on a sequentional computer can be achieved by decreasing the time which is necessary for a byte comparison to only a half, which amounts to e.g. a doubling of the clock frequency.

Selection

Table 8.3 gives the execution time, in microseconds, for an attribute size of 16 and 64 bytes. It also gives ESC, in nanoseconds (!).

| b / N | 128 | 1 k | 8 k | 32 k |
|-------|-----|-----|-----|------|
| 16 | 32 | 32 | 32 | 32 |
| 64 | 128 | 128 | 128 | 128 |
| ESC | 15 | 1.9 | 0.24 | 0.061 |

Table 8.3 Execution times for Selection

No matter how small or how large a relation is, as long as it fits in the Associative Array the execution time of the Selection operation is the same. Notice the impressing speed of Selection on larger arrays.

Projection

NR2 in the timing equation of the Projection can be expressed as $p*N$, where $p$ is the probability that a given tuple will belong to the result, and $N$ is the cardinality of the operand relation. Figure 8.23 shows the execution time for $p=0.1$, $p=0.5$ and $p=1$ for the tuple size $b=64$. The cardinality of the operand relation is the same as the number of processors in the Associative Array.

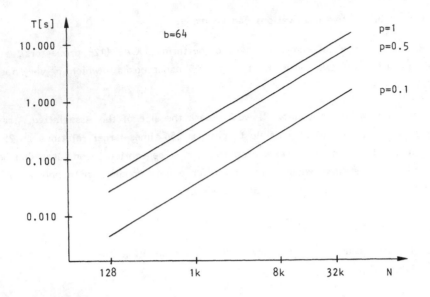

Figure 8.23 Execution time of Projection.

Figure 8.24 shows ESC of the Projection operation.

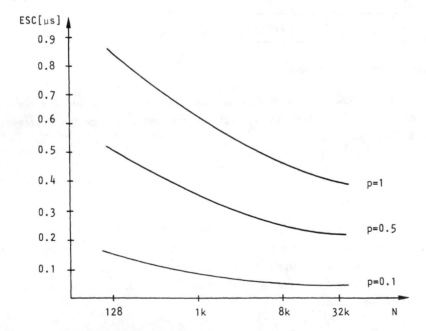

Figure 8.24 ESC for Projection.

Figure 8.24 indicates that for small p, an Associative Array perform much more cost effectively than sequential computers. For example, if a sequential computer is to perform the Projection in the situations where p=0.1 as fast as an Associative Array with 1k processors, it must be able to compare 2 bytes more than $10^7$ times/second.

## Division

Figure 8.25 shows the execution time, and Figure 8.26 shows ESC of the Division operation for b=16 bytes and for N2=0.5*N and N2=0.1*N

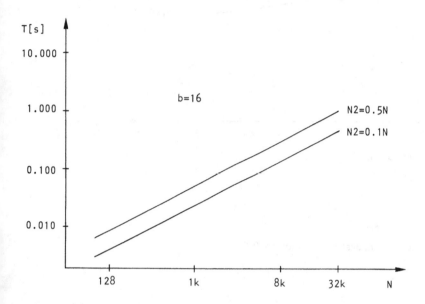

Figure 8.25 Execution time of Division.

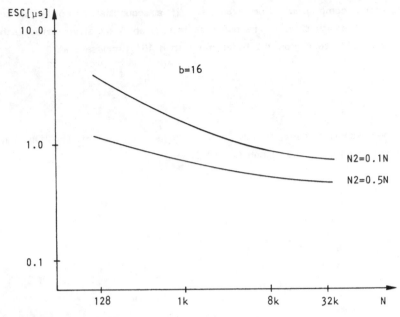

Figure 8.26 ESC for Division.

## Join

We will discuss the Join operation in Section 8.5.

## Union

Both the timing equation and ESC are similar to those of the Projection.

## Product

The advantage of using an Associative Array is that it can execute operations in parallel, e. g. by making comparisons one to many. The Product operation requires only a transfer of tuples and this transfer must be performed serially. In Table 8.2 we can see that the transfer of one byte calls for 22 clock cycles, thus with a 5 MHz clock frequency it makes approximately 4 microseconds. It is quite a slow rate when compared to execution on a sequential computer. But it does not mean that it is not a useful operation. In an Associative Array, the operands to be concatenated may be a result of some previous operation and they are identified associatively, by their Markbitslices. Also, the destination of the result of the Product operation, i.e. those memory words where the result tuples will be assembled, can be determined associatively.

## 8.2.6 Comparison of LUCAS with alternative designs

There are only a few Associative Arrays of the same type as LUCAS on which timing data for relational operations are reported. We will compare LUCAS only with STARAN, RELACS [Oliver79], and with RDB (Relational Database Machine) [Shaw79].

A search operation in STARAN [Berra and Oliver 79], which is equivalent to the Selection operation in LUCAS, takes $1 + 0.2*n$ microseconds where n is the number of bits in the argument. This is roughly equal to 1.6 microseconds/byte. In LUCAS this operation takes 10 clock cycles, with a clock frequency of 5 MHz we obtain 2 microseconds/byte. STARAN is slightly faster. We can also compare the reading times. It takes 16 microseconds to read one 256-bit word from the array of STARAN, it is 0.5 microseconds/byte. In LUCAS, to copy one byte from a memory word into an I/O Register takes 8 clock cycles which is 1.6 microseconds. STARAN is 3 times faster. If a whole 128-bytes byteslice is to be read from LUCAS it takes $128 + 8$ clock cycles which is 0.2 microseconds/byte, and this make LUCAS twice as fast as STARAN. The maximum size of the attribute on STARAN is 256 bits, on LUCAS it is over 500 bytes.

This relative similarity of performance between STARAN and LUCAS with respect to I/O and search processing makes it possible to apply many conclusions about the usefuleness of STARAN to LUCAS as well. For example, Berra and Oliver [Berra and Oliver 79] have convincingly demonstrated the great potential of STARAN in a database management environment.

In RELACS, which is a paper machine, an Associative Unit has an assumed size of between 1k and 100k words and a width of 1k bits. The search operation has an assumed speed of half that of STARAN, 3.2 microseconds/byte, 1.6 times that of LUCAS. More complex operations, such as Join, are implemented in RELACS with the help of a Comparand Register array, providing for parallel comparison many to many. In principle, this feature can be implemented [Digby73], but because of the complexity of connections we believe it will never be practically feasible.

RDB is also a paper machine. Its central part is a Primary Associative Memory, PAM, which could be realized with a large-scale distributed logic memory, or with a bit-serial or word serial design. It has a capacity of between 10k and 1M bytes (the capacity of LUCAS is 128*512=64k bytes). The time for the Selection operation is more than 0.8 microseconds/byte.

The capabilities of PAM are satisfied by LUCAS. For example a command of PAM such as

        parallel set <flag> in all <tuple variable> of <relation> with <conditions>

corresponds to the Selection operation in LUCAS. A control structure

for each ⟨tuple variable⟩ with ⟨conditions⟩ set ⟨flag⟩ and do ⟨statement⟩

of PAM can be implemented with the help of the Select first and remove operation in LUCAS.

This makes RDB algorithms comparable to algorithms on LUCAS.

For example, in LUCAS, the number of searches needed for the Project operation is equal to the cardinality of the result relation. In PAM, the number of searches is twice the cardinality of the result relation. This is because one of the two searches in the main loop of the RDB algorithm, is executed as a simple Select first and remove operation on LUCAS. This makes our algorithm faster. Similar observations can be made when analyzing algorithms for the Intersection and Difference operations. While the RDB algorithm for Join makes it necessary to perform search three times for each tuple of one of the operand relations, our alghorithm makes it necessary to do search only twice for each unique value of a joining attribute of one of the relations! The number of searches is thus considerably smaller on LUCAS than on PAM.

## 8.3 INTERNAL QUERY EVALUATION IN A SIMPLE DATABASE COMPUTER

### 8.3.1 Introduction

In this section we will demonstrate a method for evaluating queries in a simple database computer which is equipped with an Associative Array.

The method is based on decomposition of a query into a sequence of algebraic operations which are serially executed on relations in the Associative Array.

As a general environment for query evaluation we will assume the system configuration shown in Figure 8.27. This configuration forms a simple database computer consisting of: a Master Processor, a Disk memory, a Console and an Associative Array. We assume that the cardinality of relations necessary for answering a query is such that they fit inside the Associative Array.

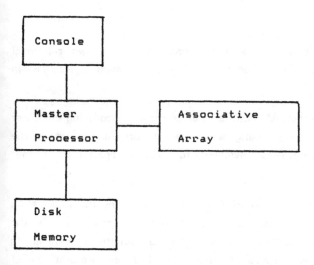

Figure 8.27 A simple database computer.

The database computer operates in the following way. A query to the database is parsed and translated by the Master Processor into a sequence of algebraic operations. The Master Processor determines which relations are needed for answering the query and if they are not present in the Associative Array, it allocates a free area in the Associative Array and loads these relations from the disk memory. The Master Processor maintains two directories, a disk directory with information about relations on the disk and an array directory with information about relations currently in the Associative Array. The array directory provides the Master Processor with information about addresses of attributes and Workfields, types and sizes of attributes, etc. The execution of a query is governed by a sequence of instructions issued by the Master Processor. Before each instruction, some necessary parameters are sent to the Control Unit of the Associative Array. The result of an instruction is always a new relation created in the Associative Array. The final relation in this sequence is the answer to the query. This relation can subsequently be saved on the disk and added to the database or submitted to some application program (computing e.g. averages) or it can simply be displayed on the Console.

The database computer must perform many other functions in addition to those described above, but we will concentrate our interest only on the use of the Associative Array in answering queries.

### 8.3.2 Database

We demonstrate the evaluation method by using the probably best known relational database in the world, the Suppliers-Parts-Projects (S-P-P) database which is described in [Date81].

The S-P-P database, used by a hypothetical multinational corporation producing computer hardware, contains the information concerning a number of projects in which the corporation is involved. All the information available to users is represented in four relations S, P, J and SPJ.

Relation S , one instance of which is shown in Figure 8.28, contains the information about suppliers of different parts to current projects. It has four attributes: S# the unique supplier number, SNAME the suppliers' names, STATUS with the integers giving status of each supplier, and CITY with names of cities. The intended interpretation of the attribute CITY is the location of the suppliers. The key of this relation is the attribute S#.

| S | | | |
|------|-------|------|--------|
| S# | SNAME | STAT | CITY |
| S1 | SMITH | 20 | LONDON |
| S2 | JONES | 10 | PARIS |
| S3 | BLAKE | 30 | PARIS |
| S4 | CLARK | 20 | LONDON |
| S5 | ADAMS | 30 | ATHENS |

Figure 8.28 Relation S.

Relation P , shown in Figure 8.29, contains the information about parts supplied to different projects. It has five attributes: P# the unique part number, PNAME the names of parts, COLOR the colours of parts, WEIGHT the integers giving the weights of parts, CITY names of cities. The intended interpretation of the attribute CITY is the location where the parts are stored. The key of this relation is the attribute P#.

| P |  |  |  |  |
|---|---|---|---|---|
| **P#** | **PNAME** | **COLOR** | **WEIGHT** | **CITY** |
| P1 | NUT | RED | 12 | LONDON |
| P2 | BOLT | GREEN | 17 | PARIS |
| P3 | SCREW | BLUE | 17 | ROME |
| P4 | SCREW | RED | 14 | LONDON |
| P5 | CAM | BLUE | 12 | PARIS |
| P6 | COG | RED | 19 | LONDON |

Figure 8.29 Relation P.

Relation J , shown in Figure 8.30, contains the information about current projects. It has three attributes: J# the unique project numbers of each project, JNAME the names (probably covert) of projects, and CITY the names of cities. The intended interpretation of the attribute CITY is the location of plants where the projects are developed. The key of this relation is the attribute J#.

| J |  |  |
|---|---|---|
| **J#** | **JNAME** | **CITY** |
| J1 | SORTER | PARIS |
| J2 | PUNCH | ROME |
| J3 | READER | ATHENS |
| J4 | CONSOLE | ATHENS |
| J5 | COLLATOR | LONDON |
| J6 | TERMINAL | OSLO |
| J7 | TAPE | LONDON |

Figure 8.30 Relation J.

Relation SPJ , shown in Figure 8.31 connects the information about the specified suppliers supplying the specified parts to the specified projects in the specified quantity. It has four attributes: S# the supplier numbers (same as in relation S), P# the part numbers (same as in relation P), J# the project numbers (same as in relation J), and QTY the integers standing for delivered quantity. The key of this relation is the combination of the S#, P# and J# attributes.

| SPJ | | | |
|-----|-----|-----|-----|
| S#  | P#  | J#  | QTY |
| S1  | P1  | J1  | 200 |
| S1  | P1  | J4  | 700 |
| S2  | P3  | J1  | 400 |
| S2  | P3  | J2  | 200 |
| S2  | P3  | J3  | 200 |
| S2  | P3  | J4  | 500 |
| S2  | P3  | J5  | 600 |
| S2  | P3  | J6  | 400 |
| S2  | P3  | J7  | 800 |
| S2  | P5  | J2  | 100 |
| S3  | P3  | J1  | 200 |
| S3  | P4  | J2  | 500 |
| S4  | P6  | J3  | 300 |
| S4  | P6  | J7  | 300 |
| S5  | P2  | J2  | 200 |
| S5  | P2  | J4  | 100 |
| S5  | P5  | J5  | 500 |
| S5  | P5  | J7  | 100 |
| S5  | P6  | J2  | 200 |
| S5  | P1  | J4  | 1000 |
| S5  | P3  | J4  | 1200 |
| S5  | P4  | J4  | 800 |
| S5  | P5  | J4  | 400 |
| S5  | P6  | J4  | 500 |

Figure 8.31 Relation SPJ.

As an example of how to interpret a tuple of the SPJ relation we can look at the first tuple which is <S1, P1, J1, 200>. It says that the supplier S1 has delivered 200 units of part P1 to project J1.

The connection between different relations in the S-P-P database is mediated by the fact that the attributes S#, P# and J# in the relation SPJ have the same domains as the key attributes in the relations S, P and J and also that the attributes called CITY in the S, P and J relation have values drawn from the same domain. The fact that the attributes have the same name in different relations is just incidental.

## 8.3.3 Evaluation of a query

A query is executed as a series of operations on relations in the Associative Array. Each operation creates a new, temporary, relation from one or two old relations. The final relation in this sequence is the result of the query. The execution is guided by the Master Processor issuing instructions and their parameters to the Control Unit of the

Associative Array. In the case of the Selection operation, a value to be compared with the contents of some attribute of a relation in the Associative Array is loaded directly into the Comparand Register.

We demonstrate our method in two examples, showing steps in which queries to the S-P-P database are executed. An accompanying figure will display all relevant original relations and all temporary relations created during the execution. The Markbitslices will be given to the right of the relations, whereas their actual position in the Associative Array is determined by the Master Processor.

To understand how the information in the figures should be interpreted we can study Figure 8.32. It shows data of three relations J, T1 and T2 in the Associative Array together with their associated Markbitslices. Above the relations we indicate which attributes belong to which relations. Relations J and T1 have three attributes (J#, JNAME, CITY) each, and relation T2 has one attribute (JNAME). Relation J is one of the original relations of the S-P-J database, T1 is a derived relation obtained by the operation Selection on J where the value of the attribute CITY is LONDON. T2 is the result of the Projection of T1 on the attribute JNAME, it only consists of two tuples with the values TAPE and COLLATOR. The information about names of relations, addresses to attributes and Workfields is maintained by the Supporting Processor.

| J# | JNAME | CITY | TTJ 21 |
|----|-------|------|--------|
| J1 | SORTER | PARIS | 1 |
| J2 | PUNCH | ROME | 1 |
| J3 | READER | ATHENS | 1 |
| J4 | CONSOLE | ATHENS | 1 |
| J5 | COLLATOR | LONDON | 111 |
| J6 | TERMINAL | OSLO | 1 |
| J7 | TAPE | LONDON | 111 |

Figure 8.32 Relations J, T1, and T2.

QUERY 1: Get names of projects supplied by supplier S1.

There is no relation connecting the supplier numbers with the names of the projects which they supply. Hence, the information from two relations, SPJ connecting the supplier numbers with the project numbers and J connecting the project numbers with the project names, is needed. To answer the query, the numbers of the projects supplied by supplier S1 must be extracted from SPJ and used in J to look up the names of those projects.

The execution of the query in the Associative Array consists of the following four steps:

1) T1:= SPJ WHERE S#='S1'
2) T2:= T1[J#]
3) T3:= J SEMIJOIN T2 ON J#
4) T4:= T3[JNAME]

Figure 8.33 illustrates the execution. In step 1 , the value S1 is loaded into the Comparand Register above the attribute S# of SPJ and the Selection is performed, creating the relation T1. Relation T1 consists of tuples of SPJ pointed out by the Markbitslice of T1. In step 2 , the Projection2 of T1 on the attribute J# is performed creating the relation T2. In step 3 , relation T3 is created by the Semi-join between J and T2 on the attribute J# with a domain common to both relations. Data of relation T3 are physically a subset of J. In step 4 , the result of the query, the relation T4, is produced by the Projection2 of T3 on the attribute JNAME.

| T1 / SPJ | | | | S TTP 21J | T3 / J | | | TTJ 43 |
|---|---|---|---|---|---|---|---|---|
| S# | P# | J# | QTY | | J# | JNAME | CITY | |
| S1 | P1 | J1 | 200 | 111 | J1 | SORTER | PARIS | 111 |
| S1 | P1 | J4 | 700 | 111 | J2 | PUNCH | ROME | 1 |
| S2 | P3 | J1 | 400 | 1 | J3 | READER | ATHENS | 1 |
| S2 | P3 | J2 | 200 | 1 | J4 | CONSOLE | ATHENS | 111 |
| S2 | P3 | J3 | 200 | 1 | J5 | COLLATOR | LONDON | 1 |
| S2 | P3 | J4 | 500 | 1 | J6 | TERMINAL | OSLO | 1 |
| S2 | P3 | J5 | 600 | 1 | J7 | TAPE | LONDON | 1 |
| S2 | P3 | J6 | 400 | 1 | | | | |
| S2 | P3 | J7 | 800 | 1 | | | | |
| S2 | P5 | J2 | 100 | 1 | | | | |
| S3 | P3 | J1 | 200 | 1 | | | | |
| S3 | P4 | J2 | 500 | 1 | | | | |
| S4 | P6 | J3 | 300 | 1 | | | | |
| S4 | P6 | J7 | 300 | 1 | | | | |
| S5 | P2 | J2 | 200 | 1 | | | | |
| S5 | P2 | J4 | 100 | 1 | | | | |
| S5 | P5 | J5 | 500 | 1 | | | | |
| S5 | P5 | J7 | 100 | 1 | | | | |
| S5 | P6 | J2 | 200 | 1 | | | | |
| S5 | P1 | J4 | 1000 | 1 | | | | |
| S5 | P3 | J4 | 1200 | 1 | | | | |
| S5 | P4 | J4 | 800 | 1 | | | | |
| S5 | P5 | J4 | 400 | 1 | | | | |
| S5 | P6 | J4 | 500 | 1 | | | | |

Figure 8.33 Execution of Query 1.

215

The result of Query 1 is the relation T4 with one attribute, JNAME, consisting of two tuples, <SORTER> and <CONSOLE>.

The execution of Query 1 called for creating four temporary relations from two original relations. But the only new space in the Associative Array used during the execution was the space used by the four Workfields of temporary relations. Four algebraic operations, one Selection, two Projections and one Semi-join were executed.

QUERY 2: Get J# values for projects not supplied with any red part by any London supplier.

The information from all four relations in the database is needed to answer this query. In S the information about the supplier numbers and the names of the cities are given, in P the part numbers and the part colour are located, J gives the project numbers of all current projects and finally, SPJ connects the part numbers, the project numbers and the supplier numbers.

The execution consists of the following nine steps:
1) T1:= S WHERE CITY='LONDON'
2) T2:= S[S#]                                    ;key
3) T3:= P WHERE COLOR='RED'
4) T4:= T3[P#]                                   ;key
5) T5:= SPJ SEMIJOIN T2 ON S#
6) T6:= T5 SEMIJOIN T4 ON P#
7) T7:= T6[J#]
8) T8:= J[J#]                                    ;key
9) T9:= T8 DIFFERENCE T7

Figure 8.34 illustrates the execution. Steps 1 and 2 produce from S the relation T2 consisting of the supplier numbers of the suppliers in London. Steps 3 and 4 produce T4 consisting of the part numbers of the red parts. Steps 5 and 6 produce T6 with tuples from SPJ including the information about the London suppliers of red parts. The Projection2 of T6 on the attribute J# in step 7 gives T7 consisting of the project numbers of the projects supplied by the London suppliers with red parts. Step 8 gives T8 from J by the Projection1 on the attribute J#. T8 contains the project numbers of all current projects. Finally, in step 9 the Difference between T8 and T7 creates the result relation T9.

**T2**

**T1**

**S**

| S# | SNAME | STAT | CITY | TTS 21 |
|----|-------|------|------|--------|
| S1 | SMITH | 20 | LONDON | 111 |
| S2 | JONES | 10 | PARIS | 1 |
| S3 | BLAKE | 30 | PARIS | 1 |
| S4 | CLARK | 20 | LONDON | 111 |
| S5 | ADAMS | 30 | ATHENS | 1 |

**T4**

**T3**

**P**

| P# | PNAME | COLOR | WEIGHT | CITY | TTP 43 |
|----|-------|-------|--------|------|--------|
| P1 | NUT | RED | 12 | LONDON | 111 |
| P2 | BOLT | GREEN | 17 | PARIS | 1 |
| P3 | SCREW | BLUE | 17 | ROME | 1 |
| P4 | SCREW | RED | 14 | LONDON | 111 |
| P5 | CAM | BLUE | 12 | PARIS | 1 |
| P6 | COG | RED | 19 | LONDON | 111 |

**T7**

**T6**

**T5**

**SPJ**

| S# | P# | J# | QTY | S TTTP 765J |
|----|----|----|-----|-------------|
| S1 | P1 | J1 | 200 | 1111 |
| S1 | P1 | J4 | 700 | 1111 |
| S2 | P3 | J1 | 400 | 1 |
| S2 | P3 | J2 | 200 | 1 |
| S2 | P3 | J3 | 200 | 1 |
| S2 | P3 | J4 | 500 | 1 |
| S2 | P3 | J5 | 600 | 1 |
| S2 | P3 | J6 | 400 | 1 |
| S2 | P3 | J7 | 800 | 1 |
| S2 | P5 | J2 | 100 | 1 |
| S3 | P3 | J1 | 200 | 1 |
| S3 | P4 | J2 | 500 | 1 |
| S4 | P6 | J3 | 300 | 1111 |
| S4 | P6 | J7 | 300 | 1111 |
| S5 | P2 | J2 | 200 | 1 |
| S5 | P2 | J4 | 100 | 1 |
| S5 | P5 | J5 | 500 | 1 |
| S5 | P5 | J7 | 100 | 1 |
| S5 | P6 | J2 | 200 | 1 |
| S5 | P1 | J4 | 1000 | 1 |
| S5 | P3 | J4 | 1200 | 1 |
| S5 | P4 | J4 | 800 | 1 |
| S5 | P5 | J4 | 400 | 1 |
| S5 | P6 | J4 | 500 | 1 |

**T9**

**T8**

**J**

| J# | JNAME | CITY | TTJ 98 |
|----|-------|------|--------|
| J1 | SORTER | PARIS | 11 |
| J2 | PUNCH | ROME | 111 |
| J3 | READER | ATHENS | 11 |
| J4 | CONSOLE | ATHENS | 11 |
| J5 | COLLATOR | LONDON | 111 |
| J6 | TERMINAL | OSLO | 111 |
| J7 | TAPE | LONDON | 11 |

Figure 8.34 Execution of Query 2.

## 8.3.4 Discussion

The method which we have developed is very simple, straightforward and has a number of advantages. One advantage is the speed of evaluation of a query. The Associative Array can be seen as a high-level language architecture. A number of powerful set-oriented operations are implemented directly in the hardware and their execution is very fast because the algorithms take advantage of the parallelism in the Associative Array. Another factor speeding up the evaluation is the one-to-one correspondence between commands defining evaluation of the query and the operation of the Associative Array. Because there is no need for layers of software making tests, translation, interpretation, iteration counts, etc, there is no software overhead slowing down the execution.

Another advantage is the opportunity for simple implementation of the user's views and access privileges. The only way to identify a tuple of a relation in the Associative Array is by using the Markbitslice. A number of users may use the same relations but, having been assigned different Markbitslices, they have access to only a subset of the tuples.

A very advantageous feature of our method is that it saves space in the Associative Array. Except for the Join operation, operations executed during the evaluation of a query do not create new data. The result of an operation is just a new Markbitslice, and even the little space it occupies can be released after the Markbitslice is used by some subsequent operation and no longer is needed.

The main disadvantage of our method is the processing of Joins on relations. The execution of a Join operation is not only slow but it might be the case that its result is larger than both the source relations, with the unhappy consequence that the result cannot be stored in the Associative Array. Fortunately, there is a large class of queries which can be handled without requiring the Join operation, where the much faster Semi-join can be used instead [Bernstein and Chiu 81].

## 8.4 COMPARATIVE PERFORMANCE EVALUATION OF DATABASE COMPUTERS

## 8.4.1 Introduction

In this section we will compare the performance of a backend database computer which contains an Associative Array with a number of other well known database computer designs.

The assumed system, shown in Figure 8.35, consists of a host computer, a disk memory

and an Associative Array with its Master processor.  In the following,  we will refer to
the    combination    of    the    Associative    Array    and    the    disk    as    LUCAS.

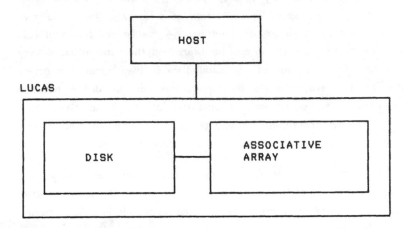

Figure 8.35 LUCAS Database computer.

We will determine a response time of LUCAS to three benchmark retrieval queries.   The
times will be compared with response times reported in [Hawthorn and Dewitt 82],   in a
performance analysis study of alternative database computers.

Hawthorn  and  DeWitt  analyzed  the  performance  of  several  database  computers  with
respect  to  typical  queries  to  a  real  database.    Three  classes  of  relational  queries  were
identified:  overhead-intensive,    data-intensive,    and multirelational queries.   From each
category  one  ´average query´  was  selected  and  it  was  submitted  to  the  following  database
computers:  Associative  Disks  [Slotnick70,     Langdon78],     RAP  (Relational  Associative
Processor)  [Ozkarahan  at  al.75,    Ozkarahan  and  Sevcik  77,    Schuster  at  al.78],    CASSM
(Context  Addressable  Segment  Sequential  Memory)  [Su  and  Lipovsky75,    Lipovski  and  Su78,
Hong  and  Su  81],    DBC  (Data  Base  Computer)  [Banerjee  at  al.78,    Banerjee  at  al.79],
CAFS  (Content  Addressable  File  Store)  [Maller79],    and  DIRECT  [DeWitt79],    and  also  to
a  conventional  computer  system  with  the  INGRES  relational  database  management  system
[Held  at  al.75,    Stonebraker  at  al.76].

All  database  computers  were  assumed  to  function  as  backends  to  a  host,    a  PDP  11/70.
Each  backend  is  a  cellular  system:  data  are  stored  in  cells,    with  one  processor  per  cell.
Operations  on  the  cells  take  place  in  parallel.    The  backends  rely  on  the  host  to  format
the  results  for  printing  and  to  move  the  results  to  the  user´s  terminal.    Those  backends
which  are  not  able  to  carry  out  arithmetic  operations  (included  LUCAS)  rely  on  the  host
to  perform  the  arithmetic  functions  as  well.

## 8.4.2 Specification of characteristics of database machines

Since all of the designs, except CAFS, are paper machines or rudimentary prototypes, Hawthorn and DeWitt made certain assumptions about their characteristics in order to make the performance comparisons fair and meaningful. We will make corresponding assumptions about LUCAS characteristics.

The data storage medium of all designs is assumed to be moving-head Ampex 9200 disk drives. Table 8.4 summarizes its parameters.

| PARAMETER | MEANING | VALUE |
|-----------|---------|-------|
| BSIZE | block size | 512 bytes |
| BTRACK | block/track | 22 blocks |
| DROT | disk rotation time | 16.7 ms |
| DAVAC | average access time | 30 ms |
| DREAD | read time | 0.8 ms/block |
| DCYL | blocks/cylinder | 418 blocks |
| DTRACK | data tracks/cylinder | 19 |

Table 8.4 Disk parameters

Associative Disks, CASSM, DBC, and CAFS are assumed to have cell processors associated with read/write heads of the disks; RAP, DIRECT, and LUCAS are caching systems to which data must be loaded from the disks.

The size of the database computers were assumed to be the following: Associative Disks, CASSM, CAFS, and DBC contain 19 cell processors (one processor/track), RAP contains 16 cells with a capacity of 16k bytes each, and DIRECT contains 8 processors and 16 data cells with a capacity of 16k bytes each. The sizes indicate that we are discussing rather large systems.

Our assumption about LUCAS is that the size of the Associative Array is SIZE=2k processors and the clock frequency is 6 MHz. All other properties are the same as those of the real LUCAS. The width of a memory word of a processor in LUCAS is WIDTH=512 bytes. We will see that it is more than enough for storing the data necessary for answering our particular queries. Since data are read from the disk at 1.5 microseconds/byte, we assume that the time for loading data into the Associative Array is the same as the time for reading them from the disk. When tuples are serially read out from the Associative Array, we assume that it takes DO=2 microseconds/byte (10 clock cycles = 8 for shifting byte into the I/O Register + 2 for copying it into the I/O Buffer Register). A byte in the Comparand Register can be compared with a byteslice in all words in the Associative Array in CPBC=2 microseconds (10 clock cycles), a byte in a selected memory word can be compared with a byteslice in CPB=6 microseconds, and a byte in a selected word can be transferred into all other words in TB=4 microseconds.

The LUCAS parameters are summarized in Table 8.5.

| PARAMETER | MEANING | VALUE |
|-----------|---------|-------|
| f | clock frequency | 5 MHz |
| WIDTH | bytes in memory word | 512 bytes |
| SIZE | processors | 2048 processors |
| DI | data rate in | 0.0015 ms/byte |
| DO | data rate out | 0.002 ms/byte |
| CPBC | compare byte to CR | 0.002 ms |
| CPB | compare byte in word | 0.006 ms |
| TB | transfer byte | 0.004 ms |

Table 8.5 LUCAS parameters

There is one further parameter to take into account in the timing equations for the total response time to a query. This is the host overhead time, HOV, which is due to query compilation and communication with the backend. HOV was carefully analyzed by Hawthorn and DeWitt who estimate that it is 0.042 s in the best case and 0.22 s in the worst case.

8.4.3 Database and queries

The database for the three queries is the University of California at Berkeley Department of Electrical Engineering and Computer Science's course and room scheduling database. This database contains 24704 pages of data (12.6 Mbytes) in 102 relations. The data are information about courses taught: instructor's name, course name, room number, type of course, etc.

The queries are actual queries.

Query  Q1  is  representative  for  a  class  of  short  overhead-intensive  queries.

Q1:  retrieve(QTRCOURSE.day,  QTRCOURSE.hour)
     where  QTRCOURSE.instructor="despain,a.m."

The relation QTRCOURSE contains 1110 tuples. Each tuple has 24 attributes and is 127
bytes long. The relation is stored as a heap in 274 pages (blocks on disks). The
attribute "day" is a character field,  7 bytes long; "hour" is 14 bytes long; the size of
"instructor" is not specified in the paper,  we assume that it is 30 bytes long.

In the test run at Berkeley,  three tuples satisfied this query.

It shall be assumed that the following algorithm is used in processing query Q1 in LUCAS:

1) The relation QTRCOURSE is loaded into the Associative Array. The size of the
relation is such that the whole relation can be loaded into the Array.

2) The values of the attribute "instructor" are compared in parallel with
´despain,a.m.´ in a Comparand Register. As a result,  three tuples are selected.

3) The values of "day" and "hour" of the selected tuples are output to the host.
Since obviously each combination (day,hour,instructor) is unique,  it is not necessary
to check the result for redundancy.

Query  Q2  is  representative  for  a  class  of  data-intensive  multirelational  queries.

Q2:  retrieve(ROOMS.building,  ROOMS.roomnum,
              ROOMS.capacity,  COURSE.day,  COURSE.hour)
        where  ROOMS.roomnum=COURSE.roomnum  and
               ROOMS.building=COURSE.building  and
               ROOMS.type="lab"

The relation COURSE contains 11436 tuples in 2858 pages (1.4 Mbytes) with information
about all the courses taught in the last four years. It requires 130 tracks (7 cylinders) of
disk space. The relation ROOMS contains 282 tuples in 29 pages with information about
every room that EECS Department can use for teaching courses. The (roomnum,building)
attribute pair is 20 bytes long,  the sizes of the attributes "capacity" and "type" is not
specified,  we assume they are 5 and 3 bytes long respectively.

There are 22 labs,  and they were used 422 times in total. The result of this query is a
list which contains the building,  room number,  capacity,  day,  and hour of use of any
lab for the last four years.

The algorithm used by LUCAS is the following:

1) The relation ROOMS is loaded into the Associative Array.

2) The 22 tuples with the information about labs are selected.

3) Cylinders of pages of the COURSE relation (1634 tuples each) are successively loaded from disks into the Associative Array, joined with the 22 tuples of the ROOMS relation and the result is output to the host. (This type of external Join evaluation will be discussed in Section 8.5.)

Query Q3 is representative for a class of data-intensive queries on a single relation. It includes an aggregate function.

Q3: retrieve(GMASTER.acct, GMASTER.fund,
             encumb=sum(GMASTER.encumb by
             GMASTER.acct, GMASTER.fund))

The relation GMASTER contains 194 tuples in 97 pages. The sizes of the attributes are not specified, we assume that they are each 10 bytes long.

There are 17 unique values for the (acct,fund) pair. The query returns to the user the 17 unique (acct,fund) pairs along with their associated sums of values of the attribute "encumb".

This query can be executed in LUCAS in the following steps:

1) The relation GMASTER is loaded into the Associative Array.

2) By an operation similar to Projection, all tuples with identical (acct,fund) pairs are selected. Then, for each such partition, one (acct,fund) pair is output to the host together with "encumb" values of all tuples.

3) The host accumulates the sum of "encumb" values.

## 8.4.4 Response times of LUCAS

The response time to a query is the sum of the time spent in all components of the machine that cannot be overlapped.

### Q1-Short query

The response time of LUCAS to query Q1, AAWORK, is given by

AAWORK= HOV + DAVAC + 274*DREAD + AAPROC + AAOUT

where HOV is the host overhead time, DAVAC is the access time to the first track on disks with data of QTRCOURSE, 274*DREAD is the time for reading 274 pages of the QTRCOURSE relation from the disk, AAPROC is the time spent on processing in the Associative Array and AAOUT is the time spent on returning the result to the host.

Since the size of the attribute "instructor" is 30 bytes, AAPROC is equal to

AAPROC= 30*CPBC = 0.060 ms.

Since the attribute "date" and "hour" are 21 bytes long together and since 3 tuples are read out,

AAOUT= 3*21*DO = 0.126 ms.

The worst case value of AAWORK is then

AAWORK= 0.22 + 0.03 + 274*0.0008 + 0.000060 + 0.000126 = 0.46 s

Notice that the time spent on processing data in the Associative Array is negligible when compared to the overhead time or to the data transfer time.

The best case value of AAWORK is obtained if the Associative Array already holds the relation QTRCOURSE at the time when the query is issued and loading time is 0

AAWORK= 0.042 + 0.000060 + 0.000126 = 0.042 s.

The situation that the relation is already in the Associative Array when a query is issued is in fact quite realistic. It is often the case that the same set of data is interrogated over and over again.

## Q2-Multirelation query

The response time to query Q2 is given by:

```
AAWORK= 2*HOV              ;host overhead, it is 2*HOV because
                          ;two relations will be accessed
  + DAVAC + 29*DREAD       ;time for loading ROOMS
  + 7*(DAVAC + 412*DREAD)  ;time for loading 7 cylinders
                          ;of COURSE


  + 3*CPBC                ;selection on ROOMS
  + 7*(22*20*CPB)         ;7 times join of 22 tuples of ROOM
                          ;with one cylinder load
  + 7*(22*5*TB)           ;7 times transfer of 22 values of
                          ;"capacity"
  + 7*(60*50*DO)          ;7 times output of result tuples

  = (2.71-3.07) s         ;best case and worst case times,
                          ;depending on HOV
```

The last term gives the time spent on outputting the 422 tuples of the result. We have assumed that they are uniformly distributed in the 7 COURSE loads, thus giving 60 tuples/load.

## Q3-Aggregate Functions

The response time to query Q3 is given by:

```
AAWORK= HOV
  + DAVAC + 97*DREAD    ;time for loading GMASTER

  + 17*20*CPB           ;time to select 17 partitions
  + 17*20*DO            ;time to output (acct,fund) pairs
  + 194*10*DO           ;time to output encumb values
  + HDP                 ;time for computing 17 sums in the host

  = (0.16-0.34) s + HDP
```

We estimate, rather conservatively that HDP, which is the time to compute 17 times the sum of 11 numbers is 0.01 s. Hence,

AAWORK= (0.16-0.34) s.

## 8.4.5 Performance comparisons

Response times to Q1, Q2, and Q3 for each system studied by Hawthorn and DeWitt and for LUCAS are plotted in Figures 8.36, 8.37, and 8.38.

The systems are ordered along the horizontal axis on the basis of "increasing complexity".

LUCAS has the largest number of processors - therefore it can be considered to be more complex than the other designs. The processors consist of RAM memory with simple bit-serial processing elements. They are much simpler than the cell processors in the other designs. The whole Associative Array may be implemented with a few chips (cf Chapter 10) - therefore it can be argued that LUCAS is less complex than other designs. Thus, somewhat arbitrarily, we place LUCAS between CAFS anf CASSM.

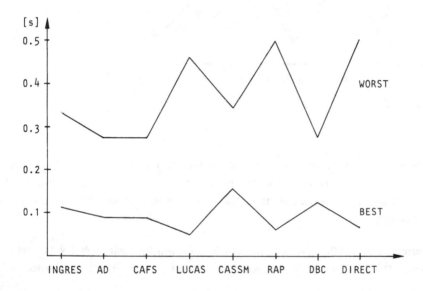

Figure 8.36 Query Q1.

Figure 8.36 shows that LUCAS exhibits the shortest best case time of all studied systems. It is also 3 times faster than INGRES. In the worst case the performance of LUCAS, though approximately the same as that of the other systems is actually worse than the performance of a conventional database management system. In processing query Q1, INGRES uses the fact that QTRCOURSE is hashed on instructors name. It is apparent that for simple queries of this type, none of the specialized database computers gives any significant increase in performance.

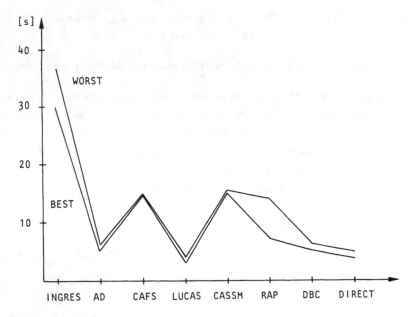

Figure 8.37 Query Q2.

LUCAS shows the best performance to query Q2 of all the studied systems. If compared with INGRES, it is also 12 times faster in the worst case and 11 times faster in the best case. It is also 1.3 times faster than the second best design which is the much more complex DIRECT.

The poor performance of RAP, CASSM and CAFS is caused by their inability to perform a Join operation. The host had to decompose query Q2 to a series of 22 subqueries.

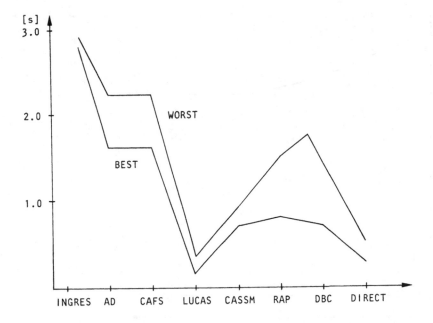

Figure 8.38 Query Q3.


LUCAS is the fastest of all designs in executing Query 3. Also, it is 5 times faster than INGRES and 1.5 times faster than DIRECT.


## 8.4.6 Influence of the size of the Associative Array

In previous sections it was assumed that the size of the Associative Array in LUCAS is 2k processors. We will now examine how the response times to queries Q1, Q2, and Q3 are influenced by an increase or decrease of this size.

Figure 8.39 shows the worst case response time for LUCAS with 0.5k, 1k, 2k, and 4k processors. The timing data were obtained by a simple modification of the equations in Section 8.3. For example, in AAWORK for query Q2 in a 1k-case, instead of loading a cylinder 7 times, (7 times DAVAC), we load a half-cylinder 14 times (14 times DAVAC), etc.

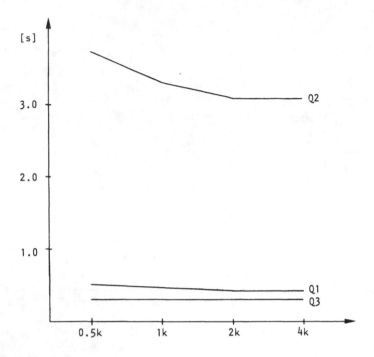

Figure 8.39 Response times for different Array sizes.

If we inspect Figure 8.39, we can make the following observations:

1) Even with a smaller array the performance with respect to queries Q2 and Q3 is still very good. As a matter of fact it continues to be better than that of the other designs.

2) The increase of the size of the Associative Array from 2k to 4k for query Q1, and from 0.5k to 4k for query Q3, does not lead to an improvement of performance. The reason is that the interrogated relation in query Q1 can be stored in the Associative Array of the size 2k, and the relation used in query Q3 can be stored in the Associative Array of the size 0.5k. The computing potential of the excess processors in the Associative Array do not contribute in the computation.

3) There is no apparent improvement in response time to query Q2 if the number of processors in the Associative Array is increased from 2k to 4k. The reason is not the idleness of processors - they are all utilized - but simply that the Associative Array operates too fast compared to the I/O time. The Associative Array of size 2k can store one cylinder load, the Array of 4k stores 2 cylinder loads. Because the main component of execution time of this query is the time to load data from the disks, a decrease of the total processing time in the Associative Array in the 4k-case (as compared to a 2k-case) is negligible when compared to the I/O time.

## 8.4.7 Conclusions

Our results indicate that in an environment of overhead-intensive queries, using an Associative Array does not give any advantage over a conventional database management system. On the contrary, the conventional system which uses standard techniques of hashing and indexing and thus can access only those pages on the disk which contain the result, in fact performs much faster.

The Associative Array must search through the whole relation indiscriminatly. All its pages must be loaded, at the speed determined by the speed of disk, and even if they are then searched in an infinitesimally short time, the damage is already done and the execution time is too large.

The potential of the Associative Array can best be exploited in an environment of data-intensive multirelational queries, where its performance is better by an order of magnitude than that of a conventional system.

The performance of the Associative Array, if compared to INGRES and to other designs of database computers we have discussed, would probably be even much more impressive if we had used queries involving more than two relations. We have assumed an array width of 512 bytes, which is the current size of LUCAS. It was much more than was necessary and it would even allow for having more than two pages in the Array at the same time. We had no use for this feature when we evaluated queries Q1, Q2, and Q3. But in the case that a query involves more than two relations, or in the case that in the process of evaluation a series of algebraic operations creating intermediate relations must be performed, then the large width of the Array could be efficiently utilized.

## 8.5 EXTERNAL EVALUATION OF JOIN

### 8.5.1 Introduction

In Section 8.4, we evaluated the performance of a database computer containing an Associative Array of LUCAS type, in a real world situation. We assumed a system consisting of an Associative Array connected to an Ampex 9200 disk drive. This system performed remarkably well in comparison to other designs.

If we analyze different components of the response times, we can see that the times are determined largely by the properties of the disk drive: average access time, block read time, number of blocks/track, and number of tracks/cylinder. If, in our experiment, the Associative Array could process data ten times faster, it would have only a negligible influence on the total response time. Also, if the Associative Array were ten times slower (assuming constant I/O time), it would not have any significant influence on the execution time either. This observation indicates that the system is not properly balanced.

In this section, we will study a similar system as the one in Section 8.4, but noe we will assume that the properties of the disk are perfectly matched to the properties of the Associative Array. The rationale is that if we are going to design a database computer with such a powerful processing component as the Associative Array, then we will surely not want to rely on the properties of a standard disk drive primarily aimed to be used with a sequential computer. We will instead modify the disk drive to achieve the highest system efficiency.

This 'ideal' Disk-Associative Array combination can be analyzed from many points of view. We will restrict our investigation to a study of the cost efficiency of the execution of one of the most important operations in query processing, the join operation.

In conventional systems, there are two basic approaches to evaluate the join [Yao79].

1) Use of a nested loop algorithm. Tuples from the two argument relations are compared and matching tuples are output. This algorithm is very inefficient, since for two relations of size N, it gives execution time proportional to N*N.

2) Use of sorting and merging, cf. Section 8.2, when the number of necessary comparisons of tuples is theoretically proportional to only N*logN.

The second method is seemingly a much faster approach than the first one. The algorithms with the complexity growing as N*logN are in general considered to be good algorithms [Knuth73]. But in reality, in the case of very large relations where data are stored on the disk and must be brought into the CPU in pages, even the sort-merge algorithm is inherently slow due to large overheads. For example, DeWitt and Hawthorn in [DeWitt and Hawthorn 81] analyze the execution of the join of two relations, with 30000 and 3000 tuples respectively, on a VAX 11/780 with an IBM 3330 disk drive, using sophisticated merge and sort algorithms. Examining the timing equation for e.g. the merge phase shows that 55 percent of the execution time is due to loading of pages to the main memory and only 45 percent is due to proper 'merging' in the CPU. Merging of two pages in the CPU is afflicted by further overheads and all this together gives inherently long total execution times.

This is an unsatisfactory situation. Fortunately, the performance of the join can be greatly improved by parallel join processors and many proposals can be found in the literature [Tong and Yao 82]. We will not try to prove that our configuration is better, we simply investigate some consequences of our design choices.

We will determine the execution time and also whether there is an optimal size of the Associative Array for given statistical properties of relations.

We assume that the join will be performed on very large relations which typically contain $10^4$-$10^6$ tuples. We must stress that what is considered to be a large relation is a function of time. Large relations in the future will be much larger than large relations today.

Since it is highly unlikely that in the reasonably near future it will be economically feasible to build Associative Arrays that are able to store large relations, we will assume that the size of the Array is less than one tenth of the cardinality of the larger of the two argument relations.

## 8.5.2 System description

We will assume the system configuration shown in Figure 8.40. The operand relations are stored on the disk. They are partitioned into pages of equal size. The disk will function as a large addressable memory where the basic unit of data which is accessed is a page.

In commercial disk systems, the average access time is not much larger than a block read/write time. Since, as we will see, processing data in the Associative Array and returning the result to the host takes much longer time than loading data, we will assume that the time to locate pages of data can be overlapped with the processing time.

The Associative Array has the same capabilities as LUCAS. For example to compare one byte in a memory word with a byteslice in all memory words takes 48 clock cycles.

Figure 8.40 Database computer.

This architecture is similar to the LUCAS system in Section 8.4. The main difference between these two systems are:

1) The data transfer rate, r, is now determined by the speed with which it can be input

into the Associative Array - in Section 8.4 we only made sure that data coming from a disk <u>could</u> be loaded into the Array

2) The size of a page is determined by the size,  c,  of the Associative Array,  a large Array means large pages,  a small Array means small pages - in Section 8.4,  the size of a page was equal to the size of a block on the disk.

First,  we will determine r.  We assume that the page is stored on the disk as a sequence of columns of bytes.  When read from the disk,  the first byte of the first tuple comes first and is loaded into the first I/O Register,  then the first byte of the second tuple is loaded into the second I/O Register,  and so on,  until the first byte of the last,  c-th,  tuple is loaded into the last I/O Register.  After the whole column is loaded into the I/O Registers,  it is shifted in 8 clock cycles into the proper bitaddress in the Associative Array.  This procedure is repeated for each column.  After every c bytes in the stream of bytes coming from the disk,  which takes c clock cycles,  there is a period of 8 clock cycles spent on shifting data from the I/O Registers into the memory words.  During this period the Associative Array cannot receive any new data.  For a large Associative Array,  a necessary buffering of 8 bytes presents no practical difficulty. Thus,  we assume that r is 1 byte/clock cycle.  For a very small Associative Array,  (and we will see that they must be studied too),  we will assume that we have more complex, ´double´,  I/O Registers working in a complementary fashion,  when one set is filled with data from the disk,  the content of the other is shifted into the Array.  Since we assume that r is 1 byte/clock cycle it also sets the limit on the minimal possible size of the Associative Array which is 8 processors.

Next,  we look at the value of s.  It is the rate with which the bytes of the result tuples are returned to the host.  We will assume that it is same as in Section 8.4,  10 clock cycles/byte (8 clock cycles for shifting + 2 for copying to the I/O Buffer Register). The difference in speed between loading and outputting of data is due to different modes of operation.  Data are loaded as pages,  but they are output as tuples which are selected according to their content.

## 8.5.3 Algorithm and timing equations

The algorithm which we will use is based on a tuple substitution algorithm [Wong and Youssefi 76],  where each tuple from one relation is compared with all tuples of the other,  and matching tuples are concatenated.  The advantage of using parallel hardware is that in one operation,  a tuple from the first relation can be compared with a whole page of tuples of the second relation.  In principle,  a speed up equal to the parallelism in the hardware could be achieved.

We assume that the two operand relations are of the same cardinality,  N tuples in P pages, and that the tuples have 2 attributes of b bytes each. The result relation has three attributes.

The execution proceeds in the following way, illustrated by Figure 8.41.

All pairs of pages of the operand relations are successively loaded into the Associative Array into areas I and II. For each pair, the values of joining attributes are compared in the way described in Section 8.3. Matching tuples are selected and serially output to the host.

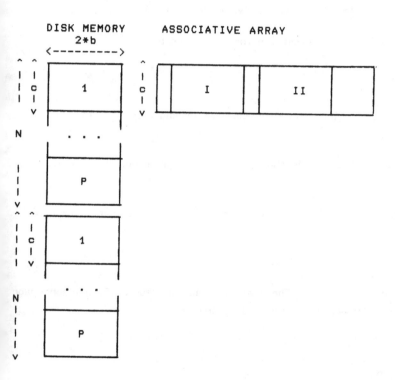

Figure 8.41 Execution of Join.

We will characterize the content of the relations by a selectivity factor g, which can be defined as the ratio between the cardinality of the result of a join of two relations and the cardinality of their product. Intuitively, g is the probability that two tuples, randomly selected from the two operand relations, will match. We will assume that the values of joining attributes are evenly distributed.

Depending on the size of g, various proposals for Join processors behave differently. There are two interesting situations which we will treat separately.

1) The case when the value of g is comparatively large. The volume of data in the result relation is then very much larger than the volume of data in the operand relations. This case is assumed in a comparative study of different hardware approaches to Join processors [Tong and Yao 82]. The study assumes a typical g being 0.5. It means that e.g. the Join of two relation of $10^3$ - $10^5$ tuples each, is a huge relation with a cardinality of $5*10^6$ - $5*10^9$ tuples.

2) The case when the value of g is small. [DeWitt and Hawthorn 81] assume g=0.0001, 0.001 and 0.01 which gives considerably smaller result relations than in the case studied by Tong and Yao.

We will analyze the performance of the Associative Array with respect to both cases.

The execution time of Join can be divided into three components:

$$T_{Join} = T_L + T_P + T_R$$

* $T_L$ is the loading time. It is the time spent on loading data from the disk into the Associative Array.

* $T_P$ is the processing time. It is the time spent on processing data in the Associative Array.

* $T_R$ is the output time. It is the time spent sending concatenated result tuples to the host.

## Loading time

The relations have P=N/c pages each. There are $P^2$ pairs of pages. To load one page takes 2*c*b clock cycles. Hence, the total loading time is

$$T_L = 2*P^2*c*b$$

## Outputing time

$P^2$ pairs of pages are compared. Each comparison of c tuples from the first relation with c tuples from the second produce in average $c^2*g$ result tuples. One result tuple is 3*b bytes long. To output one byte takes 10 clock cycles, hence,

$$T_R = 30*P^2*b*c^2*g$$

The overhead associated with selecting 'next selected tuple' for outputting is about 5 clock cycles/tuple and can be ignored.

## Processing time

a) Large g

For a large selectivity factor ($g \gg 1/N$), if $g > 1/c$ then one page with a sample of c tuples contains as many different values of the joining attribute as the whole relation. Hence, to compare two pages of the operand relations, only $1/g$ tuple comparisons must be made. Since the comparison takes 48 clock cycles/byte (cf. Section 8.2) we get,

$$T_{PG} = 48*P^2*b/g$$

b) Small g

For a small selectivity factor, we may assume that a sample of c tuples in one page contains c different values of the joining attribute. To compare a pair of pages, a tuple comparison must be made c times. Hence,

$$T_{Pg} = 48*P^2*b*c$$

The timing equations are summarized in Table 8.6. We have substituted N/c for P.

| $T_L$ | $T_R$ | $T_{PG}$ | $T_{Pg}$ |
|---|---|---|---|
| $2*N^2*b/c$ | $30*N^2*b*g$ | $48*N^2*b/(c^2*g)$ | $48*N^2*b/c$ |

Table 8.6 Timing equations for Join

### 8.5.4 Discussion

The timing equations have the same general form as the timing equations of other designs of specialized Join procesors. The dependency on the cardinality of the operand relations and the dependency on the number of processors in the Associative Array can be expressed as

$$T = N^2*A1, \quad \text{and} \quad T = A2/c + A3$$

For example, the timing equations of the Two-dimensional Join Processor Array of c processors of [Tong and Yao 81] have the form

$$T = N^2*B1, \quad \text{and} \quad T = B2/c + B3/\sqrt{c}$$

and the timing equations of a Join Processor of [Menon and Hsiao 81] have the form

$$T = N^2*C1 + N*C2, \quad \text{and} \quad T = C3/c + C4$$

We believe that - unless there will be some unexpected technological breakthrough - for very large relations, as long as data must be staged into Join processors, the timing equations for the total execution time of the Join on any hardware will always look approximately the same.

The timing equations in Table 8.5 show that the execution time decreases with increased size of the Associative Array. But we can see that the total execution time contains a term which is independent of this size, the time for outputting selected tuples, $T_R$. Obviously, above some size of the Associative Array it will dominate, which means that further incresing the size of the Associative Array does not pay. We assume that a cut point of usefulness of the size of the Array occurs when the time to output the result is 10 times larger than the sum of the time to load data and process them in the Array.

We will analyze the timing equations to see at which sizes of the Array the cut point occurs for different values of g.

Large g

To simplify our discussion, we will make the same assumption as the one made in [Tong and Yao 82], i.e. g=0.5.

Hence, the timing equation is

$$T_{TJoinL} = N^2 * b * (96/c^2 + 15 + 2/c)$$

The following formula defines the cut point:

$$96/c^2 + 2/c = 1.5$$

We can see that the cut point occurs at c=8, and a further increase of the Array size above 8 processors gives only marginal improvement of performance.

We have assumed that to output a byte from the Associative Array takes ten times longer time than to load it (ten clock cycles versus one clock cycle) and we might suspect that this is the reason why the cut point value is so small. Let us assume that we could somehow speed up the time for outputting data from the Array, e.g. to 1 clock cycle/byte. The result would not be much better as the cut point is achieved already at 40 processors.

Since the idea of using the Associative Array assumes a large number of processors, our results clearly demonstrate that a bit-serially operating Associative Array is not a viable alternative as a candidate for a Join processor in the case of large values of g.

Small g

The first observation that we can make is that the loading time is 24 times shorter than the time spent on processing in the Associative Array and can thus be neglected.

After some simplification, we get the formula for the size of the cut point

c = 16/g

Table 8.76 gives the size of the cut point for different values of g.

| g | c |
|--------|------------------|
| 0.01 | $1.6*10^3$ |
| 0.001 | $1.6*10^4$ |
| 0.0001 | $1.6*10^5$ |

Table 8.7 Cut points for small g

We can draw the conclusion that for small values of g, the large Associative Array is indeed suitable. Furthermore, we can with a large degree of confidence predict its optimum size.

We could see that in an analysis of the feasibility of the use of the Associative Array it was of outermost importance to make proper assumptions about the properties of data. For large g, i.e. any two tuples will match with a high probability, the Associative Array is obviously useless.

[Tong and Yao 82], analyzing the performance of different hardware solutions assume g=0.5 as being a worst case value. If an Associative Array was investigated according to their method the result would be very unfavorable for the simple reason that the Associative Array should certainly not be used in such a case. However, for small g, the result would indeed be different.

8.6 CONCLUSIONS

The relational data model offers many advantages. To mention a few: It is very simple as seen by the user. It is symmetrical with respect to queries, so that there is no preferred format for a question to a database. It has also a very strong theoretical foundation.

There is only one problem which has been called the greatest open research question of the relational data model: can it be implemented efficiently [Chamberlin76]? According to King, [King80], the answer, based on the experience with the IBMs System R, is a definite yes. King goes even one step further, claiming not only that relational systems can be implemented with reasonable performance but also that "exotic hardware (like associative memories, etc)" is not required. King certainly knows what he is talking about and is probably right. But there is another question: could this exotic hardware improve performance, if it was available anyway?

The purpose of the research presented in this section was to study the applicability of an Associative Array in the design of a backend database computer whose function is to support a large database which utilizes the relational data model.

Our approach is exactly the one which was criticized by DeWitt and Hawthorn in [DeWitt and Hawthorn 81] who give it the name "architecture directed" research.

.  .  .  database machine designers usually begin by designing what they consider to be a good architecture which they feel will efficiently execute one or two database operations. Afterwards they develop the algorithms to support all the required database operations using the basic primitives of their architecture . . .

They advocate instead an approach where an architect of a database machine should start by first developing algorithms and then extract the primitive operations which are necessary for their efficient implementation. Only after these primitives are known and understood, should one attempt to design a machine.

We believe that DeWitt and Hawthorn confuse the different roles of research and development. How can an architect extract the primitive operations without (at least in the back of his head) knowing anything about the potential of different hardware solutions? Furthermore, how could it be possible to know anything about the potential of exotic hardware if there were nobody exploring it.

The Associative Arrays do not enjoy widespread use at present, and so the research and development of algorithms utilizing this device is rather limited. In Section 8.2, we described the implementation of algorithms for operations of relational algebra. The implementation consisted mainly of transferring selected tuples of operand relations into the Comparand Register, comparing their values with the contents of the Associative Array, and processing bitslices of information. The implementation of the Division operation is an example of utilizing the possibilities offered by the bitslice processing.

The execution time of an operation was typically proportional to the size of the tuple and to the cardinality of one of the argument relations. We have extrapolated our results and analyzed the performance of very large Associative Arrays. The absolute execution times, assuming a moderate 5 MHz clock frequency, were very good, and probably out of reach for present day sequential computers.

We have also discovered that the increase in performance gained by increasing the size of the Associative Array by e.g. a factor of 256 can be achieved on a sequential computer by doubling its processing speed. This is a rather negative result but it would be wrong to use it indiscriminately for refuting the Associative Arrays. Its impact can be softened by the following observations. We were comparing "ordinary" algorithms on the Associative Array with only one property of the best sequential algorithms known. For large volumes of data in the argument relations, it might be the case that overheads associated with 'preparing' data for sorting are much larger than the time for proper comparisons. Furthermore, sorting and merging of data has a disadvantage of consuming very large space in the memory of the sequential computer. We conclude this defence of an Associative Array by recalling that Date [Date83] claims that a typical software DBMS uses on the average ten machine instructions per byte in evaluating a given selection condition on a given record.

In Section 8.3, we demonstrated how algorithms from Section 8.2 can be used for evaluating complex queries entirely within the Associative Array. When large Associative Arrays will become available than for a relatively stable set of queries (referring to the same relations over and over again), this method would be advantageous.

One very interesting avenue of research, which we have only very briefly discussed is the area of optimization of query evaluation. In our examples, the sequence of algebraic operations leading to the answer was stated ad hoc. But obviously, there can be more efficient ways to do it. What is the best strategy? How to identify bad strategies? How much from the research on optimization on sequential computers applies to evaluation according to our method. What "tricks" can be used to avoid the negative effects of the Join operation?

In Section 8.4, we assumed a backend database computer consisting of an Associative Array connected to a disk. We compared its performance with the performance of other well-documented designs of database computers and also with the performance of a conventional database management system. We determined the response times to three types of queries. We could see that in an environment of overhead-intensive queries the Associative Array does not give any advantage over a conventional database management system. Comparison of response times to data-intensive or multirelational queries gave that the Associative Array is more than an order of magnitude better than the conventional system and also better than all the other studied designs. We do not want to overstate the importance of this finding, it was only one benchmark experiment, it can be the case that other tests could give different results. But still, since the Associative Array performed so remarkably well the obvious implications should not be ignored.

In Section 8.5, we went beyond the basic assumption of Sections 8.2 and 8.3, which was that the Associative Array is larger than the operand relations. We dealt with the external evaluation of algebraic operations on very large relations. As an example we chose the Join operation. In a way, we were trying to answer the following question: Why is the performance of the Associative Array in Section 8.4 so good? We identified two cases which depend on the content of the database: 1) large selectivity factor - where the Associative Array is found to be useless, 2) small selectivity factor (which is the case of queries Q2 and Q3 in Section 8.4) - where its use can be advantageous.

We have started by designing a model Associative Array, LUCAS, and one goal was to investigate its feasibility in database management applications. We consider our research being an exploratory basic research. We do not claim that we have proved that the Associative Array is a viable component of future database computers. But we claim that people who dismiss it, because they believe that its only capability is searching, are certainly mistaken.

Chapter 9

# LUCAS AS A DEDICATED PROCESSOR
# FOR IMAGE PROCESSING

Our concern in this chapter is to investigate the usefulness of LUCAS - and LUCAS-type of processors - in image processing. We first state some demands that are put on a computer for image processing. We then briefly review earlier attempts to meet these demands through the use of unconventional computer architectures. We give arguments that the kind of parallelism offered by LUCAS is the one that is most useful for some very important image operations. Next we discuss different organizations of a processor array giving arguments for and against different structures. We also treat the question of how to best map an image onto a certain processor structure. Section 9.4, which constitutes the main part of the chapter, describes how image operations are performed on LUCAS organized as a linear array of processing elements. The main concern are operations that can be performed by local processing, but also measurements and global transforms are treated. The investigation is carried out in the form of examples. Timings are given and comparisons are made both with a conventional computer and with special purpose image processors.

## 9.1 COMPUTATIONAL DEMANDS IN IMAGE PROCESSING

Image processing is characterized by large amounts of low precision data. A typical image size is 512 by 512 picture elements (pixels) of 8-bit data, i.e approximately 2 million bits. On the other hand, image processing offers possibilities to treat very many data items in parallel.

The image processing area is usually divided into image analysis and enhancement on the one hand and image coding on the other. As for the first issue, a pattern recognition task calls for analysis of a picture leading to a description of it in terms of features. The computation of features normally involves a variety of picture to picture transformations. Many of these transformations are useful in their own right as image enhancement operations.

The purpose of image coding is to compress the information in an image as much as possible. A key notion is tranformation of pictures to a form in which they are represented by less correlated data. In this representation less significant data may be removed without too much distortion being introduced. The major tools in this area are reversible linear transforms. LUCAS and similar processors are useful also for this task. However, we will not further consider the image coding area in this text.

Image enhancement and image analysis often takes place in cooperation between a human operator and a computer. This is frequent in e.g. medical applications. The operator takes the decisions which operations should be performed, the machine does the calculations. This kind of interactive use calls for processing times not longer than, typically, one second in order not to be disturbing. For most operations these demands are not met by ordinary computers.

Also in completely automatic image analysis - without human interaction - strong demands are often put on the processing time. When analysing medical samples or samples of materials it is desirable to be able to analyse as many samples as possible in as short time as possible. Normally the desire is to increase the throughput of data compared to human analysis.

Furthermore, there is a constantly increasing interest in using pictures as input information in automatic control and manufacturing. If we consider how handicapped a man would be in many such activities if he was not allowed to use his eyes, we understand that this is an attractive path of development. The dynamics in the controlled process puts certain constraints on the time available for the necessary analysis of the input picture. 100 ms for a relatively advanced analysing task may serve as a typical example.

Much image processing has been done on conventional computers. Furthermore, many special purpose designs have been made, each aimed at speeding up specific processing tasks. Thus, experience is quite large on the desirable characteristics of an image processor, and the effects of different approaches to performance enhancement. A list of desirable features of a computer designed for image processing may include the following points:

* It should be able to handle efficiently many different image transformation tasks, ranging from simple operations on binary pictures through gray scale modifications and thresholding to complex filters and global transforms.

* It should be able to handle efficiently different kinds of feature extraction tasks.

* It should provide very high efficiency in those tasks that are identified as the most frequent ones.

* It should be able to cope with widely varying image sizes and number of bits per pixel. Desirable is that the same program can be used for different values of these parameters.

* It should have an efficient input/output facility. The time for input/output should stand in reasonable proportion to the computation time.

## 9.2 DIFFERENT ATTEMPTS TO MEET THE DEMANDS

Due to the constantly increasing importance of the image processing field we see a growing number of special purpose processors built to meet the computational demands. The first proposal for a special purpose computer for image processing is due to Unger [Unger58]. However, not until the late sixties and early seventies machines were actually implemented. We will divide some of the implemented machines into different categories, based on the principles of organization. A more elaborate overview can be found in [Danielsson and Levialdi 81] and [Reeves 84]. Many of the processors are described by their designers in [Duff and Levialdi 81].

### 9.2.1 Fast neighbourhood access

The importance of local operations in image processing was early understood, as was the discrepancy between the picture geometry and the linear memory space of a conventional computer. Computing the addresses of neighbouring pixels took too much time.

Picap I [Kruse73], one of the first picture processors to be built, uses two 61-stage shift registers in order to provide parallel access to the complete 3 x 3 neighbourhood of each pixel. The pixels are operated on sequentially and the picture size is fixed to 64 x 64 4-bit pixels. Picap I has two special purpose processors, one for logic operations and one for linear filters. The "Cytocomputer" [Sternberg79] is another, more recent, design utilizing this scheme for fast neighbourhood access.

### 9.2.2 A small number of special purpose processors

Some designs use a small number of identical, carefully designed, special purpose processors working in parallel. An example of this is the filter processor FIP [Kruse et al.80] developed at Linkoping University, Sweden. The FIP processor is incorporated in a larger system, Picap II, containing many special purpose processors. FIP is used for the low level image to image transformations. Other processors serve e.g. input/output and image management functions.

Another system designed at Linkoping University incorporates another processor of this category, the GOP processor [Granlund81]. GOP and FIP each use four parallel subprocessors. The subprocessors, in turn, use pipelining. The organization of the GOP subprocessors is strongly adapted to the nature of a certain general operator type. An important feature of the FIP processor is the ability to reach the elements of an almost arbitrary sized neighbourhood very fast. This is accomplished through a quite large cache memory (32 kbyte) holding a portion of the picture.

In both these machines all subprocessors perform the same operations, thus operating in an SIMD manner.

Another processor of this type - also called FIP - is included in the FLIP system developed in Karlsruhe, West Germany [Gemmar et al.81]. The 16 identical processors in the FLIP-FIP can work in either MIMD mode or SIMD mode. Each processor has its own program memory and instruction decoding circuitry. The processors may be arranged according to the topology of the processing task.

The Picap-FIP, GOP and FLIP-FIP implementations show that carefully designed special purpose processors can give considerable prestanda although very few processors work in parallel.

## 9.2.3 A large number of conventional microprocessors

During the last years designs using a large number of standard, conventional microprocessors have been proposed. Among these are the ZMOB [Rieger et al.80] and PASM [Siegel81] systems. The number of processors used in these systems is in the order of the squareroot of the number of pixels in a picture.

With a large number of processors, the design of the interconnection structure for communication between them becomes a critical issue. ZMOB and PASM use radically different structures for interprocessor communication. ZMOB, with its 256 Z80 microprocessors, uses what is called a conveyor belt. This is a 257 stage, ring formed 8-bit wide shift register with one stage ('mailbox') for each processor and one for the host computer. The PASM system with $2^n$ processors (typically 1024) is planned to be equipped with an n-stage interconnection network. Considered in particular are "the generalized cube" and "the augmented data manipulator". An important feature of these networks is their partitionability. This means that the system can be configured to work as several subsystems of parallel machines, each subsystem controlled by its own program.

## 9.2.4 A very large array of simple processors

A major part of the computational burden in image processing is image to image transformations using operations of local nature. All new pixel values can be calculated independently of each other, using only the old pixel values in a small neighbourhood as arguments.

Considering this fact it becomes attractive to arrange a large number of processors in a two-dimensional structure. Two special purpose processors for image processing designed along these lines are CLIP4 designed at University College, London [Duff79] and MPP designed at Goodyear Aerospace, Ohio under contract from NASA and particularly intended to process satellite imagery at high speed [Batcher80]. The same structure is also used in the general purpose processor array DAP, a commercial product from ICL, England [Flanders et al.77].

An overview of these designs was given in Chapter 4. All three machines use an array of bit-serial processors implemented in LSI. The size of the CLIP4 array is 96 x 96 processors. MPP has a 128 x 128 array while DAP has been implemented in both 32 x 32 and 64 x 64 array versions. The processors are controlled by a central control unit which provides identical control signals and memory addresses to all PE's. The control unit in turn gets its instructions from a master computer of conventional type.

Each processor in DAP and MPP is connected to its four nearest neighbours (north, south, east, and west). In CLIP4 also diagonal neighbours are connected resulting in eight directly connected processors.

The size of the data memory associated with each processor is for MPP typically 1 kbit and for DAP typically 4kbit. CLIP4 has a very small memory associated with each processor - only 32 bits - which is a severe limitation, especially in grey scale and colour image processing.


## 9.2.5 LUCAS compared to other machines

LUCAS is a SIMD computer composed of bit serial processing elements like MPP, CLIP4 and DAP. The number of processing elements is, however, about two orders of magnitude less than that of the above mentioned machines. This has consequences for the way pictures are best stored and manipulated. This, in turn, determines which interconnection structure between individual processors is the most suitable.

The number of processing elements is more like that of PASM and ZMOB but the processors are very different. The processors in LUCAS have no instruction decoding and sequencing circuitry. They can only work in SIMD mode. Using fully equipped microprocessors like in PASM and ZMOB is of course attractive considering the very low cost to which these can now be achieved. However, if they are primarily intended for

SIMD use - which also PASM and ZMOB apparently are - too much redundant circuitry will be present in the system. Taking into consideration a future development with integration of several processors into a single chip, the use of processing elements without redundancy appears to be a better way to follow. Availability of large scale integration technology is increasing tremendously, which makes this an important aspect.

## 9.2.6 The advantages of image parallelism

In [Danielsson and Levialdi 81], the different dimensions of parallelism open for utilization in image to image transformations of local nature (neighbourhood operations) are identified. The four possibilities are:

* Operator parallelism: The sequence of operations to be performed on the image according to a chosen algorithm is performed in parallel in a pipelined fashion.

* Image parallelism: Several pixels of the image are treated in parallel using multiple processing units.

* Neighbourhood parallelism: The processor has access to all neighbourhood pixel values simultaneously.

* Pixel bit parallelism: The bits in a pixel are treated in parallel. This is the only dimension of parallelism utilized in a conventional computer.

The range of parallelism in each of the four dimensions is between one and in the order of a hundred for all dimensions but the image coordinate dimension. Here the range is from a few thousand up to several million image points. Investments in image parallelism can almost always be utilized. This is not the case with the other types.

According to this, a processor of LUCAS type has potential to be efficient for local image operations. The main concern of this chapter is to investigate this by programming and timing several algorithms on LUCAS. First, however, the interconnection of the processing elements and the mapping of images to the processor structure will be discussed.

# 9.3 ORGANIZATION OF PROCESSOR ARRAYS FOR IMAGE PROCESSING

## 9.3.1 Introduction

Processor arrays designed to utilize image parallelism can be configured in many different ways. Besides different arrangements of the interconnection between processing elements the mapping of images to this structure can be made in different ways. Given an interconnection structure, one mapping may be favourable for certain operations, another mapping for other operations. A question of great concern is also which mapping is the most favourable for input/output. Often, different mappings require different hardware for input/output. Therefore the set of mappings available on a machine may be restricted.

When Unger first proposed utilization of image parallelism [Unger58] he used a two-dimensionally connected array of processing elements and mapped only one pixel onto each element. This mapping has obvious advantages. Firstly, it utilizes parallelism to a maximal degree. Secondly, it is very simple since the arrangement of the processors is the same as the arrangement of the pixels. This makes the step from algorithm to program straightforward and uncomplicated. The control unit, broadcasting directives to the processing elements, can also be kept fairly simple.

However, not even with the largest arrays implemented can we count on having as many processing elements as pixels. A very common image size, 512 times 512 pixels, is sixteen times the size of the largest array implemented - the 128 times 128 array of MPP. This means that with the one-pixel-per-processing-element mapping, we are obliged to resort to dividing large pictures into smaller parts, something that often gives cumbersome rand effects. Furthermore, the mapping also results in very small directly accessible neighbourhoods. Given a two-dimensional configuration of the processors, a mapping giving one subimage per processor is probably preferrable [Danielsson and Levialdi 81].

For arrays with a very large number of processing elements a two- dimensional organization is very natural and probably the best. For smaller arrays, however, other configurations may be equally favourable. A linear organization, often combined with some other interconnection scheme, is one example. Having chosen a linear organization, the mapping of an image to the array can still be made in different ways.

## 9.3.2 Two-dimensionally organized arrays

Among processor arrays implemented and used for image processing there are three examples of two-dimensional organization, namely CLIP4, MPP and DAP. Reported implementations of image processing operations on these machines ([Fountain and Goetcherian 80] (CLIP4), [Batcher80] (MPP), [Kushner et al.81] (MPP), [Marks80] (DAP)) show different mappings of images to processor arrays. While the users of CLIP4 and MPP use the one-pixel-per-PE mapping, Marks, in his implementation on the 32 x 32 PE DAP, loads a 6 x 6 pixels subimage into the memory of each processing element when processing 192 x 192 pixels pictures.

Users of CLIP4 have no true possibility of choosing other mappings since the machine was built for one-pixel-per-PE. The input/output system is made for 96*96 pixels frames from TV pictures. Furthermore, the processing elements of CLIP4 are equipped with strictly combinatorial parts that allow a signal to flow through a series of elements during one clock cycle. With the very slow clock rate of CLIP4 this is an important feature. However, it loses sense if other storage methods than one-pixel-per-PE are used. Finally, the very small memories of the processing elements do not allow many pixels to be stored in one processing element.

DAP, on the other hand, was not built for image processing. No image input/output system is built into the machine. A signal is not allowed to pass through many PEs in a single clock cycle. Therefore, Marks as a user is free to adopt any storage method. The one he finds best is to store a square subimage in each PE, although it gives some problems with irregular addressing schemes.

On MPP, with its fully synchronous processing elements and powerful input/output reformatting hardware, use of other storage schemes than one-pixel-per-PE should be possible. However, in [Kushner et al.81] the analysis is limited to 128*128 images, because the memory of each PE is considered too small for working on a larger subimage than 3*3 pixels. The reason for this is that, evidently, not only the subimage but also its immediate neighbourhood are stored in the same memory. This seems to be unnecessary.

## 9.3.3 Linearly organized arrays

Like DAP, the STARAN computer [Batcher74] was not primarily designed for image processing, but its use in this field of application has been thoroughly investigated [Goodyear76], [Potter78]. STARAN uses a linear ordering of the 256 processing elements of an array. In addition to this the so called flip network provides further possibilities for communication between processors.

The image to processor array mappings used with STARAN follow roughly the approach one-pixel-line-per-processing element. When the number of lines exceeds 256, two or more lines are stored in each processor's memory as shown for a 512 x 512 pixels image in Figure 9.1. Lines stored in the same memory word will thus be 256 lines apart in the image. Two adjacent lines along the cut in the image will reside in the memories of the bottom and top processor respectively. If a "wrap-around" neighbour communication is used this should give no access problems. However, the addresses to neighbouring pixels will be different for these lines. This may very well double the computation time for local operations.

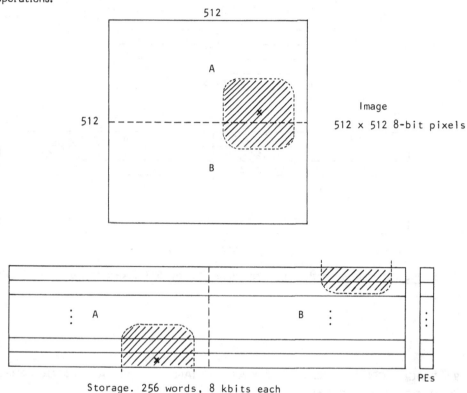

Figure 9.1 Storage of a 512 x 512 x 8 image in a 256 PE STARAN.

Another approach to storing a 512 lines picture in a 256 processors array is to store two adjacent lines in the same memory word. The major advantage with this method is the larger immediately accessible neighbourhood that automatically follows. The method is illustrated in Figure 9.2. A 5 x 5 neighbourhood is directly accessible only with up/down communication. (In fact a 5 x 512 neighbourhood). Of course, the method can be generalized to any other ratio between image height and number of processing elements. The larger the ratio, the larger will the size of the immediately accessible neighbourhood be.

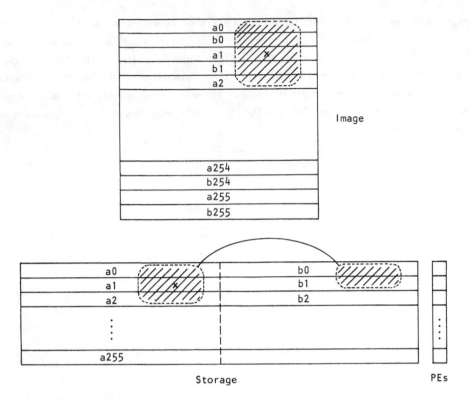

**Figure 9.2** Alternative method for storing a 512 by 512 pixels image in a 256 PE array.

## 9.4 IMAGE OPERATIONS ON LUCAS ORGANIZED AS A LINEAR ARRAY OF PROCESSING ELEMENTS

### 9.4.1 Introduction

In this section we will use LUCAS as a model machine in order to examine the applicability of bit-serial SIMD machines with up to a few hundred processors in the field of image processing . Algorithms are programmed and analysed with regard to execution time and possible changes in the hardware that would make execution faster.

We do not claim any particular novelty for the algorithms presented, but rather our interest centers on the techniques of implementation and the level of performance achievable using this specific type of hardware.

The interprocessor communication structure of LUCAS is reconfigurable. Therefore different organizations can be tested. However, we will assume a linear organization of the processor array with communication one and two steps up and down in addition to a perfect shuffle/exchange network (Figure 9.3). Furthermore, we will assume that the size of the image side agrees with the number of processing elements so that one line of the image exactly occupies a field of the memory as shown in Figure 9.4. Only in the last subsection (9.4.8) will we depart from this assumption and discuss the consequences for neighbourhood size and input/output.

The main concern in our investigation is the set of operations that takes images into images. Firstly, this is the kind of operations for which a processor array is best suited. Secondly, they are normally the most time consuming operations on ordinary computers. But we will also briefly examine the use of LUCAS for extraction of picture properties of different kinds.

In the investigations to follow we will group operations according to the characteristics of their execution on LUCAS. In association with each operation treated, we will indicate in what context of image processing it is normally used. In most cases similar operations are described in [Rosenfeld and Kak 76] where more background material can be found. Unless otherwise stated, the presented algorithms have been microprogrammed and tested on LUCAS. Timings presented are made using a clock cycle of 200 ns. The microprograms are, with a few exceptions, general with regard to image width and pixel precision. These are specified as input parameters to the microprograms.

In connection with the presentations of the algorithms we will sometimes indicate changes in the hardware of LUCAS that would improve the performance.

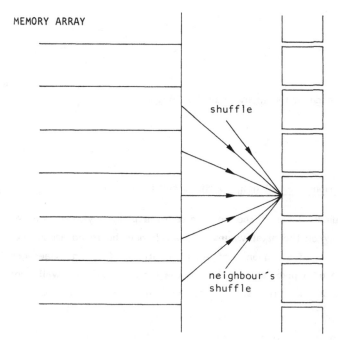

MEMORY ARRAY

shuffle

neighbour's shuffle

Figure 9.3 Available data inputs to a PE

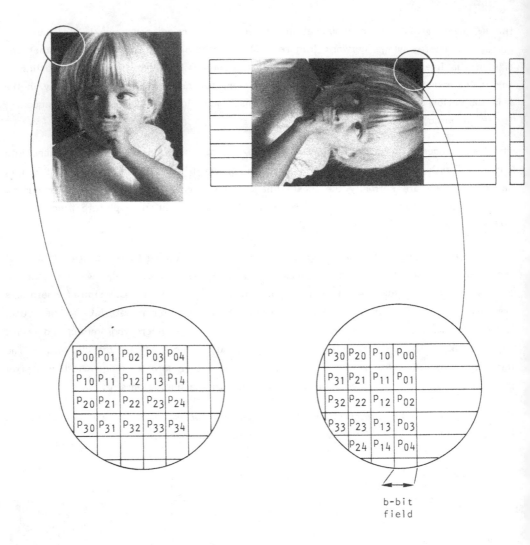

**Figure 9.4** Storage of an image in the memory of LUCAS.

### 9.4.2 Genuinely local operations. Small neighbourhood sizes

We call an operation genuinely local if the new value of a pixel $(x,y)$, as the result of the operation, depends only on the pixel values in a small neighbourhood around $(x,y)$. If O is an operator that consists of a sequence of such operations, O is no longer genuinely local, since the new value of a pixel at one side of the picture may very well depend on the old value of a pixel at the other side. This kind of operations are treated in a separate section below.

In this section we treat local operations with neighbourhood sizes smaller than or equal to 5 in one direction, arbitrarily large in the other direction. (Usually, the neighbourhood is approximately quadratic). This means that all pixel values of the neighbourhood are immediately available over the interconnection network (Figure 9.3).

## 9.4.2.1 Binary images

EXAMPLE 1: Salt-and-pepper noise removal

A binary picture obtained from a grey scale picture by thresholding often has scattered white points in black regions and scattered black points in white regions as a result of noise in the original picture. This is called salt-and-pepper noise and can be detected by counting the number of neighbours of a pixel that differ from the value of the pixel itself. If this number is large, the value of the pixel is changed. An algorithm that changes a pixel value if it differs from seven or more of its eight nearest neighbours proceeds on LUCAS as follows.

The image is swept over pixelcolumn-wise, from right to left. Matches are counted instead of non-matches. A two bit field is reserved for a counter in each word. For each pixel column, the counter is first initiated to zero. Then, for each neighbouring point that matches, the counter is incremented. After the counter has reached binary 10, the most significant bit is locked to one. This bit will serve as a mark bit for noise points. Finally, the value of these points are changed and written into a separate result image, and the scan proceeds to the next pixel column.

The execution time for an image width of $w$ pixel columns is $71w + 7$. An image with width 128 pixels is treated in 9095 clock cycles, i.e. 1.82 ms.

A dramatic time gain would of course be achieved if a counter were included in each processing element. A counter that could be incremented and tested in one clock cycle would save 56 percent of the processing time.

For the task at hand we can also manage very well without actually counting the matches or mismatches. Instead of adding the mismatch indicator (1 or 0) to the counter field for each neighbour checked, we can just save the indicator in an 8-bit mismatch vector, which can be analyzed after the whole neighbourhood is gone through. If the mismatch vector contains two or more zeroes, the point is not considered a noise point. This analysis can be done in 24 clock cycles. Compared to the 48 cycles used for counting in the above solution, we have reached a significant improvement. The total time is decreased by almost 35 percent.

EXAMPLE 2: Border finding

A point in a binary image is called a border point if it has the value '1' and is adjacent to a point with the value '0'. Depending on whether we use 8-adjacency or 4-adjacency (see Figure 9.5) we get slightly different borders (Figure 9.6).

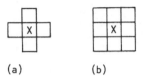

(a)          (b)

Figure 9.5 a) the points 4-adjacent to x

b) the points 8-adjacent to x.

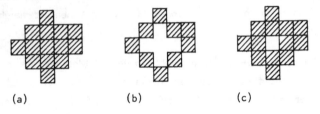

(a)               (b)               (c)

Figure 9.6 a) object

b) border using 4-adjacency

c) border using 8-adjacency.

A microprogram to mark border points is very straightforward. The image is swept over column-wise. For each column the logical product of the neighbourhood (4- or 8-) of each pixel is formed. If the product is zero and the pixel value is one the pixel is a border point. The logical product of a 3 times 3 pixels neighbourhood can be formed in only four AND-operations, two "horizontal" and two "vertical". Therefore, the 8-adjacency case gives only slightly longer execution time than the 4-adjacency case: $9w+6$ and $8w+6$, respectively. In time this means 0.23 and 0.21 ms, respectively, for $w=128$.

EXAMPLE 3: Shrinking and expanding

The operations of shrinking and expanding in binary images have many applications [Rosenfeld and Kak 76]. One or a few shrinks followed by the same number of expansions will clean up "ragged" borders and delete small objects. Shrinking and expanding can also be used to obtain the skeleton of an object or to detect clusters of points.

Shrinking is the same as deleting border points. Thus, the microprogram becomes very similar to the border finding program. The time for 4-adjacency shrink is 7w+6 and for 8-adjacency shrink 8w+6. The times are a little shorter than for border finding because, in the logical expression for the new value of a point, the point itself plays the same role as its neighbours. This is not the case for border finding. The times for expansion are the same as for shrinking.

EXAMPLE 4: Gap filling

As an example of an operation with a larger neighbourhood than 3 x 3 we use the following one [Iliffe82], useful for filling in gaps in thin curves:

If some point in X and some point in Y have the value '1', let point 'Z' have the value '1'. (See Figure 9.7).

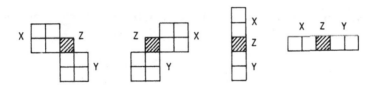

Figure 9.7 Mask configuration for gap filling.

A straightforward approach to solve this on LUCAS is to take the four cases one after the other, OR-ing the results together:

Start by clearing a scratch pad bit-slice SP. For each case:
```
        OR-sum of X-field -> R -> T
        OR-sum of Y-field -> R
        R AND T -> R
        R OR SP -> SP
  Then: SP OR Z -> Result image
```

The time for the execution of the microprogram is 45w+6 cycles. w=128 gives 1.15 ms.

9.4.2.2  Grey scale images

Many local operations on grey scale images include additions and subtractions of whole images. Often, the two images in such an operation are identical except for one of them being shifted one step. This is the case in averaging and differentiating operations, to name two examples. Therefore, our first examples will be these, generally useful, operations. Later examples will combine these to compound operations.

EXAMPLE 5: Addition/subtraction of images

Addition (or subtraction) of two pictures takes three cycles per bitslice and four additional cycles for each pixel column (for test and reloading of bit counter). Including initial parameter loading this makes

w(3b+4)+6 cycles,

where w is the image width in pixels and b is the number of bits per pixel, both specified through parameters. (The additional 4 cycles per pixel column can be reduced to one if the operation is made as a single w*b bits wide addition with markers in the mask register for pixel-slice limits).

Addition of two 128 pixel wide images with 8 bit data takes 3590 clock cycles, i.e. 0.72 ms.

EXAMPLE 6: Point by point maximum of images

A point by point maximum operation on two images A and B replaces all pixels of A, that are smaller than the corresponding pixels of B, with the B-pixels. The operation proceeds in two phases: In the first phase a pixel slice of B is subtracted from the corresponding pixel slice of A without storing the result. The signs of the result is moved to the Tag registers. In the second phase the B-slice is written tag-masked into the A-image slice. The time for subtraction is two cycles per bitslice (two reads). The time for move is also two cycles per bit-slice (one read, one write). The total time is

w(4b+10)+4 cycles.

w=128 and b=8 gives 5380 cycles, or 1.08 ms.

EXAMPLE 7: Thresholding

The most common operation used for segmentation of grey scale images is thresholding. It produces a binary image that has ones in those coordinates of the original picture where the value exceeds a certain threshold. In the implementation on LUCAS, two cycles are used per bit slice. This is because the threshold value is stored in each memory word. An alternative is to store the threshold in the Common Register. Since the ALU has one input from Common and one from the memory word, the comparison could then be made faster. However, the Common Register receives the same address signals as the memory. Hence the threshold must be stored repeatedly along the Common Register. A base register for Common Register addressing would be a good thing to include in the Control Unit.

The implementation of thresholding made on LUCAS takes

$$w(2b+5)+7 \text{ cycles.}$$

w=128 and b=8 gives 2695 cycles, or 0.54 ms.

EXAMPLE 8: Roberts' cross-difference operator

Difference operators are widely used for the detection of edges. One variation of the so called Roberts' operator [Roberts65] has the following form (j and k are image coordinates):

$$R(j,k) = \max( |I(j,k)-I(j+1,k+1)| , |I(j,k+1)-I(j+1,k)| )$$

The microprogram for this can be divided into two subtractions, two formations of absolutes, and one maximum. Subtraction and maximum were treated above. Absolute value formation on a 128 x 128 8-bit image takes 2820 cycles, or 0.56 ms. Thus, the execution time for Roberts' cross-difference operator is

```
2 subtractions:      2 x 0.72 ms
2 absolutes:         2 x 0.56 ms
1 maximum:           1 x 1.08 ms

Total execution time:    3.64 ms
```

An example showing the effect of the operator is given in Photo 9.4 under example 16 below.

EXAMPLE 9: The Laplacian operator

The derivative of an image in the x-direction can be approximated by the expression

$$df/dx = f(x+1,y) - f(x,y)$$

The second order derivative, then, becomes

$$d^2f/dx^2 = [f(x+1,y) - f(x,y)] - [f(x,y) - f(x-1,y)] =$$
$$= f(x+1,y) + f(x-1,y) - 2f(x,y)$$

The Laplacian operator is defined as

$$L(f) = d^2f/dx^2 + d^2f/dy^2 =$$
$$= f(x+1,y) + f(x-1,y) + f(x,y+1) + f(x,y-1) - 4f(x,y)$$

The application of the Laplacian to a pixel whose four neighbours all have the same value as the pixel itself, gives a zero result. If some of the neighbours have smaller values but none has larger, $L(f)$ will be negative. This is the case, for example, at one side of an edge in the image, At the other side of the edge, some values have a larger value than the center pixel, but none has smaller. There the result will be positive.

The function

$$f(x,y) - L(f(x,y)) = 5f(x,y) - [f(x+1,y)+f(x-1,y)+f(x,y+1)+f(x,y-1)]$$

will take on the value $f(x,y)$ at all points where the mean value of the 4-pixel neighbourhood is the same as the center pixel value. It will take on a value smaller than $f(x,y)$ if $f(x,y)$ is smaller than that mean value, and it will take on a larger value if $f(x,y)$ is larger than the mean value of the neighbourhood. Thus, application of this function has the effect of increasing the contrast in the image.

The Laplacian operator applied in the way described above can be used for enhancement of blurred pictures and also for detection of edges, lines and spots. Alternative digital "Laplacians" can be defined by using different neighbourhoods, or by using a weighted average over the neighbourhood.

We will consider the implementation on LUCAS of two operations of this kind, $L_4$ and $L_8$. $L_4$ is the inverse of $L$ as defined above. $L_8$ uses all pixel values of a 3x3 neighbourhood. $L_4$ and $L_8$ are linear filters that can be described as in Figure 9.8.

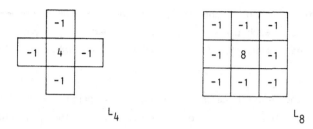

<u>Figure 9.8</u> The operators $L_4$ and $L_8$.

Photo 9.1 illustrates the effect of using $L_4$ on an image. The upper left image shows the original image, reproduced with only 4-bit grey scale. Upper right is the result of applying $L_4$. Negative values are put to zero. Addition of the result to the original image gives the result shown lower left. The contrast has increased compared to the original image. Subtraction instead of addition gives the result shown lower right. Here the edges have been blurred.

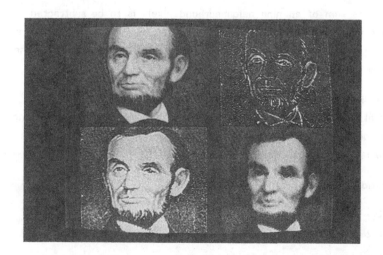

<u>Photo 9.1</u> Illustration of the effect of the Laplacian operator $L_4$. Upper left: original. Upper right: $L_4$ applied. Lower left: $L_4$ added to original. Lower right: $L_4$ subtracted from the original. Negative values have been set to zero. 4-bit grey scale is used.

Computation of $L_4$ is done by first multiplying all pixel values by the factor 4, then subtracting the values of the four neighbouring pixels, one after the other. Multiplication by 4 takes no time at all, since it only means changing the address when bits of the pixel are fetched. Thus, the total time is the time of four subtractions. We can reduce this to the time of two additions and one subtraction with the following method: First, the sum of each pixel and its upper right neighbour is formed and stored in a temporary area. Then, each pixel in this area is added to its upper left neighbour. The result obtained is finally subtracted from the original image value immediately to the right multiplied by 4.

If the full dynamics of the b-bit fields is to be used, extension of the field length to b+2 bits must be made. Thus, the time to compute $L_4$ is the following (time for addition and subtraction was given in example 5 above):

$$T(L_4) = 3*[w(3(b+2)+4)+6] = w(9b+30)+18 \text{ cycles.}$$

w=128 and b=8 gives $T(L_4)$ = 13074 clock cycles, i.e. 2.61 ms.

To compute $L_8$, the sum of all nine elements of the neighbourhood is first computed, which can be done in just four additions. First, the neighbour above is added to each element, then the neighbour below in the original image is added to this sum. In the new image obtained in this way the process is then repeated, using the left and right neighbours, respectively, instead of those above and below.

To give $L_8$, the sum of all nine neighbourhood pixels is to be subtracted from the value of the center pixel multiplied by 9. Multiplication by 9 is performed as an addition of the pixel value with itself shifted left three positions. The total sum for the computation of $L_8$ becomes the sum of:

a) Vertical addition: 1 addition using b bits, 1 using b+1 bits
b) Horizontal addition: 1 addition using b+2 bits, one using b+3 bits
c) Multiplication by 9: 1 addition using b+3 bits
d) Subtraction: 1 subtraction using b+3 bits

The computation times are:

a) w(6b+11)+12
b) w(6b+23)+12
c) w(3b+13)+12
d) w(3b+13)+12

The total time is

$$T(L_8) = w(18b+60)+48 \text{ cycles.}$$

w=128 and b=8 gives $T(L_8)$ = 26160 clock cycles, i.e. 5.23 ms.

EXAMPLE 10: Mean value filtering

In some pictures, replacing the value of each point with the average pixel value in some neighbourhood of the point (including the point itself) may be a useful way to reduce noise. This is called local averaging or mean value filtering.

Mean value filtering means addition of all pixels in the neighbourhood followed by a division by the size of the neighbourhood. We consider mean value filtering over neighbourhoods of size 3x3 and 5x5. Division by 9 can be approximated by a multiplication by 7/64 with an error of about 1.5% only. (Anyhow, with limited data length, division by 9 cannot be done exactly). Similarly, multiplication by 5/128 is an approximation of division by 25 with an error of 2.3%. Multiplication of a value by 7 can be implemented as a multiplication by 8 (which takes no time) followed by a subtraction of the original value. Division by 64 takes no time, which means that division by 9 can in fact be done as a single subtraction. Similarly, division by 5 will be a single addition.

The sum of all pixels in a 3x3 neighbourhood is obtained by four additions, as described in example 10 above. The time for this is $w(12b+34)+24$. The subsequent division by 9, which is realized as a single subtraction, takes $w(3b+13)+6$ cycles if truncation to b bits is postponed till after the division. In total, the time to compute the mean value of each 3x3 neighbourhood in an image is

$$T(M_9) = w(15b+47)+30 \text{ cycles.}$$

$w=128$ and $b=8$ gives $T(M_9) = 21406$ clock cycles, i.e. 4.28 ms.

In the case of a 5x5 neighbourhood, the sum of all elements in the neighbourhood can be obtained in six additions - three vertical and three horizontal. The three horizontal additions can be reduced to two using the fact that the image is swept over columnwise from right to left during computation. The sum over the neighbourhood of a specific pixel can be computed from the one obtained for a pixel in the preceding column by subtracting the rightmost contribution and adding a new contribution from the left.

The time to compute the sum of the neighbourhood for each pixel of the image is $w(15b+62)+30$ cycles. The final multiplication by 5 is done as a single addition on $b+5$ bits data. This takes $w(3b+20)+6$ cycles. Thus, the total time required to compute the average over 5x5 neighbourhoods is

$$T(M_{25}) = w(18b+82)+36 \text{ cycles.}$$

$w=128$ and $b=8$ gives $T(M_{25}) = 28964$ clock cycles, i.e 5.79 ms.

The time to do averaging over a 5x5 neighbourhood is only 35% longer than the time required for a 3x3 neighbourhood.

EXAMPLE 11: Median filtering

For suppression of noise in images, the use of non-linear filters, like the median filter, is considered to have many advantages over linear filters, e.g. taking the average. Perhaps the most important is the ability to preserve sharp edges [Justusson80].

Median filtering means replacing a pixel value by the median of the neighbourhood. Danielsson has devised an algorithm that utilizes bit-serial scanning of the arguments [Danielsson81]. The algorithm has been implemented on LUCAS for a 3*3 neighbourhood. It starts by analyzing the set of most significant bits of the neighbourhood points. If there are more zeroes than ones in this set, it can be concluded that the median value has a zero as its most significant bit. It proceeds with the following bits, successively refining the hypothesis.

When traversing the neighbourhood, scanning a bit slice of the arguments, certain conditions have the effect that a counter of each point is incremented, while certain other conditions have the effect that the counter is decremented. Since this operation on the counter is done bit-serially on LUCAS, it takes a considerable part of the total execution time - around 70 percent. The execution time for a w-column picture with b-bit pixel values is

$$w(154+324b) \text{ cycles.}$$

Our example w=128, b=8 yields 351,488 cycles, i.e 70 ms. If the processing elements were provided with counters that could be incremented or decremented in one cycle, the time would decrease to around 20 ms.

### 9.4.3 Genuinely local operations. Larger neighbourhood sizes

The communication network on LUCAS permits a processing element to access data from words one or two steps up or down. When data is needed from words at a larger distance from the PE, it must be temporarily loaded in words in between. The larger the distance is, the larger number of temporary storage steps are needed. When the distance is very large - 20 or more, approximately - it may be favourable to use the perfect shuffle/exchange network to route data to the desired PEs. Shift of data an arbitrary number of steps up or down can be made in $\log_2 N$ passes through the network, where N is the number of PEs [Lawrie75]. Such long distances hardly occur in local operations.

In this section we will give one example of a local operation that uses a larger neighbourhood than is directly accessible. The example given concerns filtering of a grey-scale image; according to [Kruse77] the need for larger neighbourhoods is stronger on grey-scale images than on binary images. The calculations involve multiplications, therefore the computation time will dominate strongly over the time to fetch data to the correct PEs.

EXAMPLE 12: Linear filtering

The mean value filter described in example 10 above is an example of a convolution of the image matrix with a smaller matrix, in that case a 3x3 or 5x5 matrix with all values equal to 1. The convolution was followed by a division by the total weight of the convolution matrix in order to keep the overall grey-scale level in the image unchanged.

Linear filters are often specified as convolution matrices of larger size than this. Cross correlating the image with small template images also involves the same computations.

As our example we will take a linear filter specified by a convolution matrix of size 9x9. b bit data are used, both for image pixel values and filter constants.

The convolution is computed as iterations over (a) the pixel-columns of the image and (b) the 81 values of the convolution matrix. Depending on which one is chosen as the outer loop variable, two different computation strategies are obtained:

(1): For each of the 81 values of the convolution matrix, do the following: Multiply the entire image by the value. The product obtained in a specific point, p, is to contribute to the result of another point, located at a certain distance from p. This distance corresponds to where the currently used filter constant is located in the convolution matrix. In 36 of the 81 cases (see Figure 9.9) the transfer of the product must be done in two steps because of the limitations of the interconnection network. However, the overhead from this can be reduced if the products are stored closer to the final destination already when they are formed. In fact, this reduces the overhead to one clock cycle for each bit to be transferred.

(2): For each of the pixel columns: Multiply the column and its 8 neighbouring columns (4 on each side) by 9 values each. (In total 81 multiplications). After each multiplication, transfer the result to the PE that needs it and accumulate it. The overhead due to the limitations in interconnections is the same as above.

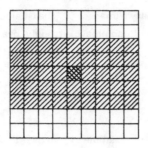

<u>Figure 9.9</u> The area whose values are needed to compute the result at the center
position. The shaded area shows which values are directly accessible.

Measuring only pure computation time, the two approaches are equivalent. An advantage
of method (2) is that computation can start as soon as a few columns of the image are
input, and output can start as soon as the result of one column is obtained. Thus,
computation and input/output can be overlapped. In the following, we will use method
(1), but the timing for the other method will be the same, disregarding overhead.

In each of the 81 iterations, the entire image is multiplied by a scalar. Preferrably,
the scalar is in canonical signed digit code (see Section 3.4.2). The time for the
multiplication is, on the average, equal to $b^2 + 4b - 3$ cycles. The products obtained
are accumulated using an increasing number of bits, on the average $2b+5$ bits. This
takes $3(2b+5)+4 = 6b+19$ cycles. Thus, the treatment of a pixel slice takes

$b^2 + 10b + 16$ cycles per iteration.

This is done for all w columns in each of 81 iterations. The total time, then, becomes

$81w(b^2+10b+16)$ cycles.

With the values w=128 and b=8 this makes 1,658,880 cycles. To this value we should add
the extra time required to pass data between the memory and the PEs due to the
limitations of the interconnection network. This is the case in 36 of the 81 iterations,
and the extra time is one clock cycle per bit to be transferred. This makes a total of
36 x w x 2b cycles, which for w=128 and b=8 is 73728 cycles. This is small compared
to the computation time.

The total execution time for an 8-bit 9x9 linear filter on a 128x128 image of 8-bit data
amounts to 1,732,608 cycles, on the average, i.e 0.42 seconds. There is some

uncertainty this value,    since this algorithm has not been programmed on LUCAS.


## 9.4.4 Semi-local operations

Operations consisting of repeated applications of local operations until some specific criterion is reached form an important class of image processing algorithms.    Although such operations are made up of local operations they can not be called genuinely local, since the result at some point in the image may depend on pixel values at a large distance from the point.    We use the term "semi-local operations" to describe these operations.

Semi-local operations can be used for such tasks as counting the number of objects in an image,    labeling objects or following curves and borders.    We will take four examples, all on binary images.


EXAMPLE 13: Connectivity preserving shrinking to a point

A method for counting the connected components (the objects) of a binary image is to shrink every object to a point and then count the number of '1's in the image.

We assume that the 4-adjacency relationship is used to define connectedness.    We further assume that the components are without holes,    otherwise the algorithm that we present here will not shrink them to a point.    (There are algorithms [Rao et al.76] that also shrink objects with holes to single points).

The shrinking process is not allowed to disconnect any object.    Therefore,    the simple shrinking operator used in Example 3 cannot be used.    It would delete thin parts of the objects and thereby disconnect them.    Instead,    the operators shown in Figure 9.10, found in [Danielsson82],    will be used.    The operators change the center pixel (underlined) from 1 to 0 if the neighbourhood is as specified.    Repeated application of the operators will shrink objects to single points.

```
    1           0           0          1 1          0
0 1 1       0 1 1       0 1 1       0 1 1       0 1 0
    1           0           1 1          0           1

    A           B           C            D           E


1               0          1 1           0          1
1 1 0       1 1 0       1 1 0       1 1 0       0 1 0
1               0            0         1 1          0

    F           G           H            I           J
```

Figure 9.10 Connectivity preserving shrinking operators.

As usual, the image will be swept over columnwise. All the operators are applied to a column before stepping to the next one. We will use what is often called "sequential" or "recursive" operating mode, meaning that the very input image is changed as the result of an operator. Thus, when applying the next operator on the same slice, the slice may have changed. This also motivates repeated application of the same operator on a slice before taking the next operator.

The algorithm that we use works as follows:

Scan the image from left to right.
For each pixel column:

  1) Apply operator A.
  2) Apply operators B, C and D in sequence.
  3) Apply operator E, repeat until no more changes occur.
  4) Apply operator J, repeat until no more changes occur.
  5) Repeat steps 2,3 and 4 until no more changes occur.

Then, scan the image from right to left.
For each pixel column:

  6) Apply operator F.
  7) Apply operators G, H and I in sequence.
  8) Apply operator J, repeat until no more changes occur.
  9) Apply operator E, repeat until no more changes occur.
  10) Repeat steps 7, 8 and 9 until no more changes occur.

Repeat the scanning procedures until a whole scan is made without any changes.

Before a new pixel column is treated a test to see if there are any '1's at all is performed. If there are no '1's in the column, applying the operators is a waste of time. Also, with the application of the operators A, B, F or G, a column may become blank. Therefore, after each of these operators, the test is performed.

The order between the individual operators is crucial. The operators A and F have the potential to delete a whole string of '1's in one application. Therefore, they are used first on each column. Once applied on a column, there is no sense in applying them once more, since no result from the other operators can make them applicable on new pixels.

The execution time for the procedure strongly depends on the characteristics of the objects in the image. On some images, one pass over the image is sufficient to delete all pixels but one per object. Normally, however, two passes or more are needed. Objects formed like spirals are the most difficult to shrink and require many passes.

An example where three passes are needed is shown in Figure 9.11. Pixels deleted in the first pass are marked by a '1', Those deleted in the second pass by a '2', etc. In the fourth pass no deletions are made. When this is discovered the procedure ends.

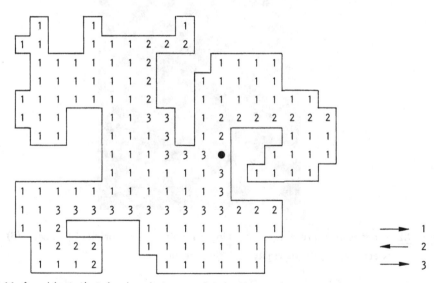

Figure 9.11 An object that is shrunk to a point in three passes.

Photos 9.2 (a) - (c) show the shrinking of 13 objects in a 128 x 128 binary picture. (a) shows the original image, (b) shows the image after one sweep from left to right and (c) shows the final 13 points. The total execution time is 10 ms.

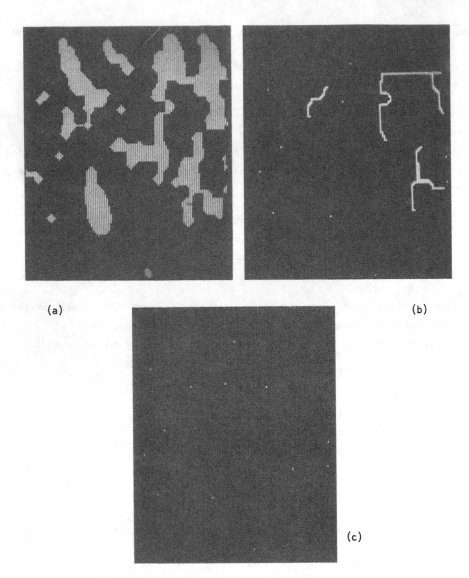

Photo 9.2 Connectivity preserving shrinking to points. (a) original image, (b) after one sweep from left to right, (c) final result

EXAMPLE 14: Finding the outer perimeters of objects

A method for finding the outer perimeter of each connected component (object) in a binary image is to propagate a marker from a point at the edge of the picture over the image area, until they reach an object. When this procedure is completed, those pixels of the objects that have markers as neighbours are marked as outer perimeter pixels.

As a matter of fact, the procedure can equally well be used for finding the holes or inner contours of objects. Hole points are those "background" pixels that have not been marked, and inner contours are those object pixels that have a hole point as a neighbour.

Different strategies can be used in order to spread the marker over the background as fast as possible. Figure 9.12 illustrates two approaches. We assume that 4-adjacency is used to define connectedness of objects. In both strategies the image is scanned back and forth. For each column, a background pixel is marked if it has any 8-neighbour that has been marked. In (a) a new column is taken all the time, whereas in (b) a column is not left until no more pixels can be marked. The starting point at the edge is marked by a *. The numbers at the image points show in which step of the procedure a particular pixel is marked. In (a) the last pixel is marked in step no. 32, in (b) all pixels are marked after 15 steps. Furthermore, many of the steps in (b) can be shortened: when acting on a certain bit-slice, the horizontal and diagonal neighbours need be considered only in the first step. During the following steps, only the neighbours below and above can affect the result. Thus, it seems that the strategy that spreads the marker vertically to a maximal degree before continuing in the horizontal direction is the best one.

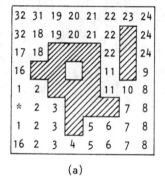

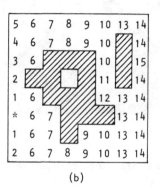

(a)                                      (b)

Figure 9.12 Different strategies for propagation of marker.

It can be noted that propagations like this are very efficiently performed on the CLIP4 processor. The reason is that CLIP4 is equipped with a propagation function that is entirely combinatorial. Thus, the entire propagation is achieved by a single instruction. On LUCAS, we could imagine a similar function, working only in one dimension - vertical. It would be easy to implement.

Strictly synchronous twodimensional arrays (as to our knowledge, MPP is such) that store one pixel per PE will of course perform well on this operation, however not as many times better than a linear array as could be expected. On the example of Figure 9.12 a twodimensional array of 64 processors would need 9 steps to reach the last pixel, compared to 15 steps needed by a linear array of 8 processors. Each step requires looking at all eight neighbours. Larger examples that we have studied show that this tendency holds - the increase in performance falls far below the increase in amount of hardware.

A microprogram on LUCAS for finding the outer perimeters of objects [Svensson83a] was applied to the image in Photo 9.3(left). The processing of the 128 x 128 image shown took 1.4 ms. In Chapter 6 the algorithm is specified in the notation of Pascal/L.

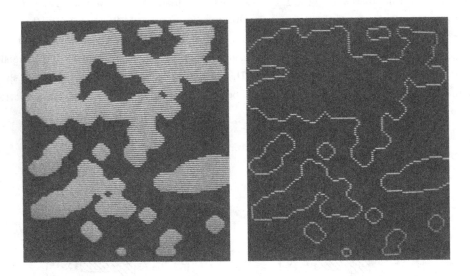

Photo 9.3 Finding the outer perimeter of objects

EXAMPLE 15: Component labeling

Component labeling in binary pictures is the process of assigning different labels to different components of the image; in other words, for any component C, we want all points of C to have the same value, and no point not in C to have that value. The best method for doing this on LUCAS is probably to start off with a connectivity preserving shrinking operation, as suggested in [Danielsson and Ericsson 82]. After the shrinking process, the image is scanned once more. For each pixel with the value '1' a new label is stored in the result image - the labeled image - at the corresponding position. Now, the labels of the points are propagated to all points belonging to the same object in the original image. This is a process similar to the propagation described in the previous example. However, in this case not only a marker bit is propagated, but also - in a different memory area - a multi-bit label.

As with the previous examples, the processing time strongly depends on the shape of the objects in the image. The operation has not been programmed on LUCAS. A qualified guess is that the time for propagating labels is approximately the same as for connectivity preserving shrinking, assuming at most 64 different labels.


EXAMPLE 16: Tracking

For the detection of edges in an image some kind of gradient operator (e.g. Roberts' cross difference operator, described in example 8) is often applied. (Possibly, some kind of preprocessing, e.g. median filtering, is first done in order to suppress the influence of noise). The derived picture is then typically thresholded at some appropriate lavel. A too high level will lead to some edge points being missed, while a too low threshold will give many "false" edges. A method that can be used to remove these drawbacks is "tracking". We then start with the "safe" edge points obtained by thresholding with a high threshold value (see image A in Figure 9.13). Then we propagate these points along connected edges in a picture that has been obtained by thresholding at a lower level (image B) and obtain an image of true edges (image C).

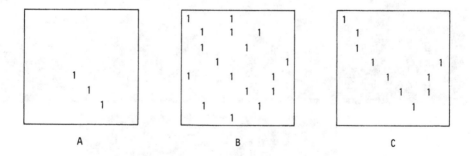

A       B       C

Figure 9.13 Result of thresholding at high level (A) and at low level (B). Result of tracking the '1's of A in B is shown in C.


The technique used for propagation is exactly the same as in Example 15. An example is shown in Photo 9.4 (a) ... (e). (a) shows the original image, (b) shows the result of Roberts' gradient operator (see Example 8) applied to the image, (c) and (d) show the result of thresholding (b) using two different levels. (e) finally, shows the result obtained when the points in (c) are tracked along the edges of (d). The processing times to reach the different results are

b) 3.64 ms (Roberts´)
c) 0.54 ms (Threshold)
d) 0.54 ms (Threshold)
e) 0.77 ms (Tracking)

The image size is 128 x 128 8-bit pixels.  However,  in the illustration in Photo 9.4 (a) and (b) only 4-bit grey scale is used.

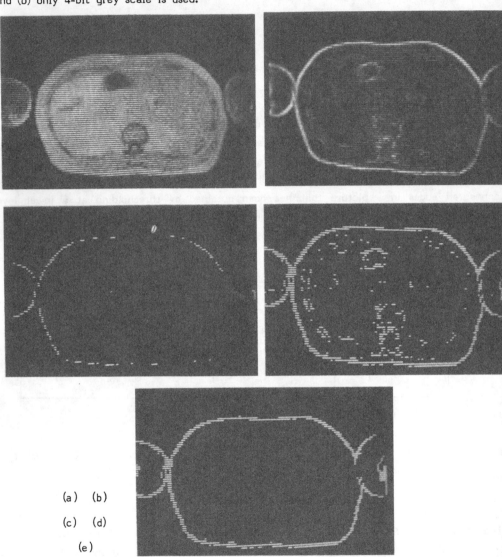

(a)  (b)

(c)  (d)

   (e)

Photo 9.4 (a) original,  (b) result of Roberts´ cross difference operator applied to (a),  (c) result of thresholding (b) at level 10,  (d) result of thresholding (b) at level 4, (e) result of tracking the points in (c) along the points in (d).

## 9.4.5 Measurements

The operations that we have looked at so far have all been of the kind that transforms images to images. Often, we instead want to measure things in the image, e.g. count the number of objects, determine the area of the perimeter of an object, etc. This is also known as feature extraction.

Looking closer at such measurements, one finds that many rely upon a count of the number of '1's in a binary image, e.g. those mentioned above do. Another measurement that is sometimes useful for pattern analysis is the following: Apply a shrinking operator to a binary picture repeatedly. After each step, count the number of remaining '1's. The successive counts will form a "feature vector" that will have quite different characteristics if the objects are small or large, elongated or not, etc.

As a matter of fact, a quantitative measure of the "elongatedness" of an object can be obtained through a study of shrinking. Let t be the number of shrinking steps required in order to erase the object totally. This means that the width of the object is 2t. Now, if the object has a quadratic form, the area is $4t^2$. Let A be the true area of the object. The quotient $A/(4t^2)$ is then a measure of the elongatedness of the object. Thus, we first measure the area of the object, i.e. we count the number of '1's in the binary image. Then we shrink the object until it vanishes and count the number of shrinking steps required. These two measures can then be used to get a value of the elongatedness of the object.

Counting the number of '1's in a binary picture is one example that we will consider in this section. Another is finding the maximum pixel value of an image, together with the coordinates of that pixel. The third example that we will treat is histogram collection.

EXAMPLE 17: Counting the number of ones

We will discuss two methods for counting the number of '1's in a binary picture. The second method assumes additional hardware, not implemented on LUCAS.

Method 1.

The first step in this method is the summing of each row of the image separately. This is of course done in parallel for all rows (words). The fastest way is the following (assume a 128x128 binary picture): First, sum pixels pairwise so that 64 sums, each with a value between 0 and 2, are formed. Then sum these sums pairwise, giving 32 sums with values between 0 and 4, etc. The reason for this method being efficient is the circumstance that the initial additions use very few bits, although the additions are many, and that the longer additions towards the end of the procedure are very few. In total, a little less than one thousand clock cycles are needed to sum over the rows.

Now, the row sums can be added fastly over the perfect shuffle/exchange network. Seven addition steps are required to add all 128 row sums. The number of bits increases from 8 to 14 during the process, which requires approximately 300 clock cycles.

In total, then, 1300 clock cycles are needed to count the number of '1's in a binary 128x128 picture. With a cycle time of 200 ns, this takes 260 microseconds.

Method 2.

If LUCAS is equipped with special purpose hardware to count the number of responders (number of Tag registers with value one), the number of '1's in a picture can of course be obtained faster.

An adder tree according to Figure 9.14 can serve this purpose. Using standard PROMs and adder circuits the summing time is 160 ns, thus smaller than the clock cycle time. The values of consecutive counts are accumulated in the "Count Accumulator", a register that can be read from the Master Processor.

The time needed to count the number of '1's in a binary image is then equal to the time needed to put the bit-slices in the Tag flip-flops. This can be done at the speed of one slice per cycle. Thus, the total count time for a 128x128 image becomes 128 cycles, i.e 25.6 microseconds using a 5 MHz clock. This is ten times faster than by method 1.

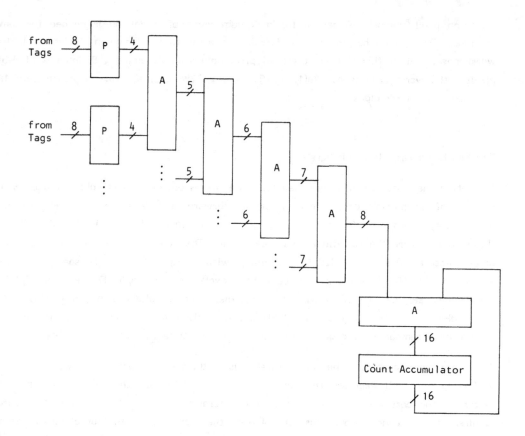

<u>Figure 9.14</u> Part of an adder tree to count the number of responders. A=Adder, P=PROM. The total number of PROMs required is 16, the total number of 4-bit adders is 34.

EXAMPLE 18: Maximum value of image

An algorithm to locate the maximum-valued element in a matrix was described in Section 3.3.4. It starts off by finding the maximum element of the first column, then examines the next column to see if there are larger elements. If there are, the largest one is taken as a new candidate, etc. A bit-slice in the associative array and a register in the Address Processor are constantly updated to keep track of where the maximum value so far can be found.

The computation time is data dependent. One search for "larger than Common" is needed for each pixel column. A search for maximum value of a column is needed for some columns. Also, data has to be moved from the array to the Common Register. In the worst case, all of this is needed for all pixel columns. Assuming 128 columns of 8-bit pixels, the worst case takes $128(12 + 29 + 16) = 7296$ cycles, i.e. approximately 1.5 ms, using a 5 MHz clock.


EXAMPLE 19: Grey level histogram

Collecting the histogram of a grey level picture means counting the number of occurences of each of the possible grey levels. A straightforward method is the following: For each of the grey levels, search the entire picture and produce a binary picture with ´1´s in those points where the specific grey level occurs. Then count the number of ´1´s in the binary picture. Assuming a 128 by 128 image with 256 grey levels, the search will take approximately 1500 cycles and the count 1300 cycles (see Example 17, method 1), i.e. 3800 cycles per grey level. Thus, the total histogram is collected in $256 \times 3800 = 972$ 800 cycles, i.e. 195 ms using a 5 MHz clock. This is quite a long time, in fact the Master microcomputer could gather the histogram in a time that is close to this.

There are ways to shorten the time. First, using the count responders network described in Example 17 will decrease the time to 133 ms. Second, the search can be made faster at the cost of having to reserve some scratch pad area for intermediate search results. The following is one possibility: Divide the grey values into four classes based on the two most significant bits. Create binary maps showing which pixels belong to each of these classes. Twelve cycles per pixel slice are needed to create these maps, i.e. 1536 cycles in total. A similar division of grey values is made based on the next two bits, etc. This gives 16 maps in total, created in $4 \times 1536 = 6144$ cycles. Now, the points having a certain grey value can be obtained through logical AND between four maps. This takes four cycles per bit-slice, i.e. 512 in total for each grey value. The result is obtained in the Tags, and the number of ones can be calculated in the adder tree at once. Thus the total time for histogram collection using this method will be $6144 + 256 \times 512 = 137\ 216$ cycles, i.e. 27 ms.

Histogram collection is not one of those tasks that an array of this kind performs best. With increased capabilities of the processing elements, that allow them to perform one histogram collection each on the pixels stored in their respective memories, it is possible to do well also on this task, as shown in [Danielsson and Ericsson 82]. We can also choose the possibility to compute the histogram outside the array. A fairly simple device "listening" to the input or output stream of pixels can be designed for this task. Each pixel value that passes the device is used as an address pointer to a memory, and the corresponding memory word is incremented by one. The maximum I/O rate with LUCAS is one 8-bit pixel every 200 nanoseconds. A histogram collection device following this rate is realistic, and would collect a histogram for an $128 \times 128 \times 8$ image in 3.3 ms.

## 9.4.6 Global transforms

There are many two-dimensional global transforms that are used in image processing, primarily for the purpose of image enhancement and restoration and image encoding. In this study we will restrict ourselves to a brief discussion of how the two-dimensional Fourier transform can be calculated on LUCAS and the implications of this for the Walsh-Hadamard transform.


EXAMPLE 20: Two-dimensional FFT

In Section 7.3 we studied the implementation of the one-dimensional discrete Fourier transform using the FFT algorithm. The two-dimensional discrete Fourier transform of an image, I, can be obtained in the following way [Nussbaumer81]: First, transform each row of I to produce an intermediate matrix, G, then transform the columns of G to produce the final result, F.

With an image stored in LUCAS, transforming the rows means making an entire FFT calculation within one Processing Element. 128 such computations are done simultaneously. Assuming a 128 x 128 image, the time for the row transforms will be the same as for the column transforms. This is because the same number of arithmetic operations are performed in the two cases, the only difference being the way data is accessed. During the row transforms, data is accessed by means of "butterfly addressing" within the Memory Module. In the column transforms, the shuffle/exchange network automatically provides the correct data.

The result matrix is obtained with its rows bit-reversed. When the image is output this is corrected through the use of a bit-reversed address buffer, as described in Section 7.3.

The total time for a Fourier transform of a 128 x 128 x 8 bit picture will be 256 times the required time for a 128 point one-dimensional FFT. Since this was 1.1 ms, the total time will be around 300 ms.

Another transform frequently used in image processing is the Walsh-Hadamard transform (WHT). The principle for the computation of the FFT can be applied also to the WHT [Gonzalez and Wintz 77]. The difference is that the trigonometric functions are reduced to plus one and minus one. This reduces the computation time with approximately 90 percent. Thus, a two-dimensional WHT could be performed on a 128 x 128 x 8 picture in 30 ms.

## 9.4.7 Input/output

Finally, we want to investigate how long time is needed for input/output of images.

The I/O rate of the Processor Array itself is very high. The bottleneck is outside the array. Data is transferred between the I/O data registers and the Memory Modules at a rate of 128 bits per clock cycle, i.e. $128 \times 5 \times 10^6 = 640$ Mbits/second. However, data can not be written into or read from the I/O data registers at that speed. This is what puts the limit on I/O data speed: how fast can the rest of the system communicate with the I/O data registers?

When no special purpose I/O processor is used, the fastest way for the Master Processor to communicate with the I/O data registers is through the use of the system's DMA unit. The total time required for input/output of a 128x128 matrix of 8-bit data by this method is 19.9 ms. A binary image requires 1/8 of this time, i.e. 2.5 ms.

The I/O processor is capable of writing or reading an I/O register with maximal speed, i.e. 5 MHz, and can thus fill the 128 I/O registers in 25.6 microseconds. The time to transfer the contents of the I/O registers to the Memory Array is 2.2 microseconds. The time required for input or output of a $128 \times 128 \times 8$ image is then $128(25.6 + 2.2)$ microseconds $= 3.6$ ms. A binary image requires 0.45 ms.

One further comment on the input/output time should be made: Filling (or reading) the I/O data registers from the Master Processor or I/O processor can be done at the same time as computations take place in the array. Thus, for tasks that are computation bound, the effective input/output time is in fact 2.2 microseconds per 8-bit slice, i.e. 282 microseconds for a whole $128 \times 128 \times 8$ bit image.

## 9.4.8 Larger images

Throughout Section 9.4 we have assumed that the size of the image side agrees with the number of Processing Elements, so that one line of the image exactly occupies a field of the memory.

When the number of pixels per line in the image is greater than the number of PEs we propose that each PE takes care of more than one column of the image. For example, a $512 \times 512$ pixels image is stored with four columns per Memory Module. We propose neighbouring columns because this is advantageous from neighbourhood access point of view. (Larger accessible neighbourhood). Each memory module would receive $512 \times 4 = 2048$ pixels. Since the MMs are only 4096 bits wide, only two bits per pixel can be stored. This means that LUCAS is not large enough to hold larger pictures than that. To equip this kind of machine with larger memories is one of the easiest things to do and we feel it is highly recommendable if the machine is to be used for image processing.

We disregard the memory length problem for a while and concentrate on how the pixels should be individually ordered within the MM. As an example we take a 16 x 16 pixels image to be stored in a 4 PE machine. Figure 9.15 shows which pixels of the image are stored in each Memory Module. We propose a storage ordering according to Figure 9.16. It simplifies ~~makes~~ the addressing required to access neighbouring pixels simple. For each pixel we have that its eight nearest neighbours are stored at the pixel places with addresses -16 $\pm$ 1, 0 $\pm$ 1 and +16 $\pm$ 1 relative to the pixel's own address and taken modulus64. Some neighbours are in the same MM, others in a neighbouring one.

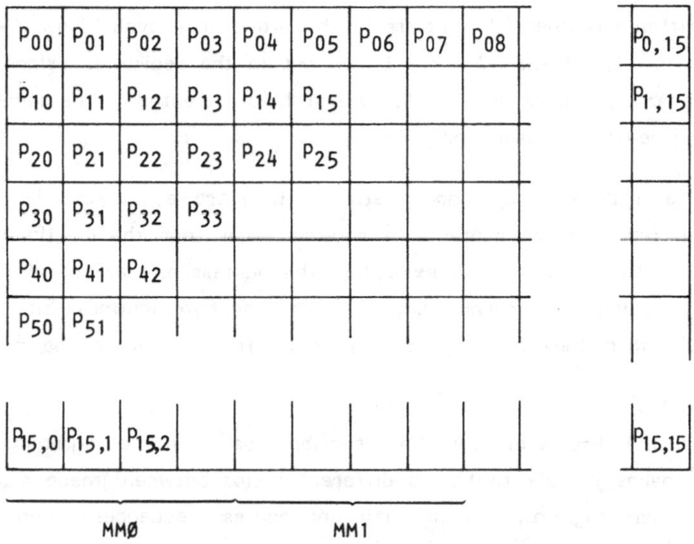

| $P_{00}$ | $P_{01}$ | $P_{02}$ | $P_{03}$ | $P_{04}$ | $P_{05}$ | $P_{06}$ | $P_{07}$ | $P_{08}$ | | $P_{0,15}$ |
|---|---|---|---|---|---|---|---|---|---|---|
| $P_{10}$ | $P_{11}$ | $P_{12}$ | $P_{13}$ | $P_{14}$ | $P_{15}$ | | | | | $P_{1,15}$ |
| $P_{20}$ | $P_{21}$ | $P_{22}$ | $P_{23}$ | $P_{24}$ | $P_{25}$ | | | | | |
| $P_{30}$ | $P_{31}$ | $P_{32}$ | $P_{33}$ | | | | | | | |
| $P_{40}$ | $P_{41}$ | $P_{42}$ | | | | | | | | |
| $P_{50}$ | $P_{51}$ | | | | | | | | | |
| $P_{15,0}$ | $P_{15,1}$ | $P_{15,2}$ | | | | | | | | $P_{15,15}$ |

MMØ          MM1

Figure 9.15 Division of a 16x16 image on four Memory Modules.

MM0: $P_{00}$ $P_{10}$ $P_{20}$ $P_{30}$ ··· $P_{01}$ $P_{11}$ $P_{21}$ $P_{31}$ ··· $P_{02}$ $P_{12}$ $P_{22}$ $P_{32}$ ··· $P_{03}$ $P_{13}$ $P_{23}$ $P_{33}$ ···

MM1: $P_{04}$ $P_{14}$ $P_{24}$ $P_{34}$ ··· $P_{05}$ $P_{15}$ $P_{25}$ $P_{35}$ ··· $P_{06}$ $P_{16}$ $P_{26}$ $P_{36}$ ··· $P_{07}$ $P_{17}$ $P_{27}$ $P_{37}$ ···

MM2: $P_{08}$ $P_{18}$ $P_{28}$ $P_{38}$ ··· $P_{09}$ $P_{19}$ $P_{29}$ $P_{39}$ ···

MM3: $P_{0,12}$...

Figure 9.16 Storage order of pixels within Memory Modules.

Input/output according to these principles is not without problems. When the number of pixels per line agrees with the number of PEs, pixels arriving one by one in TV scan mode are just written into the I/O registers in the order of arrival. Now, every fourth pixel only - no. 0, 4, 8 and 12 - are to be put in the registers. When these have been input to the array, pixels no. 1, 5, 9 and 13 are treated in the same way, etc. The procedure is repeated for each line.

What is needed is a device with enough storage to store a line and with addressing hardware that can read out the contents in another order than the one in which it was stored. In the case that served as an example, the address bits are merely shifted two steps to the left, giving the sequence 0,4,8,... when the two rightmost bits are 00, the sequence 1,5,9,... when they are 01, and so on. Thus, this can be a very simple device.

The implemented I/O Processor can be described as a microprogrammable address generator. This makes it able to handle different ratios between image size and array size. Different microprograms, giving different address sequences, can be initiated depending on the ratio at hand.

9.4.9 Comparison of execution times

Some of the tasks described have also been programmed on a conventional VAX 11/780 computer and measures of execution times have been made. For some of the special purpose image processing machines that we have mentioned in this chapter, performance results from implemented image operations have been reported. We will take a few such examples. Since we want to use the results to make comparisons with the processing times on LUCAS, we have only chosen such results that can be put directly in relation to LUCAS results.

## 9.4.9.1  VAX 11/780

The programs were written in Vax assembly language.  The comparison is summarized in Table 9.1.

As can be expected,  the greatest difference in time is found for binary images.   The simple shrinking operation takes 650 times longer time on the VAX computer than on LUCAS.  With 8-bit data the VAX computer is better off,  but LUCAS is still nearly two orders of magnitude faster.  16-bit pixel values are not very common in image processing. Comparison between 8- and 16-bit processing times show that an ordinary computer like VAX cannot take advantage of the fact that image data have low precision - the processing times for 8- and 16-bit data are nearly identical.

| Binary image | Time on VAX (ms) | Time on LUCAS (ms) | Ratio |
|---|---|---|---|
| Border8, Shrink8 | 130 | 0.2 | 650 |
| **8-bit pixel values** | | | |
| Laplace $L_4$ | 197 | 2.61 | 75 |
| Laplace $L_8$ | 290 | 5.23 | 55 |
| Roberts' cross-difference | 218 | 3.64 | 60 |
| Mean value 3x3 | 335 | 4.28 | 78 |
| **16-bit pixel values** | | | |
| Laplace $L_4$ | 203 | 4.46 | 46 |
| Laplace $L_8$ | 296 | 8.92 | 33 |
| Roberts' cross-difference | 218 | 6.80 | 32 |
| Mean value 3x3 | 374 | 7.35 | 51 |

Table 9.1 Compared processing times for VAX 11/780 and LUCAS.  Image size is 128 x 128 pixels

## 9.4.9.2  DAP

In [Marks80] the time needed for collection of histogram on the pilot DAP with 32 x 32 PEs and 200 ns cycle time is given.  The histogram of a 192 x 192 pixels image with 6-bit grey scale is obtained in 17.25 ms.

To get a comparative measure for LUCAS, we imagine a 128 x 256 pixels image with 6-bit pixel values. This is very close in size to the one Marks uses. LUCAS would require 10.8 ms to collect the histogram, provided it was equipped with an adder tree. Without an adder tree the time would be 44 ms. DAP has eight times as many processors and the same clock rate as LUCAS.

Marks further reports processing time for the following operation on an image of the same size: The image is first differentiated in two directions, the absolute values are formed, thresholding performed, and logical OR between the results is taken. The time for this is reported to be 2.9 ms.

On LUCAS, the same operation on a 128 x 256 x 6 bit image would take 5.8 ms, i.e. twice as long time. LUCAS has more powerful instructions in the PEs which probably in part accounts for the ratio being smaller than eight, which is the ratio between the numbers of processors in the two machines. Also, the addressing of neighbouring pixels within the PEs causes some overhead in DAP.

### 9.4.9.3  CLIP4

In [Fountain and Goetcherian 80] execution times for a couple of algorithms implemented on CLIP4 are reported. Addition of two images, 96 x 96 x 16 each, takes 450 microseconds on CLIP4. LUCAS adds two 128 x 128 x 16 images in 1332 microseconds. The time per pixel is 49 ns for CLIP4 and 81 ns for LUCAS. Thus CLIP4, with its 72 times as many processing elements, is only 40 % faster per pixel.

An edge detection algorithm for binary 96 x 96 pictures, similar in complexity to a shrinking operation, is reported to take 25 microseconds on CLIP4. Binary shrinking of a 128 x 128 image on LUCAS takes 180 microseconds. This is 2.7 ns/pixel for CLIP4 and 11 ns/pixel for LUCAS. Thus, in this case CLIP4 can be considered 4 times as fast.

### 9.4.9.4  Picap-FIP

The main features of the Picap-FIP processor are the use of four special purpose processors operating in parallel and the utilization of a fast cache memory to hold that portion of the image that is currently treated. In [Kruse et al.80] the execution time for Roberts´ cross difference operator performed on Picap-FIP is given. The time required is 100 ns/pixel (8-bit data). On a 128 x 128 pixels image, this makes 1.6 ms. The comparative time for LUCAS is 3.64 ms.

### 9.4.9.5  FLIP-FIP

The FLIP-FIP, using 16 identical processors, is reported to perform median filtering over a 3x3 neighbourhood in 1 second for a 512 x 512 pixels image [Gemmar et al.81]. This makes 3.8 microseconds/pixel. On LUCAS, the same operation is performed on a 128 x 128 image in 70 ms, which makes 4.2 microseconds/pixel.

Laplace-filtering using 3x3-window is reported to take 0.2 seconds for a 512 x 512 image on FLIP-FIP. This makes 0.76 microseconds/pixel. On LUCAS, a 128 x 128 image is treated in 2.61 ms, which makes only 0.15 microseconds/pixel.

### 9.4.9.6 Conclusion

We note that the processing times presented for LUCAS and those for the other machines are of the same order of magnitude. The comparisons with VAX show that the times are about two orders of magnitude shorter than the times on a sequential computer. We take these figures as an indication that LUCAS has the potential to be a useful tool in image processing.

## 9.5 CONCLUSIONS

As we noted at the beginning of this chapter, image processing is a large computational area with many different demands. The processing examples that we have treated in this chapter by necessity cover but a small part of the types of computations that an image processing system should be able to perform efficiently. The presented operations are all examples of tasks that require very long execution times when performed on conventional computers. We have shown that they can be solved on LUCAS with a considerable speed-up compared to sequential execution [Svensson83b].

More important than the usefulness of the physical machine is the usefulness of the kind of architecture that it represents. We feel quite convinced that there is a need for bit-serial processor arrays in image processing. LUCAS represents another kind of array than DAP, CLIP4 and MPP, with a number of PEs that is in the order of the squareroot of the image size instead of in the order of the image size itself. Our experience is that using a number of PEs that is equal to the image side and organizing the PEs in one dimension only, give very straightforward programming and simple input/output.

If varying image sizes are used, this organization may have some drawbacks, and it may be favourable to use a two-dimensional organization as is proposed for LIPP [Danielsson and Ericsson 82]. The two-dimensional organization gives a more intricate neighbourhood addressing scheme and thus puts stronger demands on the address generating control unit.

**Part 4**

**EPILOGUE**

# Chapter 10
## CONCLUSIONS AND CONTINUED RESEARCH

## 10.1 GENERAL

The bit-serial, word parallel working mode is the prime characteristic of the LUCAS processor.. We have found that great flexibility and generality is offered by the use of bit-serial processing elements. Treating many bits in parallel in each PE would of course give faster processing in many cases, but often that kind of parallelism could not be utilized. The instruction set would be more complex for the PEs in the bit-parallel case.

The Processing Elements have been found to have the necessary facilities for most tasks, with respect to both the number of flip-flops and the available functions. Sometimes - but surprisingly seldom - the processing would have been faster if more boolean functions had been available.

A minor change that would have improved the performance on some tasks is the following (see Figure 2.7): If the Direct input (D) and the Common input (COM) were interchanged it would still be possible to input one bit from each source simultaneously. But it would also be possible to input one bit on D and at the same time one bit on, say, the "Above" input which would make vertical differentiation faster.

To increase the processing speed of a processor array there are two ways to follow. One is to increase the number of processors. The other is to make the processors more powerful, which can be done without abandoning the bit-serial working mode.

There are application areas where the first approach is advantageous. Data base processing is probably such an area [Lindh et al.84]. However, image and signal processing may benefit more from improving the power of the processors. As we noted in some examples on image processing, a counter that could be incremented or decremented in one clock cycle would add significantly to the performance. The counter function could be integrated with an index register function. The latter would be useful to "shift" data a different number of bits in different memory words - necessary e.g. in floating point operations - and also for table look-up. Multiplication is a function often needed. In MPP [Batcher82] and PROPAL 2 [Cimsa79] it is speeded up through the use of a shift register to hold the partial products in the processing elements.

## 10.2 A PROPOSAL FOR A MORE POWERFUL PE ARCHITECTURE

### 10.2.1 The New Design

In [Ohlsson84a, Ohlsson84b] a new PE architecture to suit signal processing applications is proposed. In these applications the operation being the prime candidate for PE support is multiplication. Multiplication on LUCAS of b bit operands requires approximately $3*b^2$ bit-slices to be sent between the memory and the processors. This is quite a lot compared to the 4*b memory-processor transfers required just to read the operands and to store the result

The use of shift registers in the PEs to hold the partial products makes the constant of proportionality drop from 3 to slightly above 1, but execution time is still quadratic with respect to the number of bits which seems to be a fairly small pay-off.

Ohlsson's approach is to add some extra logic to the shift registers to make them bit-serial multipliers. A bit-serial multiplier is a cellular structure with bit-serial input and output. It uses the principle of carry save addition to compute the sum of partial products.

The proposed multiplier is shown in Figure 10.1. It is based on a carry-save adder shown in [Gosling80] for multiplication of unsigned integers, modified for two's complement represented numbers. One array of flip-flops, the M flip-flops, is used to hold the bits of the multiplicand. The partial product is contained in the S and C flip-flops. The S flip-flop of one cell holds the sum bit generated by the full adder in that cell and the C flip-flop holds the carry bit. The sum bit is propagated to the neighbouring cell to the left, whereas the carry bit is fed back into the same cell. It is operated by first shifting in the multiplicand, most significant bit first, into the array of M flip-flops. The bits of the multiplier are then successively applied to the input, least significant bit first, and the product bits appear at the output, also least significant bit first. This mode of operation, the bits of the multiplicand being applied in reversed order compared to those of the multiplier and the product, is sometimes considered unfavourable. But we assume that the address processor can deliver bitslice addresses in arbitrary order, why this argument is of no concern.

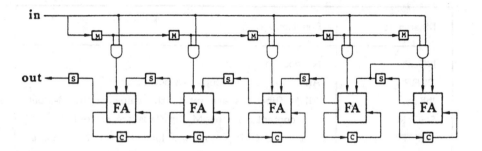

Figure 10.1. The bit-serial multiplier.


The function of the bit-serial multiplier can be described as follows: Let the cells be numbered from zero to n-1 from left to right. At time t=0 the least significant bit of the multiplier is applied at the input. The full adder function (sum and carry) computed by cell number i at time t is:

$$FA_{i,t} = s_{i+1,t-1} + c_{i,t-1} + a_i * b_t$$

The bit produced at the output at time t is thus s(0,t) which is the t:th bit of the product. Refer to [Gosling80] for a more detailed description.

If a is represented with n bits and b is represented with m bits, the time required for multplication is n clock cycles to load a plus m clock cycles to apply each of the bits of b plus (n+m-1) clock cycles to store the bits of the product. The execution time thus equals the number of required memory accesses.

Sign extension of the partial product is accomplished by letting the sign bit be fed back to one of the inputs to the (n-1):th full adder. By having a broadcast line (not shown in the figure) to all the d-elements of the multiplicand register sign extension of the multiplicand is provided. The sign bit of the multiplier is extended by letting it remain on the input while the most significant bits of the product are shifted out. This can be accomplished with an external register. The operation of the multiplier is controlled by the functions listed in Table 10.1.

| Mnemonic | Function |
|----------|----------|
| NOOP | No change |
| CLRP | All S and C flip-flops are set to zero |
| INITM | All M flip-flops are set to the value on the M-input |
| SHFTM | The contents of the M flip-flops are shifted |
| SHFTP | The S and C flip-flops are loaded from their inputs |

Table 10.1. Multiplier functions

A new PE design with hardware enough only to sufficiently support common operations in signal processing applications is also suggested. The architecture of the new PE is shown in Figure 10.2.

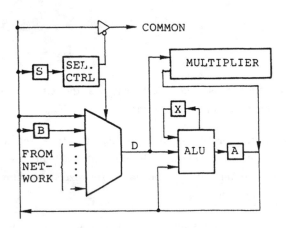

Figure 10.2. The proposed new processing element.

The ALU is smaller than the one in LUCAS. It has three inputs (A, X and D) and two outputs (A and X), which is a minimum since it must be able to perform a full adder function efficiently. The A flip-flop serves as an accumulator register by holding one of the operands (except when the multiplier is used) and storing one of the result bits. To support multiply-and-accumulate operations one of the inputs to the ALU can be taken from the output of the multiplier instead of from the A-register. The X flip-flop is an auxilliary register. In arithmetic operations it holds the carry. The third operand comes from the output of a data selector which serves as the interface to the interconnection network, which will be discussed later. One of the inputs to the data selector comes from the internal one-bit data bus that is connected to the PE's memory module and the I/O-register. The width of the I/O-register should match the width of the external I/O-channel. The bus can also be supplied with data from the A-register and from the output of the multiplier. Another input to the data selector comes from a general purpose register, the B-register. The primary use of this register is to hold the sign bit of the multiplier when the most significant product bits are being computed. The S flip-flop is the Select register. It is used to control the interconnection network and will be described below.

The PE instruction set contains the multiplier instructions described above, the ALU-functions in given in Table 10.2. plus the instructions in Table 10.3.

| Mnemonic | A | X |
|----------|---|---|
| NOP | A | X |
| LDA | D | X |
| LDAX | DX v AX' | X |
| CLRX | A | 0 |
| SETX | A | 1 |
| LDX | A | D |
| ADD | S(A,D,X) | C(A,D,X) |
| SUB | S(A,D',X) | C(A,D',X) |

Table 10.2  ALU-functions

In Table 10.2. $S(x,y,z)$ denotes the sum function: $(x+y+z)$ modulo two and $C(x,y,z)$ is the carry function: $(x+y+z)$ integer divided by two. In the three last functions the A-input can be taken from the multiplier instead of from the A-register. This is denoted by adding a "P" to the mnemonic, e.g. ADDP.

The remaining PE instructions listed in Table 10.3. all require only one parameter. The instructions LDB and LDS can have either "AREG" (A-register), "IOREG" (I/O-register) or a memory address as parameter. The instructions STA and STP can have either "IOREG" or a memory address and IN and OUT can only have a memory address as parameter.

| Mnemonic | Function |
|----------|----------|
| LDB | Load the B-register |
| LDS | Load the S-register |
| STA | Store the content of the A-register |
| STP | Store the output of the multiplier |
| OUT | One bit is shifted into the I/O-register |
| IN | One bit is shifted out of the I/O-register |

Table 10 3. Other PE instructions

We give a few examples of microprograms to illustrate the use of the bit-serial multiplier.

The first microprogram loads one of the multiplication operands, the multiplicand, into the multiplier. The sign bit is first copied into all positions with the INITM-operation. Then the remaining bits are shifted in, most significant bit first. NoOfBits is assumed to be less or equal to the number of cells in the multiplier.

```
Microprogram LoadMultiplicand(Source,NoOfBits);
begin
    Source:=Source+NoOfBits-1;
    INITM(Source,Direct) Source:=Source-1;
    iterate NoOfBits-1 times begin
        SHFTM(Source,Direct); Source:=Source-1;
    end;
end;
```

When the multiplicand has been loaded into the multiplier, the actual multiplication can take place. The bits of the other operand are successively applied at the input of the multiplier. The product bits then appear at the output. To avoid transferring the sign bit of the operand several times from memory it is saved in the B-register, and is from there applied to the multiplier input when the most significant bits of the product are shifted out.

```
Microprogram IntegerMultiply(Source,Dest,NoOfBits);
begin
  CLRP;
  iterate NoOfBits-1 times begin
    SHFTP(Source,Direct); Source:=Source+1;
    STP(Dest);             Dest:=Dest+1;
  end;
  SHFTP(Source,Direct); LDB(Source);

  iterate NoOfBits-1 times begin
    STP(dest); Dest:=Dest+1; SHFTP(Dummy,B);
  end;
  STP(dest);
end;
```

The last example demonstrates how multiplication of a field can be combined with addition to another field.

```
Microprogram FixMultiplyAdd(MulSource,AddSource,Dest,NoOfBits);
begin
  CLRP; CLRX;
  iterate NoOfBits-1 times begin
    SHFTP(MulSource,Direct); MulSource:=MulSource+1;
  end;
  SHFTP(MulSource,Direct); LDB(MulSource);

  ADDP(AddSource,Direct); AddSource:=AddSource+1;
  LDA(One,Direct); SHFTP(Dummy,B);
  iterate NoOfBits-1 times begin
    STA(Dest): Dest:=Dest+1; SHFTP(Dummy,B);
    ADDP(AddSource,Direct);  AddSource:=AddSource+1;
  end;
  STA(Dest);
end;
```

## 10.2.2 Execution times with the new design

With the new design, application programs involving multiplications are executed significantly faster. The execution time for one iteration of an n-point FFT on a n/2 PE array is now 26*b clock cycles [Ohlsson84a], and the total execution time is thus $26*b*\log_2 n$ cycles (b is the number of data bits). On a 128 PE array the execution time for a 256-point FFT with 16-bit data becomes 0.66 ms assuming a 5MHz clock. The time on the existing LUCAS with 5 MHz clock is 9.1 ms.

Multiplication of two 128 by 128 element matrices of b-bit data on the new architecture takes $2^{14}*4b$ clock cycles, compared to $2^{14}*(b^2+10b)$ on the existing LUCAS. For b=8 the time is reduced from 0.5 to 0.1 seconds. For b=16 the time is reduced from 1.4 seconds to 0.2 seconds.

In [Ohlsson84a] the execution times for FFT, convolution and matrix multiplication on both the existing LUCAS and the proposed new architecture are compared with those of a pipelined sequential processor capable of performing one multiplication and one addition/subtraction on 16-bit data words every clock cycle. Provided that the problem size is large enough, a parallel machine can of course be made faster than the sequential processor by equipping it with sufficiently many processing elements. Table 10.4 shows the number of PEs required to make the parallel processor - the LUCAS architecture or the proposed new one - as fast as the sequential processor when the precision is 16 bits.

| | LUCAS | Improved architecture | Ratio |
|---|---|---|---|
| FFT | 1135 | 69 | 16.3 |
| FIR-filter | - | 48 | - |
| IIR-filter | - | 128 | - |
| Matrix mult  p x p | 416 | 64 | 6.5 |
| Matrix mult. $\sqrt{p}$ x $\sqrt{p}$ | 944 | 192 | 4.9 |

Table 10.4 The number of PEs required to make the parallel processor as fast as a pipelined sequential processor with the same clock rate

It should be noted that the comparison is coarse: the wordlength is chosen to fit the pipelined processor and the problem size is chosen to fit the parallel architecture. However, it can be concluded that, in spite of its bit-serial working mode, the kind of architecture that we discuss in this book is competitive also in signal processing applications of moderate size if special care is taken to make multiplication faster.

## 10.3 VLSI IMPLEMENTATION OF THE PROCESSOR ARRAY

An important feature of today's technology as compared to the technology at hand when the von Neumann computer model was suggested is that memory and processing logic are now made using the same technique. Therefore there is no reason to distinctly separate memory from logic. In other words, from a pure technological point of view the use of data processing memory is reasonable. In a processor of LUCAS kind the distinction between memory and processing logic is not as distinct as in sequential computers. This suggests that the use of large scale integration technology has extraordinary advantages in such processors.

Due to its regular structure the kind of processor that we discuss in this book is very well suited for VLSI implementation. As part of a multi-project chip the logic of one Processing Element (excluding memory) was in fact implemented in CMOS/SOS by the project group in 1981.

We will investigate what the consequences of integrating many processing elements on one chip would be in terms of number of gate functions and number of pins per chip.


## 10.3.1 Off-chip memory

We first consider the consequences of using ordinary read/write memory chips for the memory modules. We further assume that we want exactly the facilities now implemented in LUCAS. This means that for interconnection each processing element needs one input from above, one from below, one for shuffle and one for shuffle+exchange. We further assume that the control signals for I/O data registers, multiplexer and ALU functions are gathered to a single "instruction code", k bits wide. 8 bits would be appropriate to implement the present possibilities. Finally, we assume b bits wide I/O data registers. In LUCAS, b is 8.

Table 10.5 describes the number of pins needed on a chip comprising n processing elements. Table 10.6 lists the function for different values of n for two different combinations of b and k.

The first combination, b=8 and k=8, represents what is implemented on the current LUCAS. b=16 means improving the I/O rate by a factor of two. k=12 means increasing the number of ALU functions significantly.

| Specification | pins |
|---|---|
| I/O data bus | b |
| I/O write | 1 |
| I/O data register address | $\log_2 n$ |
| Chip select | 1 |
| Select First chain | 2 |
| Data in/out | n |
| Common Register output | 1 |
| Shuffle input | n |
| Above/Below | 2 |
| Instruction code | k |
| Power,Ground,Clock | 3 |

Sum: $b+k+10+2n+\log_2 n$

Table 10.5 The number of pins of an n processor chip

|  | (I) | (II) |
|---|---|---|
|  | b=8<br>k=8 | b=16<br>k=12 |
| n=1 | 28 | 40 |
| n=2 | 31 | 43 |
| n=4 | 36 | 48 |
| n=8 | 45 | 57 |
| n=16 | 62 | 74 |
| n=32 | 95 | 107 |
| n=64 | 160 | 172 |

Table 10.6 The number of pins for different values of n assuming (I) 8-bit data and 8-bit instruction code and (II) 16-bit data and 12-bit instruction code

The number of gate functions needed to implement the processors is totally dominated by the logic required to implement the arithmetic/logic unit. Assuming $k_1$ bits, out of the k instruction bits, are needed to specify the function and assuming f flip flops in each PE, one bit from Memory and one from Common,

$$G_1 = f * 2^{f+k_1+1+1}$$

memory cells are needed to implement the ALU of one PE as a ROM. (This is an upper limit, since the number can be reduced considerably if a PLA structure is used instead of a ROM.) In LUCAS, we have f=4 and $k_1$=5, which gives

$$G_1(\text{LUCAS}) = 4 * 2^{11} = 2^{13}$$

In an n processor chip, $nG_1$ memory cells are required. Table 10.7 lists $nG_1$ for different values of f and $k_1$.

Using these tables we can now choose parameters and a value of n that give values of cell count and number of pins within the limit of available technology.

| $nG_1$ | $f=2$ $k_1=4$ | $f=4$ $k_1=5$ | $f=4$ $k_1=7$ |
|---|---|---|---|
| n=1 | $2^9$ | $2^{13}$ | $2^{15}$ |
| n=2 | $2^{10}$ | $2^{14}$ | $2^{16}$ |
| n=4 | $2^{11}$ | $2^{15}$ | $2^{17}$ |
| n=8 | $2^{12}$ | $2^{16}$ | $2^{18}$ |
| n=16 | $2^{13}$ | $2^{17}$ | $2^{19}$ |
| n=32 | $2^{14}$ | $2^{18}$ | $2^{20}$ |
| n=64 | $2^{15}$ | $2^{19}$ | $2^{21}$ |

Table 10.7 The number of memory cells required for an n-PE chip with f flip-flops per PE and $2^{k_1}$ functions

For example

$$b=8, \quad k=8, \quad f=4, \quad k_1=5$$

as in LUCAS, would make it possible to put 32 PEs in a 95 (or maybe 96) pin chip comprising $2^{18}$ (=256k) cells which is possible with current VLSI technology.

We assumed the memory modules were outside these chips. Suppose we want a memory word length of 64 kbits. We could then use memory chips of 64 K 8-bit words. Four of these would be required to support one 32-PE chip of the above kind. A circuit board with 80 chips would then have 512 Processing Elements, each with 64 kbits of memory. Some additional chips for I/O address decoding and buffering would be needed on each board.

A particular problem appears with the perfect shuffle/exchange network - if this is the one chosen. We would like to be able to use many of the 512-PE boards together, and be able to perform shuffle permutation on the total of PEs. Can this be implemented without rewiring the whole network when new boards are added?

The answer is yes - with some loss in efficiency. If each 512-PE board is equipped with an internal perfect shuffle/exchange network, a 1024 PE shuffle permutation can be performed in twice the time if the two boards can exchange data over a 512 bit bus. In general, if m boards are used, a 512 x m shuffle can be made in a time of m shuffles. (It is assumed that an individual PE can choose the shuffle or the shuffle/exchange input based on e.g. the tag contents).

## 10.3.2 On-chip memory

We next consider the case of including the memory modules in the PE chips. If we want to equip the PEs with index registers for addresses, this alternative should probably be chosen. Otherwise, the PEs must output the memory addresses.

To provide an address for the bit slice of the memory, address pins are needed. We assume $2^m$-bits memory words, requiring m address bits. Furthermore, a write control signal is needed. Thus, the pin count exceeds what we had in Table 10.6 with m+1.

With m=16, the 16 processors/chip case would require 79 pins/chip. A board with 64 such chips would thus have 1024 processors in total.

The number of gates needed for the memory modules would dominate the gate count in such a chip. Assuming n processors with $2^m$ bits of memory each, $n2^m$ memory cells are needed. For n=16 and m=16, this makes $2^{20}$, which is one million. The cell count for the PE part, according to Table 10.7, ranges between $2^{13}$ and $2^{19}$, depending on complexity.

We conclude that, with memory on the chip, it is probably the number of gate functions that puts the limit on how many processors can be implemented on one chip.

Before leaving this example we also point to the attractive possibility of using read/write memory to implement the arithmetic/logic unit. Loading of the ALU memory can e.g. be done using the memory address pins and I/O data pins.

## 10.3.3 No interconnection network

In the cases considered above we have assumed that communication is needed between processing elements. In some applications this is not required. Relational data base management is the prime example. We end up by considering the consequences of this for VLSI implementation.

The number of pins required for an n-PE chip will be (cf. Table 10.5)

$$b + k + 10 + \log_2 n + m + 1$$

where b is the I/O data bus width, k is the instruction code length, and m is the memory address length. (We assume memory on chip).

Table 10.8 lists this number for different values of the parameters. We can see that the pin count is very low, even with very many PEs on the chip.

|  | b=8<br>k=8<br>m=12 | b=16<br>k=8<br>m=16 | b=32<br>k=8<br>m=16 |
|---|---|---|---|
| n=1 | 39 | 51 | 67 |
| n=4 | 41 | 53 | 69 |
| n=16 | 43 | 55 | 71 |
| n=64 | 45 | 57 | 73 |
| n=256 | 47 | 59 | 75 |
| n=1024 | 49 | 61 | 77 |

Table 10.8 The number of pins of an n-processor chip without external interconnection. b is the I/O data width, k is the length of the instruction code, and m is the length of the memory address.

Clearly, it is the number of gate functions that puts the limit on what is implementable in this case. The number of memory cells per processor is $2^m$ for the memory words and $f * 2^{f+k_1+1}$ for the PEs. Assuming f=4, i.e. each PE having four flip-flops, the two counts have the same value if $m=k_1+7$. Assuming f=2, which is probably sufficient for data base processing, the two counts are equal if $m=k_1+4$. $k_1=4$ is probably sufficient in this case. Thus, we conclude that the number of gate functions to implement the memory modules will again be totally dominating. Assuming we can have $2^{20}$ (1 million) memory cells on a chip, and that the word length is chosen to be $2^{12}$ bits. Then 256 processors could be implemented on a single chip. A data base processor with thousands of processing elements would be easily implemented with these circuits.

10.4 FINAL WORDS

The research presented in this book is intended to explore the possibilities offered by the concept of an Associative Array in different application areas. We feel that it has been a great advantage to have available a working associative array computer. In the course of the project we have found that the range of applicability is wider than we first expected. We have found effective solutions to many problems that were not considered when the architecture was decided. Surprisingly, it has often been very easy to map the problems on the structure of the machine, contradicting the opinion that a parallel architecture with a parallel interconnection scheme is effective only on a very limited range of applications.

Appendix 1

## ALU Functions

The ALU implements 32 different functions. Some functions are listed  more than once, under different mnemonics, since they naturally belong to more than one function group.

Registers not mentioned are left intact. XO=M leaves the X-register intact if, by the Data Select code, M is chosen to be X. + is mod 2 addition. v is OR.

<u>No operation</u>

| NOP | No operation (=LXMA) | | XO=M | |
|-----|----------------------|--|------|--|

------------------------------------------------------------------------------

<u>Set, Clear, Complement</u>

| SETT | Set tags | TO=1 | XO=T |
|------|----------|------|------|
| COT | Complement tags | TO=T' | XO=M |
| | | | |
| SCA | Set C, all | CO=1 | XO=M |
| CCA | Clear C, all | CO=Ø | XO=M |
| | | | |
| CRA | Clear R, all | RO=Ø | XO=M |
| CORA | Complement R, all | RO=R' | XO=M |
| CORT | Complement R, tagmasked (=XORRTA) | Where T=1 do RO=R' elsewhere RO=R XO=M | |

------------------------------------------------------------------------------

<u>Load Registers</u>

| LRMA | Load R from M, all | RO=M | XO=R |
|------|--------------------|------|------|
| LRMT | Load R from M, tagmasked | Where T=1 do RO=M elsewhere RO=R | |
| LRCA | Load R from C, all | RO=C | XO=M |
| LRTA | Load R from T, all | RO=T | XO=M |
| | | | |
| LTMA | Load T from M, all | TO=M | XO=T |
| LTMT | Load T from M, tagmasked (=CMOT =ANDTMA) | Where T=1 do TO=M elsewhere TO=T=Ø XO=T | |
| LTRA | Load T from R, all | TO=R | XO=M |
| LTRT | Load T from R, tagmasked (=CROT =ANDTRA) | Where T=1 do TO=R elsewhere TO=T=Ø XO=M | |
| LTMIT | Load T from M inverted, tagmasked (=CMZT =ANDTMIA) | Where T=1 do TO=M' elsewhere TO=T=Ø XO=T | |
| LTRIT | Load T from R inverted, tagmasked (=CRZT =ANDTRIA) | Where T=1 do TO=R' elsewhere TO=T=Ø XO=M | |
| | | | |
| LCRA | Load C from R, all | CO=R | XO=M |
| | | | |
| LXMA | Load X from M, all (=NOP) | XO=M | |
| | | | |
| XRT | Exchange R and T | TO=R | RO=T  XO=M |

------------------------------------------------------------------------------

## Compare (Result in T)

CRZT     Compare R to Zero, tagmasked         Where T=1 and R=$\emptyset$ do TO=1
        (=LTRIT =ANDTRIA)                   elsewhere TO=$\emptyset$       XO=M

CROT     Compare R to One, tagmasked          Where T=1 and R=1 do TO=1
        (=LTRT =ANDTRA)                      elsewhere TO=$\emptyset$       XO=M

CRMT     Compare R to M, tagmasked            Where T=1 and R=M do TO=1
                                         elsewhere TO=$\emptyset$       XO=T

CRCT     Compare R to COM, tagmasked         Where T=1 and R=COM do TO=1
                                         elsewhere TO=$\emptyset$       XO=M

CMZT     Compare M to Zero, tagmasked        Where T=1 and M=$\emptyset$ do TO=1
        (=LTMIT =ANDTMIA)                  elsewhere TO=$\emptyset$       XO=T

CMOT     Compare M to One, tagmasked         Where T=1 and M=1 do TO=1
        (=LTMT =ANDTMA)                     elsewhere TO=$\emptyset$       XO=T

CMCT     Compare M to COM, tagmasked        Where T=1 and M=COM do TO=1
                                         elsewhere TO=$\emptyset$       XO=T

-------------------------------------------------------------------------------

## Logical

ANDTRA    AND T with R, all (=LTRT =CROT)      TO = T AND R     XO=M
ANDTMA    AND T with M, all (=LTMT =CMOT)      TO = T AND M     XO=T
ANDTMIA   AND T with M, inverted, all             TO = T AND M'    XO=T
          (=LTMIT =CMZT)
ANDTRIA   AND T With R inverted, all              TO = T AND R'    XO=M
          (=LTRIT =CRZT)

ANDRMA    AND R with M, all                     RO = R AND M     XO=R
ORRMA     OR   R with M, all                     RO = R OR   M     XO=R
XORRMA    XOR R with M, all                     RO = R XOR M     XO=R

XORRTA    XOR R with T, all                     RO = R XOR T     XO=M

-------------------------------------------------------------------------------

## Arithmetic

| | | |
|---|---|---|
| ADMA | Add M to R with carry, all | RO=M+R+C      CO=MRvMCvRC<br>XO=Overflow = MR(RO)'vM'R'(RO) |
| ADMIA | Add M inverted to R with carry, all | RO=M'+R+C     CO=M'RvM'CvRC<br>XO=Overflow = M'R(RO)'vMR'(RO) |
| ASMT | Add/sub M to/from R with carry<br>where T=1/Ø | Where T=1: same as ADMA<br>Where T=Ø: RO=M+R+C   CO=R'MvC(R+M)'<br>XO=Overflow = R'M(RO)vRM'(RO)' |
| ACMA | Add COM to M with carry, all | RO=COM+M+C     CO=(COM)Mv(COM)CvMC<br>XO=Overflow = M(COM)(RO)'vM'(COM)<br>(RO) |
| ACIMA | Add COM inverted to M with carry, all | RO=(COM)'+M+C  CO=(COM)'Mv(COM)'CvMC<br>XO=Overflow = M(COM)'(RO)'vM'(COM)<br>(RO) |
| ACMIA | Add COM to M inverted with carry, all | RO=COM+M'+C     CO=(COM)M'v(COM)CvM'C<br>XO=Overflow = M'(COM)(RO)'vM(COM)'<br>(RO) |

--------------------------------------------------------------------------------

**Appendix 2**

**LUCAS Microprogramming Language**

## COMPILATION UNIT, MODULES AND MICROPROGRAMS

\<compilation unit\> ::=
   \<module\> .

\<module\> ::=
   module \<identifier\>; \<declaration part\> \<submodule part\> endmod

\<declaration part\> ::=
   \<empty\> I \<constant declaration\> I
   \<variable declaration\> I \<subroutine declaration\> I
   \<constant declaration\> \<variable declaration\> I
   \<constant declaration\> \<subroutine declaration\> I
   \<variable declaration\> \<subroutine declaration\> I
   \<variable declaration\> \<subroutine declaration\>
                            \<subroutine declartion\>

\<submodule part\> ::=
   \<empty\> I \<module\> /;\<module\>/ I \<microprogram\> /;\<microprogram\>/

\<microprogram\> ::=
   \<microprogram heading\> \<local declartion part\> \<statement part\>

\<microprogram heading\> ::=
   microprogram \<identifier\>; I
   microprogram \<identifier\>(\<formal microprogram parameter list\>);

\<formal microprogram parameter list\> ::=
   \<microprogram parameter\> /,\<microprogram parameter\>/$^3$

\<microprogram parameter\> ::=
   \<empty\> I \<identifier\>

## DECLARATIONS

```
<constant declaration> ::=
   const <identifier>=<sign><constant>
            /; <identifier>=<sign><constant>/;
```

```
<variable declaration> ::=
   var <identifier> /,<identifier>/;
```

```
<subroutine declaration> ::=
   <subroutine heading><local declaration part><statement part>

<subroutine heading> ::=
   subroutine <identifier>; |
   subroutine <identifier>(<formal subroutine parameter list>);

<formal subroutine parameter list> ::=
   <identifier> /,<identifier>/

<local declaration part> ::=
   <empty> | <constant declaration> | <variable declaration> |
   <constant declaration> <variable declaration>
```

## STATEMENT PART

```
<statement part> ::=
   begin <statement list> end

<statement list> ::=
   <statement> /;<statement>/

<statement> ::=
   <empty> | <subroutine call> | <assignment> | <stack operation> |
   <if statement> | begin <statement list> end | <exit statement> |
   <loop statement> | <PE instruction>
```

```
<PE instruction> ::=
    <PE0 identifier> | <PE1 identifier> (<address>) |
    <PE2 identifier> (<address>,<permutation>)


<PE0 identifier> ::=  <identifier>


<PE1 identifier> ::=  <identifier>


<PE2 identifier> ::=  <identifier>


<address> ::= <variable> | <constant>


<permutation> ::=
    DIRECT | SHUFFLE | NSHUFFLE | ABOVE | BELOW



<subroutine call> ::=
    call <identifier> | call <identifier>(<actual parameter list>)


<actual parameter list> ::=
    <actual parameter> /,<actual parameter>/


<actual parameter> ::=
    <variable identifier> | <sign><constant>



<assignment> ::=
    <variable1>:=<sign><constant> |
    <variable1>:=<variable2> |
    <variable1>:=<variable1><arithmetic operator><constant> |
    <variable1>:=<variable1><arithmetic operator><variable2>



<stack operation> ::=
    SPUSH (<variable identifier>) | SPOP (<variable identifier>)


<if statement> ::=
    if <condition> then <statement> |
    if <condition> then <statement> else <statement>
```

```
<exit statement> ::=
    exit | exit (<loop identifier>)

<loop identifier> ::=
    <identifier>


<loop statement> ::=
    <loop label part> <while statement> |
    <loop label part> <repeat statement> |
    <loop label part> <iterate statement>

<loop label part> ::=
    <empty> | <identifier> :


<while statement> ::=
    while <condition> do <statement>


<repeat statement> ::=
    repeat <statement list> until <condition>


<iterate statement> ::=
    iterate <value> times <statement>


<condition> ::=
    <variable><Boolean operator><variable> |
    <variable><Boolean operator>0 |
    TRUE | FALSE | SOME | NONE |
    ZMASK(<address>) | NZMASK(<address>)

<constant> ::=   <number> | <constant identifier>

<value> ::=  <constant> | <variable identifier>

<constant identifier> ::=  <identifier>

<variable identifier> ::=  <identifier>
```

<sign> ::=  <empty> | -

<arithmetic operator> ::=   + | -

<Boolean operator> ::=   = | <>

# PE INSTRUCTION SET

The PE instructions embrace operations performed on the registers and on the memory in the Processing Elements. The instructions are of three kinds:

Without parameters. These instructions use the PE registers as operands and leave the result in the registers.

With one parameter. These instructions either use the Common Register as an operand or store the R register in the PE memory. The parameter specifies the PE memory address.

With two parameters. These are instructions where one of the operands comes from the interconnection network. The first parameter gives the PE memory address of the source bit. The second parameter specifies the permutation of data over the network.

The PE instruction set may be changed by reprogramming the ALU PROMs. The instruction list below describes the current instruction set. In the list the following conventions are used:

* Several of the instructions exist in two versions: A tag-masked instruction (the instruction name ends with the letter "T"), which affects only the selected PEs. A non-tag-masked instruction (the name ends with the letter "A", for "all"), which affects all PEs.

* Arithmetic operations: R receives the result, C the carry and X the arithmetic overflow (used only when the last bit has been processed). The previous value of the C register is used as incoming carry.

* The results of the compare instructions affect the Tag in the following way: A Tag which has the value "zero" is not affected. A Tag which is "one" gets the value "zero" if the compare fails.

## PE INSTRUCTIONS WITHOUT PARAMETERS

### Load/Exchange Register

| | |
|---|---|
| LTRA | Load T from R |
| LTRT | Load T from R |
| LTRIT | Load T from R´ (R´ stands for R-inverted) |
| LTXA | Load T from X    T to X |
| LTXT | Load T from X    T to X |
| LTXIT | Load T from X´   T to X |
| LRTA | Load R from T |
| LRCA | Load R from C |
| LRXA | Load R from X    R to X |
| LRXT | Load R from X    R to X |
| LCRA | Load C from R |
| XRT | Exchange R and T |

### Set/Reset/Complement Register

| | |
|---|---|
| STA | Set T |
| SCA | Set C |
| CCA | Clear C |
| CRA | Clear R |
| COTA | Complement T |
| CORA | Complement R |
| CORT | Complement R |
| SELF | SELECT FIRST. Clear T in all PEs with number > i, where PE no. i is the first PE where T is One |

### Compare

| | | |
|---|---|---|
| CRZT | Compare R to Zero | |
| CROT | Compare R to One | |
| CRXT | Compare R to X T to X | |
| CXOT | Compare X to One | T to X |
| CXZT | Compare X to Zero | T to X |

### Logical

| | |
|---|---|
| ANDTRA | T AND R to T |
| ANDTRIA | T AND R´ to T |
| ANDRXA | R AND X to R   R to X |
| ANDTXA | T AND X to T   T to X |
| ANDTXIA | T AND X´ to T   T to X |
| ORRXA | R OR X to R    R to X |
| XORRTA | R XOR T to R |
| XORRXA | R XOR X to R   R to X |

Arithmetic

| | |
|---|---|
| ADXA | Add X to R |
| ADXIA | Add X' to R |
| ASXT | Add/Subtr X To/From R where T=1/0 |
| SUXA | Subtr X from R |

PE INSTRUCTIONS WITH ONE PARAMETER

The parameter specifies a bit address to the PEs.

| | | |
|---|---|---|
| WRRA | Write R into PE memory | |
| WRRT | Write R into PE memory | |
| CRCT | Compare R to Common | |
| CXCT | Compare X to Common | T to X |
| ACXA | Add X to Common | |
| SCXA | Subtr Common from X | |

PE INSTRUCTIONS WITH TWO PARAMETERS

The first parameter specifies a bit address to the PEs. The second parameter specifies a permutation of the bit-slice, which is performed before the data enters the PE ALU. In the instruction list below, "M" is used to denote incoming data from the Interconnection Network.

Possible permutations are:

| | |
|---|---|
| DIRECT | No permutation |
| SHUFFLE | The bit-slice is shuffled (see section 1.6.2) |
| NSHUFFLE | The bit-slice is shuffled, then exchanged |
| ABOVE | The bit-slice is rotated one step down. |
| | Data to PE no.i comes from PE no. (i-1) mod 128 |
| BELOW | The bit-slice is rotated one step up |

Load Register

| | | |
|---|---|---|
| LRMA | Load R from M | R to X |
| LRMT | Load R from M | R to X |
| LTMA | Load T from M | T to X |
| LTMT | Load T from M | T to X |
| LTMIT | Load T from M' | T to X |
| LXMA | Load X from M | |

## Compare

| | | |
|---|---|---|
| CMOT | Compare M to One | T to X |
| CMZT | Compare M to Zero | T to X |
| CMCT | Compare M to Common | T to X |
| CRMT | Compare R to M T to X | |

## Logical

| | |
|---|---|
| ANDRMA | R AND M to R    R to X |
| ANDTMA | T AND M to T    T to X |
| ANDTMIA | T AND M′ to T    T to X |
| ORRMA | R OR M to R      R to X |
| XORRMA | R XOR M to R    R to X |

## Arithmetic

| | |
|---|---|
| ADMA | Add M to R |
| ADMIA | Add M′ to R |
| ACMA | Add M to Common |
| ASMT | Add/Subtr M To/From R where T=1/0 |
| ACIMA | Add Common′ to M |
| ACMIA | Add Common to M′ |

**Appendix 3**

**Pascal/L - SYNTAX IN BNF**


DATA DECLARATIONS

&lt;selector type&gt;  ::=
    selector[&lt;range&gt;] |
    selector[&lt;range&gt;] := &lt;Boolean aggregate&gt;

&lt;range&gt; ::=
    &lt;constant&gt;..&lt;constant&gt;

&lt;Boolean aggregate&gt; ::=
    &lt;choice&gt; =&gt; &lt;Boolean value&gt;

&lt;choice&gt; ::=
    &lt;constant&gt; | &lt;constant&gt;..&lt;constant&gt; |
    &lt;constant&gt;..&lt;constant&gt; step &lt;constant&gt;

&lt;Boolean value&gt; ::=
    true | false


&lt;parallel array type&gt; ::=
    parallel array[&lt;range&gt;] of &lt;parallel type&gt; |
    parallel array[&lt;range&gt;,&lt;constant&gt;..&lt;constant&gt;]
                                    of &lt;parallel type&gt;

&lt;parallel type&gt; ::=
    &lt;parallel type identifier&gt; | &lt;parallel standard type&gt; |
    record &lt;parallel field list&gt; end

&lt;parallel type identifier&gt; ::=
    &lt;identifier&gt;

&lt;parallel standard type&gt; ::=

integer(<constant>) I unsigned integer(<constant>) I Boolean I
fixed(<constant>.<constant>) I char I string(<constant>)

<parallel field list> ::=
   <parallel record section> /;<parallel record section>/

<parallel record section> ::=
   <field identifier> /,<field identifier>/ : <parallel standard type>

<field identifier> ::=
   <identifier>

## MICROPROGRAM DECLARATION

<microprogram declaration> ::=
   microprogram <identifier> <microprogram parameter list>; external;

<microprogram parameter list> ::=
   <empty> I
   ( <microprogram parameter> /,<microprogram parameter>/ )

<microprogram parameter> ::=
   <empty> I <identifier>

## INDEXING

<indexed parallel variable> ::=
   <parallel variable identifier> I
   <parallel variable identifier>[ <first index>] I
   <parallel variable identifier>[ <first index>,<expression>]

<parallel variable identifier> ::=
   <identifier>

```
<first index> ::=
    * | <constant> | <constant>..<constant> | <selector expression>
```

## STATEMENTS

```
<where statement> ::=
    where <selector expression> do <statement> |
    where <selector expression> do <statement> elsewhere <statement>


<parallel case statement> ::=
    case where <parallel expression> of
            <case list element> /; <case list element>/; <others part> end

<case list element> ::=
    <case label> /,<case label>/ : <statement>

<others part> ::=
    <empty> | others : <statement>


<while and where statement> ::=
    while and where <selector expression> do <statement>
```

# REFERENCES


[Anderson74]        Anderson, G.A. "Multiple Match Resolutions: A New Design Method",
                    IEEE Trans. on Computers, Dec. 1974.

[Astrahan et al.79]
                    Astrahan M.M. et al., "System R, A Relational Database Management
                    System", IEEE Computer, Vol. 12, No. 5, May 1979

[Baba and Hagiwara 81]
                    Baba, T. and Hagiwara, H. "The MPG System: A Machine-
                    Independent Efficient Microprogram Generator", IEEE Trans. on
                    Computers, Vol C-30, No. 6, June 1981.

[Banerjee at al.78]
                    Banerjee J., Baum R.I., Hsiao D.K., "Concepts and Capabilities of a
                    Database Computer", ACM TODS, Vol. 3, No. 4, December 1978.

[Banerjee at al.79]
                    Banerjee J., Hsiao D.K., Kannan K., "DBC - A Database Computer
                    for Very Large Databases", IEEE Trans. on Computers, Vol. C-28,
                    No. 6, June 1979.

[Barnes et al.68]   Barnes, G.H., Brown, R.M., Kato, M., Kuck, D.J., Slotnick,
                    D.L., Stokes, R.A. "The ILLIAC IV Computer", IEEE Trans. on
                    Computers, Vol. C-17, pp. 746-757, Aug. 1968.

[Batcher74]         Batcher, K.E. "STARAN parallel processor system hardware", Proc of
                    the 1974 National Computer Conference, pp. 405-410.

[Batcher76]         Batcher, K.E. "The Flip Network in STARAN", Proc. of the 1976
                    Int. Conf. on Parallel Processing, 1976.

[Batcher77]         Batcher, K.E. "The multidimensional access memory in STARAN",
                    IEEE Transactions on Computers, Vol. C-26, No. 2, 1977, pp.
                    174-177.

[Batcher79]         Batcher, K.E. "The STARAN Computer", Infotech State of the Art
                    Report Supercomputers, Infotech Intl. Ltd., Maidenhead, Berks.,
                    UK, 1979.

[Batcher80]         Batcher, K.E. "Design of a massively parallel processor", IEEE
                    Transactions on Computers, Vol. C-29, 1980, pp. 836-840.

[Batcher82]         Batcher, K.E. "Bit-serial parallel processing systems", IEEE
                    Transactions on Computers, Vol. C-31, 1982, pp. 377-384.

[Bentley79]        Bentley, J.L. "A parallel algorithm for constructing minimum spanning trees", Seventeenth Annual Allerton Conference on Communication, Control, and Computing, 1979, pp. 11-20.

[Bernstein and Chiu 81]
                   Bernstein P.A., Chiu D.W., "Using Semi-Joins to Solve Relationsl Queries", Journal of the Association for Computing Machinery, Vol. 28, No. 1, January 1981.

[Berra and Oliver 79]
                   Berra B.P., Oliver E., "The Role of Associative Array Processors in Data Base Machine", IEEE Computer, Vol.12, No. 3, March 1979.

[Bratbergseugen et al.79]
                   Bratsbergseugen, K., Risnes, O., Amble, T. "ASTRAL - A Structured and Unified Approach to Data Base Design and Manipulation", RUNIT Comp. Center at the University of Trondheim, Norway. Report No. STF14.A80003, 1979.

[Chamberlin76]     Chamberlin D.D, "Relational Data-Base Management Systems", Computing Surveys, Vol. 8, No. 1, March 1976.

[Cimsa79]          Cimsa, "Processeur Parallelle Associatif - PROPAL 2. Presentation", Cimsa - Compagnie d´Informatique Militaire Spatiale et Aeronautique, 781 40 Velizy, France, 1979 (in French).

[Codd70]           Codd E.F., "A relational model of data for large shared data banks", Comm. ACM, Vol. 13, No. 6, June 1970.

[Codd82]           Codd E.F., "Relational Database: A Practical Foundation for Productivity", Comm. ACM, Vol. 25, No. 2, February 1982.

[Cooley and Tukey 65]
                   Cooley, J.W. and Tukey J.W. "An algorithm for the machine calculation of complex Fourier series", Math. of Compu., Vol. 19, 1965, pp. 297-301.

[Danielsson81]     Danielsson, P.E. "Getting the median faster", Computer Graphics and Image Processing 17, 1981, pp. 71-78.

[Danielsson82]     Danielsson, P.E. "Operations on binary images", Internal Report, Linkoping University, 1982 (in Swedish).

[Danielsson84]     Danielsson, P.E. "Serial/Parallel Convolvers", IEEE Transactions on Computers, Vol.C-33, No.7, July 1984.

[Danielsson and Ericsson 82]
                   Danielsson, P.E. and Ericsson T. "Suggestions for an image processor array", Internal Report, Linkoping University, Sweden, 1982.

[Danielsson and Levialdi 81]

     Danielsson, P.E. and S. Levialdi, "Computer architectures for pictorial information systems", Computer, November 1981, pp. 53-67.

[Dasgupta and Tartar 76]

     Dasgupta, S., Tartar, J. "The Identification of Maximal Parallelism in Straight-Line Microprograms", IEEE Trans. on Computers, Vol. C-25, No. 10, Oct. 1976.

[Dasgupta80]     Dasgupta, S. "Some Aspects of High-Level Microprogramming", Computing Surveys, Vol. 12, No. 3, Sept. 1980.

[Date81]     Date C.J., An Introduction to Database Systems, Addison-Wesley Publishing Company, Reading, Mass., 1981.

[Date83]     Date C.J., An Introduction to Database Systems - Volume II, Addison-Wesley Publishing Company, Mass., 1983.

[Davidson et al.81]

     Davidson, S., Landskov, D., Shriver, B.D., Mallett, P.W. "Some Experiments in Local Microcode Compaction for Horizontal Machines", IEEE Trans. on Computers, Vol. C-30, No. 7, July 1981.

[Deo and Yoo 81] Deo, N. and Yoo, Y.B. "Parallel algorithms for the minimum spanning tree problem", Proceedings of the 1981 International Conference on Parallel Processing, IEEE New York, 1981, pp 188-189.

[DeWitt76a]     DeWitt, D.J. "A Machine-Independent Approach to the Production of Horizontal Microcode", PhD thesis, Univ. of Michigan, Ann Arbor, June 1976.

[DeWitt76b]     DeWitt, D.J. "Extensibility - A New Approach for Designing Machine-Independent Microprogramming Languages", Proc. 9th Ann. Workshop on Microprogramming (ACM), Sept. 1976.

[DeWitt and Hawthorn 81]

     DeWitt D.J.,Hawthorn P.B.,"A Performance Evaluation of Database Machine Architectures", Proc 7-th VLDB Conf., Cannes, September 1981.

[Dewitt79]     DeWitt D.J.,"DIRECT - A multiprocessor organization for supporting relational database management systems", IEEE Trans. on Computers, Vol. C-28, No. 6,June 1979.

[Digby73]     Digby D. W.,"A Search Memory for Many-to-Many Comparisons",IEEE Trans. on Computers, Vol. C-22, No. 8, August 1973.

[Dijkstra59]     Dijkstra, E.W. "A note on two problems in connection with graphs", Numerische Math., Vol. 1, 1959, pp. 269-271.

[Duff79]        Duff, M.J.B. "Parallel processors for digital image processing", in "Advances in Digital Image Processing", edited by P. Stucki, Plenum Press, New York, 1979, pp. 265-276.

[Duff and Levialdi 81]
        Duff, M.J.B. and Levialdi S. (editors), "Languages and Architectures for Image Processing", Academic Press, London, 1981.

[Feierbach and Stevenson 78]
        Feierbach, G.F., Stevenson, D.K. "The Phoenix Array Processor", Proc. 17th Ann. Tech. Symposium, June 1978.

[Fernstrom82]     Fernstrom, C. "Programming Techniques on the LUCAS Associative Array Computer", Proc. of the 1982 International Conf. on Parallel Processing, Aug. 1982.

[Fernstrom83]     Fernstrom, C. "The LUCAS Associative Array Processor and its Programming Environment", PhD thesis, Dept. of Computer Engineering, University of Lund, Sweden, 1983.

[Fernstrom et al.83]
        Fernstrom, C., Kruzela, I., Ohlsson, L., and Svensson, B. "An associative parallel processor used in real time signal processing", Proceedings of the Second European Signal Processing Conference, Sept 1983, pp. 793-796.

[Flanders et al.77]Flanders, P.M., Hunt D.J., Reddaway S.F., and Parkinson D. "Efficient high speed computing with the Distributed Array Processor", in High Speed Computer and Algorithm Organization, edited by D.J. Kuck, D. Lawrie, and A.H. Sameh, Academic Press, New York, 1977.

[Floyd62]       Floyd, R.W. "Algorithm 97: shortest path", Comm ACM, Vol. 5, 1962, p. 345.

[Flynn66]       Flynn, M.J. "Very High-Speed Computing Systems", Proc. of the IEEE, Vol. 54, No. 12, Dec. 1966.

[Foster76]      Foster, C.C. "Content Addressable Parallel Processors", Van Nostrand Reinhold Co., 1976.

[Fountain and Goetcherian 80]
        Fountain, T.J. and Goetcherian V. "Clip parallel processing system", IEEE Proceedings, Vol. 127, Pt.E., No. 5, 1980, pp. 219-224.

[Gemmar et al.81]Gemmar, P., Ischen H., and Luetjen K. "FLIP: A multiprocessor system for image processing", in [Duff and Levialdi 81] pp. 245-256.

[Golumb61]      Golumb, S.W. "Permutations by Cutting and Shuffling", SIAM Rev., Vol. 3, pp. 293-297, Oct. 1961.

[Gonzalez and Wintz 77]

        Gonzalez, R.C. and Wintz P. "Digital Image Processing", Addison-Wesley, Reading, Massachusetts, 1977.

[Goodyear76]     Goodyear Aerospace Corporation "Digital image processing and STARAN", Report GER-16336, GAC, Akron, Ohio, 1976.

[Gosling80]      Gosling, J.B. "Design of Arithmetic Units for Digital Computers", MacMillan Press Ltd, London, 1980.

[Granlund81]     Granlund, G. "GOP: A fast and flexible processor for image analysis", in [Duff and Levialdi 81], pp. 179-188.

[Hawthorn and DeWitt 82]

        Hawthorn P. B., DeWitt D., "Performance Analysis of Alternative Database machine Architectures", IEEE Trans. on Software Engineering, Vol SE-8, No. 1, January 1982.

[Held et al.75]   Held G. D.,Stonebraker M. R., and Wong E., "INGRES - A relational data base management system", Proc. AFIPS 1975 National Computer Conf., AFIPS Press, 1975.

[Hockney and Jesshope 81]

        Hockney, R.W. and Jesshope C.R. "Parallel Computers: Architecture, Programming and Algorithms", Adam Hilger Ltd, Bristol, 1981.

[Hsiao80]       Hsiao D. K., "Data Base Computers", in Advances in Computers, Vol. 19, ed. Yovits M. C., Academic Press, Toronto, 1980.

[Hong and Su 81] Hong Y.C, Su S.Y.W, "Associative Hardware and Software Techniques for Integrity Control", ACM TODS, Vol. 6., No. 3, September 1981.

[Hwang79]      Hwang, K. "Computer Arithmetic: Principles, Architecture and Design", Wiley, New York, 1979.

[IEEE G-AE 67] IEEE G-AE Subcommittee on Measurement Concepts "What is the fast Fourier transform?", IEEE Transactions on Audio Electroacoustics, AU-15(2), 1967, pp. 45-55.

[Iliffe82]       Iliffe, J.K. "Advanced Computer Design", Prentice Hall, London, 1982.

[Justusson80]    Justusson, B.I. "On the use of medians and other order statistics in picture processing", Proceedings of the First Scandinavian Conference on Image Analysis, Linkoping, 1980, pp. 84-86.

[King80]        King W.F., "Relational Database Systems: Where We Stand Today", Proc. IFIP Congress 1980, Toronto 1980.

[Knuth73]           Knuth D.,   The Art of Computer Programming,   Vol.   3,   Addisson-Wesley Publishing Company,   Reading,   Mass.,   1973.

[Kordina83]         Kordina,   S.   "An I/O Processor for LUCAS",   Master Thesis,   Department of Computer Engineering,   University of Lund,   Sept.   1983.

[Kruse73]           Kruse,   B.   "A parallel picture processing machine",   IEEE Transactions on Computers,   C-22,   1973,   pp.   1075-1087.

[Kruse77]           Kruse,   B.   "Design and Implementation of a Picture Processor",   PhD thesis,   Linkoping Studies in Science and Technology Dissertation,   No.   13,   1977.

[Kruse et al.80]    Kruse,   B.,   Gudmunsson B.,   and Antonsson D.   "FIP - the picap II filter processor",   5th International   Joint   Conference   on   Pattern Recognition,   1980,   pp.   484-488.

[Kruzela83]         Kruzela,   I.K.   "An Associative Array Processor Supporting a Relational Algebra",   PhD thesis,   Dept.   of Computer Engineering,   University of Lund,   Sweden,   1983.

[Kruzela and Svensson 81]
                    Kruzela I.,Svensson B.   A.,"The LUCAS Architecture and its Application to Relational Data Base Management",   Proc of the 6-th Workshop on Computer Architecture for Non-Numerical Processing,   INRIA,   Hyeres,   1981.

[Kuck68]            Kuck,   D.J.   "ILLIAC IV Software Application Programming",   IEEE Trans.   on Computers,   Vol.   C-17,   No.   8,   Aug.   1968.

[Kushner et al.81]  Kushner,   T.,   Wu A.,   and Rosenfeld A.   "Image processing on MPP:1",   Technical Report TR-1007,   Computer Vision Laboratory,   University of Maryland,   College Park,   MD,   USA,   1981.

[Landskov et al.80]
                    Landskov,   D.,   Davidson,   S.,   Shriver,   B.,   Mallett,   P.W.   "Local Microcode Compaction Techniques",   Computing Surveys,   Vol.   12,   No.   3,   Sept.   1980.

[Lang76]            Lang,   T.   "Interconnections Between Processors and Memory Modules Using the Shuffle-Exchange Network",   IEEE Trans.   on Computers,   Vol.   C-25,   No.   5,   May 1976.

[Langdon78]         Langdon G.   G.,   "A note on associative processors for data management",   ACM TODS,   Vol.   3,   No 2.,   June 1978.

[Lawrie74]          Lawrie,   D.H.   "Glypnir Programming Manual",   ILLIAC IV Doc.   No.   232,   ILLIAC IV Proj.,   University of Illinois at Urbana-Champaign,   Urbana,   Ill.   1974.

[Lawrie et al.75] Lawrie, D.H., Layman, T., Baer, D., Randal, J.M. "Glypnir - a Programming Language for ILLIAC IV", Comm. of the ACM, Vol. 18, No. 3, March 1975.

[Lawrie75] Lawrie, D.H. "Access and alignment of data in an array processor", IEEE Transactions on Computers, Vol. C-24, No. 12, 1975, pp. 1145-1155.

[Levialdi et al.80] Levialdi, S., Isoldi, M., Uccella, G. "Programming in Pixal", IEEE Workshop on Picture Data Description and Management, Asilomar, California, Aug. 1980.

[Lindh at al.84] Lindh G., Kruzela I., and Speck D.,"A Relational Algebra Machine", Proc. of the International Workshop On High-Level Computer Architecture 84, Los Angeles, May 1984.

[Lipovski et al.78] Lipovski G.J, Su S.Y.W, "Architectural Features of CASSM: A Context Addressed Segment Sequential Memory", Proc. 5th Annual Symposium on Computer Architecture, Palo Alto, April 1978.

[Loucks et al.82] Loucks, W.M., Snelgrove M., and Zaky S.G. "A Vector Processor Based on One-Bit Microprocessors", Computer, February 1982, pp. 53-62.

[Love75] Love, H.H. "Programming the Associative Linear Array Processor", Proc. of the 1975 Sagamore Comp. Conference on Parallel Processing.

[Maller79] Maller V.A.J, "The Content Addressable File Store - CAFS", ICL Technical Journal, Vol. 1, No. 3., November 1979.

[Marks80] Marks, P. "Low-level vision using an array processor", Computer Graphics and Image Processing, Vol. 14, 1980, pp. 281-292.

[McGee81] McGee W. C., "Data Base Technology", IBM J. Res. Develop., Vol. 25, No. 5, September 1981.

[Menon and Hsiao 81] Menon M. J., Hsiao D. K., "Design and Analysis of A Relational Join Operation for VLSI", Proc 7-th VLDB Conf., Cannes, September 1981.

[Mezzalama et al.82] Mezzalama, M., Prinetto, P., Filippi, G. "Microcode Compaction via Microblock Definition", Proc. 15th Ann. Workshop on Microprogramming (ACM), 1982.

[Mick and Brick 80] Mick, J. and Brick, J. "Bit-Slice Microprocessor Design", Mc Graw-Hill Book Company, 1980.

[Millstein73]        Millstein, R.E. "Control Structures in ILLIAC IV FORTRAN", Comm. of the ACM, Vol. 16, No. 10, Oct. 1973.

[Millstein and Muntz 75]
                     Millstein, R.E. and Muntz, C.A. "The ILLIAC IV FORTRAN Compiler", Proc. of a Conf. on Programming Languages and Compilers for Parallel and Vector Machines, March 1975.

[Mueller et al.80]  Mueller, P.T. Jr, Siegel, L.J., Siegel, H.J. "A Parallel Language for Image and Speech Processing", Proc. of the COMPSAC 80, Oct. 1980.

[Nussbaumer81]       Nussbaumer, H.J. "Fast Fourier Transform and Convolutional Algorithms", Springer-Verlag, Berlin, 1981.

[Ohlsson82]          Ohlsson, L. "Real time spectral analysis of speech on a small associative computer", Master Thesis Technical Report, Department of Computer Engineering, University of Lund, 1982.

[Ohlsson and Svensson 83]
                     Ohlsson, L. and Svensson, B. "Matrix multiplication on LUCAS", 6th Symposium on Computer Arithmetic, IEEE 1983, pp. 116-122.

[Ohlsson84a]         Ohlsson, L. "An improved LUCAS architecture for Signal Processing", Technical Report, Department of Computer Engineering, University of Lund, Sept 1984.

[Ohlsson84b]         Ohlsson, L. "An SIMD processor with bit-serial multipliers", International Conference on Computers, Systems and Signal Processing, Bangalore, India, Dec 1984.

[Oliver79]           Oliver E. J., "RELACS, An Associative Computer Architecture to Support a Relational Data Model", PhD thesis, Syracuse University, 1979.

[Orcutt74]           Orcutt, S.E. "Efficient Data Routing Schemes for ILLIAC IV - type Computers", Digital Systems Lab., Stanford University, Tech. Rep. 70, Apr 1974.

[Ozkarahan et al.75]
                     Ozkarahan E.A., Schuster S.A., Smith K.C., "RAP - An Associative Processor for Data Base Management", Proc AFIPS 1975 National Computer Conf., AFIPS Press, 1975.

[Ozkarahan and Sevcik 77]
                     Ozkarahan E.A., Sevcik K.C., "Analysis of Architectural Features for Enhancing the Performance of a Database Machine", ACM TODS, Vol 2, No. 4, December 1977.

[Ozkarahan et al.77]
                     Ozkarahan E.A., Schuster S.A., Sevcik K.C., "Performance evaluation of a Relational Associative Processor", ACM TODS, Vol. 2, No. 2, June 1977a.

[Pahrami73]       Pahrami B., "Associative Memories and Processors: An Overview and Selected Bibliography", Proc of the IEEE, Vol. 61, No. 6, June 1973.

[Parker80]        Parker, D.S. "Notes on Shuffle/Exchange-Type Switching Networks", IEEE Trans. on Computers, Vol. C-29, No. 3, Mar. 1980.

[Pease68]         Pease, M.C. "An adaptation of the fast Fourier transform for parallel processing", Journal of the Association for Computing Machinery, Vol. 15, No. 2, 1968, pp. 252-264.

[Pease77]         Pease, M.C. "The indirect binary n-cube microprocessor array", IEEE Transactions on Computers, Vol. C-2 , No. 5, 1977, pp. 458-473.

[Perrott79]       Perrott, R.H. "A Language for Array and Vector Processors", ACM Trans. on Prog. Languages and Systems, Vol. 1, No. 2, Oct. 1979.

[Presberg and Johnson 75]
                  Presberg, D.L. and Johnson, N.W. "The Paralyzer: IVTRAN's Parallelism Analyzer and Synthesizer", Proc. of a Conf. on Programming Languages and Compilers for Parallel and Vector Machines, March 1975.

[Potter78]        Potter, J.L. "The STARAN architecture and its application to image processing and pattern recognition algorithms", National Computer Conference 1978, pp. 1041-1047.

[Quinn and Deo 84]
                  Quinn, M.J. and Deo, N. "Parallel graph algorithms", Computing Surveys, Vol.16, No.3, Sept 1984, pp 319-348.

[Ramamoorthy and Tsuchiya 74]
                  Ramamoorthy, C.V. and Tsuchiya, M. "A High-Level Language for Horizontal Microprogramming", IEEE Trans. on Computers, Vol. C-23, No. 8, Aug. 1974.

[Rao et al.76]    Rao, C.V.K., Prasada B., and Sarma K.R. "A parallel shrinking algorithm for binary patterns", Computer Graphics and Image Processing, Vol. 5, 1976, pp. 265-270.

[Reddaway79]      Reddaway, S. "The DAP approach", Infotech State of the Art Report on Super Computers, Vol. 2, 1979.

[Reeves84]        Reeves, A. "Parallel computer architectures for image processing", Computer Vision, Graphics, and Image Processing, Vol.25, 1984, pp 68-88.

[Reeves et al.80] Reeves, A.P., Bruner, J.D., Poret, M.S. "The Programming Language Parallel Pascal", 1980 Internat. Conf on Parallel Processing.

[Reeves and Bruner 80]
Reeves, A.P. and Bruner, J.D. "High Level Language Specification and Efficient Function Implementation for the MPP", Internal Purdue Electrical Engineering Report TR-EE 80-32, Jul. 1980.

[Reeves et al.81] Reeves, A.P., Bruner, J.D., Brewer, T.M. "High Level Languages for the MPP", Internal Purdue Electrical Engineering Report TR-EE 81-45, Nov. 1981.

[Resnick and Larson 75]
Resnick, H.K. and Larson, A.G. "DMAP - A COBOL Extension for Associative Processors", Proc. of a Conf. on Programming Languages and Compilers for Parallel and Vector Machines, March 1975.

[Rieger et al.80] Rieger, C., Bane J., and Trigg R. "ZMOB: A highly parallel multiprocessor", 1980 IEEE Workshop on Picture Data Description and Management, pp 298-304.

[Roberts65] Roberts, L.G. "Machine perception of three-dimensional solids", in "Optical and Electrooptical Information Processing" (J.T. Tippett et al., eds.), pp.1 59-197, MIT Press, Cambridge, Massachusetts, 1965.

[Rosenfeld and Kak 76]
Rosenfeld, A. and Kak A.C. "Digital Picture Processing", Academic Press, New York, 1976.

[Schlumberger74] Schlumberger, M.L. "De Bruijn Networks", PhD thesis, Comp. Science Dept., Stanford, Cal. June 1974.

[Schomberg77] Schomberg, H. "A Peripheral Array Computer and its Applications", Parallel Computers - Parallel Mathematics, M. Feilmeier (ed.), Internat. Assoc. for Mathematics and Computers in Simulation, 1977.

[Schuster et al.78]Schuster S.A., Nguyen H.B., Ozkarahan E.A., Smith K.C., "RAP.2 - An Associative Processor for Data Bases", Proc. 5th Annual Symposium on Computer Architecture, Palo Alto, April 1978.

[Shaw80] Shaw D. E., "Knowledge-Based Retrieval on A Relational Database Machine", PhD thesis, Stanford University, 1980.

[Siegel81] Siegel, H.J. "PASM: A reconfigurable multimicrocomputer system for image processing", in [Duff and Levialdi 81], pp. 257-265.

[Slotnick82] Slotnick, D.L. "The Conception and Development of Parallel Processors - a Personal Memoir", Ann. of the History of Comp. Vol. 4, No.1, Jan. 1982.

[Slotnik70] Slotnik D. L., "Logic per track devices", in Advances in Computers, Vol. 10, ed. Alt F., Academic Press, Toronto 1970.

[Sternberg79]    Sternberg,    S.R.    "Parallel    architectures    for    image    processing",
Proceedings of the 3rd International IEEE COMPSAC,    Chicago 1979,
pp 712-717.

[Stevens75]    Stevens,    K.G.    Jr.    "CFD - A FORTRAN-Like Language for the
ILLIAC IV",    Proc.    of a Conf.    on Programming Languages and
Compilers    for    Parallel    and    Vector    Machines,    March    1975.

[Stone71]    Stone,    H.S.    "Parallel processing with the perfect shuffle",    IEEE
Transactions on Computers, Vol. C-20, No. 2, 1971, pp. 153-161.

[Stonebraker et al.79]
Stonebraker M.    R.,    Wong E.,    and Kreps P.,    "The Design and
Implementation of INGRES",    ACM TODS,    Vol 1,    No. 3,    September
1976.

[Su and Lipovski 75]
Su S.Y.W,    Lipovski G.J,    "CASSM: A Cellular System for Very Large
Data Bases",    Proc.    Int.    Conf Very Large Databases,    September
1975.

[Svensson83a]    Svensson,    B.    "LUCAS Processor Array - Design and Applications",
PhD thesis,    Department of Computer Engineering,    University of Lund,
1983.

[Svensson83b]    Svensson,    B.    "Image operations performed on LUCAS - an array of
bit-serial processors",    3rd Scandinavian Conference on Image Analysis,
July 1983,    pp.    308-313.

[Thurber and Wald 75]
Thurber K.    J.,    Wald L.    D.,    "Associative and Parallel Processors",
Computing    Surveys,    Vol.    7,    No.    4,    December    1975.

[Thurber76]    Thurber,    K.J.    "Large Scale Computer Architecture",    Hayden Book
Comp.,    Rochelle Park,    New Jersey,    1976.

[Tong and Yao 81]
Tong F.,    Yao B.    S.,    "Design of a Two-Dimentional Join Processor
Array",    Proc of the 6-th Workshop on Computer Architecture for
Non-Numerical    Processing,    INRIA,    Hyeres,    June    1981.

[Tong and Yao 82]
Tong F.,    Yao S.    B.,    "Performance analysis of database join
processors",    Proc AFIPS 1982 National Computer Conf.,    AFIPS Press,
1982.

[Unger58]    Unger,    S.H.    "A    computer    oriented    towards    spatial    problems",
Proceedings    of    IRE,    Vol.    46,    1958,    pp.    1744-1750.

[Uhr79]    Uhr,    L.    "A Language for Parallel Processing of Arrays,    Embedded in
Pascal",    Comp.    Sciences Technical Report #365,    Sept.    1979.

[Wirth71]        Wirth, N. "The Design of a PASCAL Compiler", Software-Practice
                 and Experience, 1, No. 4, 1971.

[Wong and Youssefi 76]
                 Wong E., Youssefi K., "Decomposition - A Strategy for Query
                 Processing", ACM TODS, Vol. 1, No. 3, September 1976.

[Yao79]          Yao S. B., "Optimization of Query Evaluation Algorithms", ACM
                 TODS, Vol. 4, No. 2, June 1979.

[Yau and Feng 77]
                 Yau S. S., Fung H. S., "Associative Processor Architecture - A
                 Survey", Computing Surveys, Vol. 9, No. 1, March 1977.

[Yew and Lawrie 81]
                 Yew, P-C. and Lawrie D.H. (1981) "An easily controlled network for
                 frequently used permutations", IEEE Transactions on Computers, Vol.
                 C-30, No. 4, 1981, pp. 296-298.

[Zloof75]        Zloof M. M., "Query By Example", Proc AFIPS 1975 National
                 Computer Conf., AFIPS Press, 1975.